AUTOCAD®
REFERENCE GUIDE

Second Edition

Everything You Wanted to Know About AutoCAD — Fast!

By Dorothy Kent

New Riders Publishing, Gresham, Oregon

AUTOCAD® REFERENCE GUIDE

Everything You Wanted to Know About AutoCAD — Fast!

By Dorothy Kent

Published by:

New Riders Publishing
1025 E. Powell #202
Gresham, OR 97030

Second Edition 1991

Printed in the United States of America

10 9 8 7 6

Library of Congress Cataloging-in-Publication Data

Kent, Dorothy, 1955-
    AutoCAD reference guide: everything you wanted
to know about AutoCAD--fast! / by Dorothy Kent. --
2nd ed.
        p.   cm.
    ISBN 0-934035-02-4 : $14.95
    1. AutoCAD (Computer program)   I. Title.
T385.K42   1991
620'.0042'02855369--dc20
                                90-27278
                                   CIP

Warning and Disclaimer

This book is designed to provide data about all the AutoCAD commands. Every effort has been made to make this book as complete and as accurate as possible. However, no warranty or fitness is implied.

The information is provided on an "as-is" basis. The author and New Riders Publishing shall have neither liability nor responsibility to any person or entity with respect to any loss or damages in connection with or rising from the information contained in this book.

If you do not agree to the above, you may return this book for a full refund.

Trademarks

AutoCAD, AutoLISP, and AutoShade are registered trademarks of Autodesk, Inc.

The publisher has attempted to identify other known trademarks or service marks by printing them with the capitalization and punctuation used by the trademark holders. New Riders Publishing attests that it has used these designations without intent to infringe on the trademarks and to the benefit of the trademark holders. However, the publisher disclaims any responsibility for specifying which marks are owned by which companies or organizations.

Production

Editorial Director:	B. Rustin Gesner
Managing Editor:	Ken Billing
Technical Editor:	Kevin Coleman
AREF Disk Development:	Ken Billing, Rusty Gesner
Copyediting:	Christine Steel, Margaret Berson
Page Layout:	Margaret Berson

About the Author

Dorothy Kent is a veteran AutoCAD user who has been teaching people how to be productive with AutoCAD since 1983. A graduate with an advanced degree from Adelphi University, Dorothy worked as a scale model maker and draftsperson before she became the Director of Education and Training at Synergis Technologies, Inc., in Blue Bell, Pennsylvania.

She currently teaches and develops implementation strategies for engineers and design professionals using the entire family of Autodesk products.

Acknowledgments

Dorothy would like to thank Harbert Rice, Martha Lubow, and David Sharp for providing the opportunity, encouragement, and support to write this book.

Great appreciation and thanks go to Ken Billing for his technical editing, rewriting, and guidance.

A special appreciation to Pat Haessly for his AutoLISP programming used on the AREF disk and to Christine Steel for developing the style sheet used for the second edition.

Special thanks to the entire staff at Synergis Technologies, Inc., for their understanding, support, and encouragement.

A very personal thank you goes to Martha Lubow for her guidance as a teacher, friend, and coach; and to Florence and Harry Kent for their continued love and support.

Finally, a special thanks to all the AutoCAD users who have shared their ideas, experience, and experiments throughout the years.

Autodesk, Inc., supplied AutoCAD for the book. Synergis Technologies, Inc., Blue Bell, Pennsylvania, provided a complete SYNERGIS 386 computer workstation.

Table of Contents

Introduction

Command Reference

Appendix A

Appendix B

Appendix C

Introduction

Getting Faster Answers About AutoCAD

Whether you are a beginning AutoCAD user, a part-time user, or even a long-standing user, it is virtually impossible to remember every nuance and every option for every AutoCAD command. We have all had questions like "Can I do it this way with that command?" or "How do I get this sequence to work?" It's more important to know *where* to find information about AutoCAD commands than to remember it all. This reference guide is designed to give you fast access to AutoCAD's commands. Each command is presented alphabetically and described simply and to the point. The complexities of commands are explained with tips and warnings from experienced users.

Why This Book Is Different

This guide pulls AutoCAD commands into one easy-to-use reference that brings important information about every AutoCAD command to your fingertips. The guide is not limited to just a listing of commands and what they do. It also helps you:

□ Find commands quickly to get key descriptions,

□ Get tips and warnings that will save you time,

□ See example sequences and screen shots illustrating how to use a command,

□ Identify system variables for use with menu macros, AutoLISP, and 3D.

How to Use the AutoCAD Reference Guide

We recommend keeping the reference guide right next to your computer. Or better yet, for really fast access, put it *inside* your computer. This entire reference guide is also available as a disk (called AREF), which you can load as a help file inside AutoCAD.

To order the disk, see the New Riders Publishing order card at the back of the book. For instructions on loading the disk, turn to Appendix C.

Using the guide is simple. The commands are listed in alphabetical order. Just use the handy thumb tabs (or the Table of Contents), to help you turn to the command you want, and start reading. Related commands are cross-referenced for easy location. If you are using the AREF disk, type the command name at the AREF prompt. You get the same information on command description, menu access, prompts and options, tips, warnings, and examples that you get with the book.

How to Get Information From the AutoCAD Screen

If you are new to AutoCAD, or unfamiliar with AutoCAD's screen display, take a moment to review the information that you can get directly from AutoCAD's drawing display.

Selecting the word AutoCAD at the top of the screen always takes you back to the root menu.

Selecting the * * * * (asterisks) near the top of the screen brings up a submenu of object snap and other frequently used commands. As soon as you choose an option, you are returned to the previous screen menu.

Here are some of the other quiet but important clues given to you by AutoCAD for moving around the program. Use the numbers to locate key areas on the AutoCAD screen illustrated below

① The upper left-hand side of your monitor lists the current layer. If Ortho, Snap, or Tablet is on, you will see these words on the upper left-hand side of the monitor also.

② X,Y coordinates display the location of the crosshairs as absolute X,Y values; as a distance and angle (polar); or they can be turned off.

③ The screen menu on the right-hand side of the screen gives you access to all the AutoCAD commands.

④ The menu bar at the top of the screen is activated by the crosshairs, provided your system supports AUI. The menu bar displays pull-down menus giving you access to menu commands similar to the screen menu. Menu selections followed by ... means that dialogue boxes will appear if the command is chosen. Not all AutoCAD commands are accessed from menus.

⑤ The command prompt is at the bottom of the screen when AutoCAD is waiting for a command. If you want to repeat the last command, you can press the space bar or <ENTER> key on the keyboard.

⑥ The icon in the lower left-hand corner (called the UCSICON) orients you to the current coordinate system. It shows the direction of the X,Y axis, indicates the origin and Z axis direction, and tells you whether you are in the WCS or a UCS. This icon is replaced with an icon indicating perspective projection or parallel orientation to the display screen when appropriate.

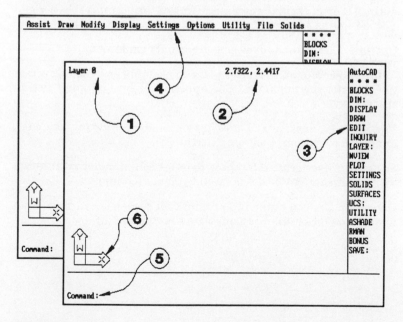

Screen

What the Guide Tells You About Each Command

We have tried to make your access to each command as straightforward as possible. Each command listing follows the same basic format:

Command name. You'll find the command names (or topics) arranged alphabetically with thumb tabs at each letter division.

Menu directions. Lists the Release 11 screen and pull-down menu selections you need to invoke the command. (Release 10 menus will look slightly different.) *Screen* refers to the screen menu on the right-hand side of the screen; *Pull down* refers to the menu bar across the top of the screen. Note: some icon menu labels are too long to print as a selection in this book. In such cases, the key word that displays in red by the icon is printed. If no screen or pull-down menu selections are possible, directions are given for using the keyboard.

Description. This is a general description of the command, including defaults.

Prompts. This section demonstrates the prompting text that AutoCAD displays in the command line at the bottom of the screen, where input is requested.

Options. The command options are briefly explained.

Related system variable(s). Lists any related or affected system variables for the command. (See Appendix B for a complete listing of system variables and their descriptions.)

Tip(s) and Warning(s). Gives key tips and warnings on using the command or options, including tips on 3D.

See also: Gives cross references to other commands that interact with or are similar to the command you are looking up.

Example. Gives a command prompt and response example or an illustration (or both) to demonstrate the command.

Quick Start Guide

If you are just beginning with AutoCAD, here are some suggestions for picking up essential information about AutoCAD from this guide.

If you want to know about:	Turn to:
An individual command	Command name
Entering drawing points	Point Entry
Pull-down menus and trivia	Appendix A
Setting drawing aids	DDRMODES (Drawing Aids)
Setting coordinate systems	UCS and WCS
Setting system variables	SETVAR and Appendix B
Using object snaps	OSNAPS
Using point filters	Point Entry and Point Filters

How the Exercises Look and Work

In our exercise format, AutoCAD's screen display text and your input are in Courier typeface on the left of the exercise. Comments and instructions are given on the right in the book's normal text font.

When you see *Pull down*, you select the indicated pull-down menu. *Screen* means to pick the menu item shown from the screen menu. The bracketed items are menu items, labels, or boxes. To select an item, highlight its label and press your mouse or digitizer pointer pick button. You can also execute commands by typing them at the keyboard and pressing <RETURN> (also known as the <ENTER> key). You'll find that AutoCAD seldom requires you to type the whole name of a cmmand. Usually, commands or options appear on the screen with the first few letters capitalized. You need only type those those key letters to execute the command.

Each exercise shows all necessary commands, prompts, and input at the left-hand side of the page. The input you need to enter as you work through the exercises is shown in boldface type. The <RETURN> is shown only when it is the sole input on the line; otherwise you should automatically press <RETURN> following any input you make.

Type input exactly as shown (followed by <RETURN>), watching carefully for the difference between the number 0 and the letter O.

The @ is the @ character, above the 2 on your keyboard. Keyboard keys are shown in angle brackets, like <RETURN>. <F9> is a function key and <^C> stands for the Control-C key combination.

Getting Started

Whether you are using the *AutoCAD Reference Guide* book or the AREF disk, there is no magic to getting started. Just look up the command you need and off you go.

AME (Advanced Modeling Extension)

A

See AMElite

AMElite (Advanced Modeling Extension LITE)

Screen **[SOLIDS] [LOAD AMElite]**
Pull down **[Solids] [Load AMElite]**

AMElite (Release 11 only) gives you limited ability to create, modify, display, and analyze solid 3D entities.

AMElite primitives consist of a box, cylinder, torus, sphere, wedge, and cone. You can extrude (add height to) or revolve (sweep about an axis) 2D entities and create your own solids. Solids can be analyzed for their physical and material properties. You can produce shaded renderings and hidden line views of solids by converting wireframe models (SOLWIRE) into surface meshes (SOLMESH) and assigning colors.

The optional AME module (Release 11 only) is a more comprehensive program giving you the ability to perform Boolean operations on solids. Although you are given the software files and documentation when you purchase AutoCAD, it is not activated with the basic AutoCAD program. Once you purchase a licensed AME, you receive a code number for unlocking the AME program files.

All the AMElite commands begin with the letters SOL. Selecting commands only available with AME results in the following message: Command requires the solid server - it's not available.

AMElite COMMANDS

SOLAREA	Calculates the surface area of a solid
SOLBOX	Creates a solid box or cube
SOLCONE	Creates a solid cone
SOLCYL	Creates a solid cylinder
SOLEXT	Extrudes 2D objects into 3D solids
SOLIDIFY	Solidifies 2D objects into 3D solids
SOLLIST	Lists solid definition information
SOLMAT	Controls material definitions used by solids
SOLMESH	Displays a solid as a mesh
SOLPURGE	Purges unused solid information
SOLREV	Revolves a polyline about an axis to create a solid
SOLSPHERE	Creates a solid sphere
SOLTORUS	Creates a solid torus or donut
SOLVAR	Maintains solid system variables
SOLWEDGE	Creates a solid wedge
SOLWIRE	Displays a solid as a wireframe

AME COMMANDS

These include all the AMElite commands plus the following:

SOLCHAM	Chamfers the edges of a solid
SOLCHP	Changes properties of a solid
SOLFEAT	Creates 2D objects from 3D model features
SOLFILL	Fillets the edges of a solid
SOLIN	Imports AutoSolid assembly files
SOLINT	Creates a new solid from the intersection of existing solids
SOLMASSP	Calculates mass properties of a solid
SOLMOVE	Moves or rotates solids according to geometric codes
SOLOUT	Outputs AutoSolid assembly files
SOLPROF	Creates a 2D profile from 3D solid models
SOLSECT	Cuts a 2D section from 3D solid models
SOLSEP	Separates composite solids
SOLSUB	Subtracts one solid from another
SOLUCS	Aligns the UCS with a solid
SOLUNION	Creates a new solid from the union of existing solids

Tips

◻ You can create elliptical solids, taper the sides of an extrusion, and perform Boolean operations with the complete AME module.

◻ AMElite remains loaded as long as AutoCAD is running, even between editing different drawings. This can lead to unnecessarily larger files even if you don't use the AMElite commands. Type the following at the command prompt to unload the AMElite executable file: XUNLOAD "AMELITE".

Warning(s)

▪ HANDLES are automatically turned on once you activate or select any AMElite function. If you aren't using AMElite solids, you should consider turning Handles off and unloading AMElite to conserve memory.

▪ The layer AME_FRZ is created as soon as you select an AMElite function.

▪ 3D objects in drawings created prior to Release 11 are represented with 3D faces and are not mathematical representations of solids.

▪ Solids included in blocks lose their solid identity. Exploding the block restores it as a solid. Issuing the SOLPURGE command's Erase option while the solid is defined in a block causes the solid to lose its identity permanently.

▪ You can use DXFOUT with files containing solids and then use DXFIN to retrieve the drawing. DXFIN works as long as there are no other entities in the drawing file. The DXFOUT Entities option cannot be used to bring solids into another drawing with DXFIN. Using the DXFOUT Entities option strips internal data required to read the solid.

See also: DXF, HANDLES, LAYER, "SOL" commands

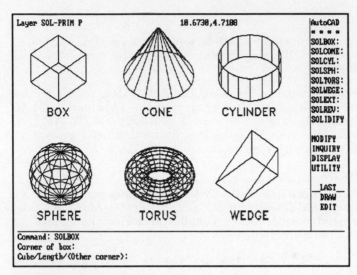

Solid Primitives Example

APERTURE

Screen **[SETTINGS] [APERTUR:]**

The APERTURE command controls the size of the target box located in the middle of the crosshairs during object snap selection. The size of the aperture box may be changed by specifying its height in pixels (1–50). A pixel is the smallest visible dot that appears on screen. The default setting is <10>.

Prompt
```
Object snap target height (1-50 pixels) <10>:
```

Related System Variable(s)
APERTURE

Tips

□ Set the default to four or six pixels for the best visibility.

□ Set the aperture and pickbox to different sizes.

Warning(s)

▪ Don't make the aperture setting so large or so small that it is difficult to pick entities.

▪ If you use a display list processing video driver, it may control the target box size. Setting the pixel height in AutoCAD may have unpredictable effects. Check your driver documentation for details.

See also: OSNAP, PICKBOX

ARC

Screen [DRAW] [ARC]
Pull down [Draw] [Arc >]

The ARC command draws any segment of a circle in one of several ways. The default draws by three points: the start, a second point, and the end.

Prompts and Options

There are eight options to the arc command. The combination of these options and the ability to continue an arc tangent to the last arc provides eleven ways to construct an arc. Prompts display the options available based on the order of the arc construction. (See examples.)

The eight options are: Start point, Second point, End point, Center, Angle, Length of chord, Radius, and Direction.

Related System Variable(s)

LASTANGLE

Tips

▢ X,Y,Z coordinates may be supplied for the first point of the arc. The Z coordinate sets the elevation for the arc.

▢ If arcs look like polygons, this may be because of a low VIEWRES setting. Regardless, the plotted output of the arcs will be smooth.

▢ Arcs are also created with the FILLET and PLINE command, or by editing a circle with BREAK or TRIM.

Warning(s)

■ All arcs, like circles, may only be constructed in the counterclockwise direction (except those created by the three-point method).

See also: FILLET, PLINE, VIEWRES

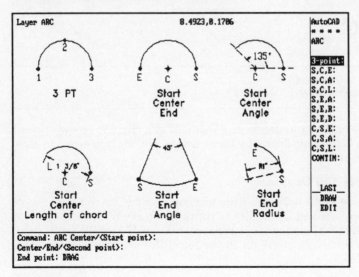

Arc Examples

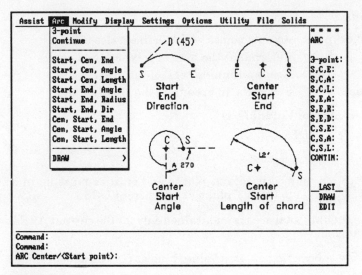

Arc Examples

AREA

Screen **[INQUIRY] [AREA:]**
Pull down **[Utility] [Area]**

The AREA command calculates the area of either an entity (circle or polyline) or a series of points that define an area. In addition to the area, the perimeter of a closed entity or the length of an open polyline is displayed. If a polyline isn't actually closed, AREA calculates the value that would result if a straight line segment passed through its two endpoints. A running total may be calculated by adding and subtracting areas. The default expects three or more points that define the area to be calculated.

Prompts

```
<First point>/Entity/Add/Subtract:
Next point:
Next point:
```

Options

First/Next point Accepts points which define a closed area.
Entity   Determines the area of polylines and circles.
Add   Keeps a running total of the area.
Subtract   Subtracts an area from the running total.

Related System Variable(s)

AREA, PERIMETER

Tips

◻ 3D points may be used, but points and entities must lie in a plane parallel to the X,Y plane of the current UCS.

◻ The running total area is maintained only for the current AREA command.

◻ Before subtracting an area value, it must first be added.

◻ An area composed of contiguous arcs and lines may be calculated by combining the entities into a polyline using the join option of the PEDIT command. If the polyline is not closed, AREA computes the polyline's area as though a straight line connected its starting and ending points.

◻ Preset OSNAP to Endpoint and Intersection when picking the boundary of an area made up of multiple entities.

See also: PEDIT (Join), LIST, DBLIST

Example

```
Command: AREA
<First point>/Entity/Add/Subtract: A
<First point>/Entity/Subtract:          Pick ①.
(ADD mode) Next point:                  Pick ②.
(ADD mode) Next point:                  Pick ③.
(ADD mode) Next point:                  Pick ④.
(ADD mode) Next point: ↵
Area = 21.44, Perimeter = 19.25
Total area = 21.44

<First point>/Entity/Subtract: S
<First point>/Entity/Add: E
(SUBTRACT mode) Select circle or polyline:
                                 Pick the rectangle.
```

```
Area = 1.53, Perimeter = 5.25
Total area = 19.91
(SUBTRACT mode) Select circle or polyline:   Pick the circle.
Area = 2.56, Circumference = 5.67
Total area = 17.35

(SUBTRACT mode) Select circle or polyline: ↵
<First point>/Entity/Add: ↵        Exit the command.
```

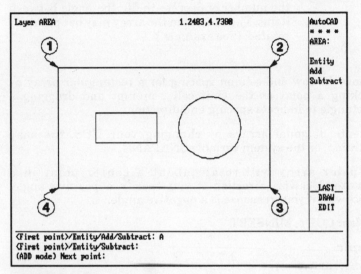

AREA Examples

ARRAY

Screen **[EDIT] [ARRAY:]**
Pull down **[Modify] [2D ARRAY]**

ARRAY copies entities in rectangular or polar (circular) patterns.

Prompt

```
Rectangular or Polar array (R/P):
```

Options

Rectangular Designate the number of rows and columns and the distance between rows and columns for a rectangular array. There must always be at least one row or one column. (See example.)

Polar Specify a center point and answer two of the following three questions: the number of items; the number of degrees to fill; the angle between items. The entities in the array may be optionally rotated. (See example.)

Tips

▫ Show the row and column spacing for a rectangular array by picking a point at the Unit cell... prompt and dragging a rectangle to indicate spacing and direction.

▫ Create diagonal arrays by changing your UCS, the snap rotation, or the system variable SNAPANG.

▫ A polar array will rotate about a center point in a counterclockwise direction if you specify a positive angle; clockwise if your response is a negative angle.

See also: COPY, MINSERT

Example

```
Command: ARRAY
Select objects:                          Select lines.
Rectangular or Polar array (R/P): R
Number of rows (---) <1>: 4
Number of columns (||||) <1>: 5
Unit cell or distance between rows (---): 20
Distance between columns (||||): 20
Command: ARRAY
Select objects:                          Select lines at ①.
Rectangular or Polar array (R/P): P
Center point of array:                   Pick point ②.
Number of items: 16
Angle to fill (+=ccw, -=cw) <360>: ↵
Rotate objects as they are copied? <Y> ↵
```

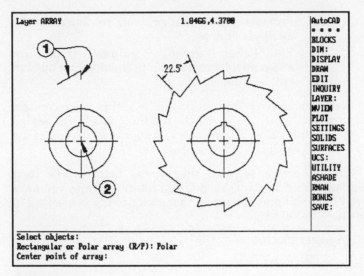

Polar Array

ATTDEF

Screen **[BLOCKS] [ATTDEF:]**
Screen **[DRAW] [ATTDEF:]**

Attributes provide you with the ability to store text data in a drawing, such as for bills of materials and schedules. ATTDEF (ATTribute DEFinition) defines how attribute text will be prompted for and stored. Attributes are saved in blocks that contain additional entities. Attribute data is specified when the block is inserted.

Prompts, Modes, and Options

Attribute modes -- Invisible:N Constant:N Verify:N
Preset:N

The following steps are necessary to create attributes:

First, define attributes with a combination of the following modes set as either Yes or No. (They default to No.)

Invisible   Controls attribute visibility.

Constant   Sets a fixed, uneditable value for the attribute.

Verify   Prompts you to confirm your responses to the
                attribute prompt.

Preset   Establishes default values that are
                automatically inserted into the drawing but can
                still be edited.

After you set the modes, you are prompted to assign a tag, create a
prompt to appear when you insert the attribute block, and assign
an optional default value. The default will appear at the end of the
prompt and will be placed in angle brackets.

Next, you are prompted with the typical text options (text
justification, insertion point, height, and rotation). Once you have
answered the text option prompts, the attribute tag is inserted in
the drawing. (See examples.)

Related System Variable(s)

AFLAGS, ATTREQ, ATTDIA

Tips

□ When creating a block with attributes, select each attribute
   individually in the order you want the prompts to appear.

□ When inserting a block with attributes, attribute prompts do
   not appear until after the normal prompts for a block insertion
   have been answered.

□ Save time by keeping the Verify option set to No. You can always
   edit the attributes after the attribute block has been inserted.

□ If you want to edit the attribute definition (ATTDEF), use the
   CHANGE, CHPROP, or DDEDIT commands before you include
   the attribute in a block.

Warning(s)

■ If you create a Constant attribute, you cannot edit it. Consider
   using Preset for greater flexibility.

■ Redefining a block with attributes causes Constant attributes
   to be lost in existing insertions unless the new block replaces
   them. The original variable attributes remain, and new variable
   attributes are ignored.

See also: ATTDIA (setvar), ATTDISP, ATTEDIT, ATTEXT,
ATTREQ (setvar), BLOCK, DDATTE, DDEDIT

Example

```
Command: ATTDEF
Attribute modes - Invisible:N Constant:N Verify:N
Preset:N
Enter (ICVP) to change, RETURN when done: ↵
Attribute tag: SIZE
Attribute prompt: What is the valve's size?
Default attribute value: 4
Justify/Style/<Start point>: C
Center point:                    Pick center of text.
Height <0.2000>: ↵
Rotation angle <0>: ↵


Command: ATTDEF
Attribute modes -- Invisible:N Constant:N Verify:N
Preset:N
Enter (ICVP) to change, RETURN when done: ↵
Attribute tag: MATERIAL
Attribute prompt: What is the valve's material?
Default attribute value: C.S.
Justify/Style/<Start point>: ↵


Command: ATTDEF
Attribute modes -- Invisible:N Constant:N Verify:N
Preset:N
Enter (ICVP) to change, RETURN when done: I
Attribute modes -- Invisible:Y Constant:N Verify:N
Preset:N
Enter (ICVP) to change, RETURN when done: P
Attribute modes -- Invisible:Y Constant:N Verify:N
Preset:Y
Enter (ICVP) to change, RETURN when done: ↵
Attribute tag: TYPE
Attribute prompt: What is the joint type?
Default attribute value: FLANGED
Justify/Style/<Start point>: ↵
Command: ATTDEF
Attribute modes -- Invisible:Y Constant:N Verify:N
Preset:Y
Enter (ICVP) to change, RETURN when done: P
Attribute modes -- Invisible:Y Constant:N Verify:N
Preset:N
Enter (ICVP) to change, RETURN when done: ↵
Attribute tag: SERVICE
Attribute prompt: What is the service?
Default attribute value: WATER
Justify/Style/<Start point>: ↵
```

Block the part and attributes, name the block VCONTROL, and make an insertion point at ①.

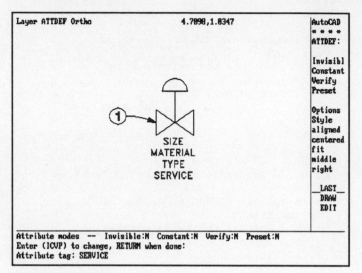

ATTDEF Example

ATTDISP

Screen **[DISPLAY] [ATTDISP:]**

ATTDISP (ATTtribute DISPlay) controls the display of all inserted attributes in the current drawing. ATTDISP overrides ATTDEF of Invisible mode. The default is <Normal> (ATTDEF).

Prompts

Normal/ON/OFF <Normal>:

Options

Normal	Displays attributes the way they are defined.
ON	Makes every attribute visible.
OFF	Makes every attribute invisible.

Related System Variable(s)

ATTMODE

Tips

▫ If you change the ATTDISP mode and REGENAUTO is off, you will need to regenerate your drawing to see the result.

▫ You may want to create all attributes as visible and control their display by placing them on different layers. Turn the layers off or freeze them if you want to have invisible attributes.

See also: ATTDEF, ATTEDIT, ATTEXT, ATTMODE (setvar), LAYER

ATTEDIT

Screen **[EDIT] [ATTEDIT:]**

ATTEDIT (ATTribute EDIT) lets you edit attributes individually, or globally if they have the same block names, tag names, or value. The default is to edit attributes one at a time. (See example.)

Prompts

```
Edit Attributes one at a time? <Y>:
Block name specification <*>:
Attribute tag specification <*>:
Attribute value specification <*>:
Select attributes:
Value/Position/Height/Angle/Style/Layer/Color/Next <N>:
```

Options

Individual   Specify the attributes to edit by their block name, attribute tag, attribute value, and selection set. If you respond with an asterisk, you can edit all attributes regardless of block name, attribute tag, and attribute value. Only attributes currently visible on the screen may be edited. You can edit the following properties:

```
Value/Position/Height/Angle/Style/Layer/
Color
```

Global   Only attribute values may be edited. You may choose to edit only those attributes visible on the screen or all the attributes regardless of visibility. A screen regeneration will be performed after the command has completed unless REGENAUTO is off. If so, you will need to wait until the drawing is regenerated or force a regeneration with the REGEN command to see the results of your editing.

Tips

▢ Edit attributes with a dialogue box by using the DDATTE command.

▢ A null attribute can be edited by supplying a backslash as the attribute value and doing a global edit.

▢ Wild-card characters "?" and "*" can be used to specify the block names, tags, and values of attributes to edit. These characters are treated literally if used within a String to change or New string prompt.

Warning(s)

■ Attributes defined as Constant cannot be edited.

■ Attribute values are case-sensitive.

See also: ATTDEF, ATTDISP, ATTEXT, DDATTE

Example

```
Command: ATTEDIT
Edit attributes one at a time? <Y> ↵
Block name specification <*>: ↵
Attribute tag specification <*>: ↵
Attribute value specification <*>: ↵
Select Attributes:          Pick attribute text.
1 attributes selected.
Value/Position/Height/Angle/Style/Layer/Color/
Next <N>: V
Change or Replace? <R>: ↵
New attribute value: 3
Value/Position/Height/Angle/Style/Layer/Color/
Next <N>: ↵
```

ATTEXT

ATTEXT (ATTribute EXTract) extracts attribute data from your drawing. This information is written to an ASCII text file in one of three possible formats, CDF, SDF, or DXF. Other programs, such as databases or spreadsheets, can read the extracted file for analysis and report generation. Either all or selected attributes can be extracted. The default format is CDF.

Prompt

CDF, SDF or DXF Attribute extract (or Entities)? <C>:

Options

The extracted data can have the following formats:

CDF	Comma Delimited Format. Extracts from the entire drawing.
SDF	Standard Format (fixed field). Extracts from the entire drawing.
DXF	Drawing Interchange Format. Extracts from the entire drawing.
Entities	Select specific entities to extract.

Tips

▫ The program you use to manipulate the extracted data will determine which format to use.

▫ In order to extract a CDF or SDF file, you must create an ASCII template file. The template file specifies the type and order of data to be extracted. Each data item is listed on its own line, specifying field name, character width, and precision for numeric fields.

▫ To have the data display on the screen, enter CON when asked for an extract file name. To send the data to a printer, specify a printer port (LPT1 or PRN) when asked for an extract file name.

▫ CDF template files can contain records to change the standard single quote and comma delimiter character to a character of your choice.

Warning(s)

- Extract file names default to the current drawing name and have the extension .TXT. Make sure you don't use the name of a file already on your hard disk.

- You will receive the error message ** Field overflow in record <number> if you don't allocate enough space for field output.

See also: ATTDEF, ATTDISP, ATTEDIT

AUDIT

Main Menu **Option 9. Recover damaged drawing**
Screen **[UTILITY] [AUDIT:]**

The AUDIT command (Release 11 only) examines a drawing's integrity, checking for errors. If executed while in the drawing editor, the errors can be automatically corrected or left uncorrected (the default). If errors are detected, recommended actions are given.

If executed from the main menu, it will automatically correct any errors. The drawing is automatically loaded into the drawing editor when this process is complete.

An ASCII report file that describes any problems and actions taken is generated. This report is in the same directory as the current drawing. Its name is the same as the drawing file with the extension .ADT.

Prompt

Fix any errors detected? <N>:

Options

No   A report is created but errors are not fixed. For each error reported, a corrective action is recommended.

Yes   A report is created and errors are fixed.

Warning(s)

■ This command only works for drawings begun with Release 11 or saved at least once within Release 11. There may be times when AUDIT will not be able to recover a corrupt drawing.

AXIS

Screen **[SETTINGS] [AXIS:]**
Pull down **[Settings] [Drawing Tools...] [Axis]**

AXIS creates ruler marks or ticks on the bottom and right side of the screen. These marks are used as visual drawing aids. The default setting is OFF with a spacing of <0.0000>.

Prompts

Tick spacing(X) or ON/OFF/Snap/Aspect <0.0000>:

Options

Tick spacing	Assigns an absolute value for the ruler spacing.
0	Sets the ruler mark spacing equal to the current snap spacing.
nX	Sets the ruler mark spacing as a multiple of the current snap spacing.
ON	Displays ruler marks.
OFF	Ruler marks are not displayed.
Snap	Sets ruler marks equal to the current snap spacing.
Aspect	Defines different horizontal and vertical tick spacing.

Related System Variable(s)

AXISMODE, AXISUNIT

Tips

□ Use the 'DDRMODES command to activate a dialogue box, change the axis value, and toggle the command on or off.

Warning(s)

■ When multiple viewports are displayed, the AXIS command is disabled and tick marks are not shown. Turn AXIS off before displaying viewports to reduce redraws.

See also: 'DDRMODES, SNAP, GRID

BASE

Screen **[BLOCKS]** **[BASE:]**

Every drawing file has a base or insertion point of 0,0,0 by default. Any drawing can be inserted into another drawing. The BASE command establishes the insertion point of the current drawing to any 2D or 3D point.

Prompt

Base point <0.0000,0.0000,0.0000>:

Related System Variable(s)

INSBASE

Tips

◻ If you need to change the insertion point of a drawing you are inserting with the INSERT command, edit the drawing directly with the BASE command rather than using WBLOCK to redefine the insertion point.

See also: BLOCK, INSERT

BLIPMODE

B

Screen **[SETTINGS] [BLIPS:]**
Pull down **[Settings] [Drawing Tools...] [Blips]**

Blips are the small temporary cross marks that appear when you enter a point or select an object. BLIPMODE controls their display. The default is <On>.

Prompt

MODE ON/OFF <On>:

Options

ON   Generates blips.
OFF   Suppresses blips.

Related System Variable(s)

BLIPMODE

Tips

◻ REDRAW, or any command like GRID that automatically creates a redraw or regeneration, will clear away blip marks.

Warning(s)

▪ You cannot OSNAP to blip marks.

See also: DDRMODES

BLOCK

Screen **[BLOCKS] [BLOCK:]**

The BLOCK command defines a group of entities as a single object within the current drawing. The INSERT command is used to place copies of blocks into a drawing. You define a block by picking entities which are deleted from the current drawing and stored as a block definition in the drawing with a name and insertion point.

Prompts

```
Block name (or ?):
Insertion base point:
Select objects:
```

Options

Block name   Up to 31 characters can be used to name a block.

?   Lists the names of blocks currently defined in the drawing in alphanumeric order. Any wild-card combinations can be used to create a more specific or partial list.

Tips

▫ Blocks can include entities on any layers with any color or linetype. Blocks created with entities on layer 0 take on the color and linetype of the layer they are inserted on. Blocks created with entities that have color or linetype set to BYBLOCK take on the current explicit color or linetype setting.

▫ Blocks can contain other blocks. There is no limit to the nesting levels.

▫ Use the EXPLODE command to convert a block back into separate entities. You cannot explode blocks that have different XYZ scale values, blocks that are inserted with a negative XYZ insertion point, or blocks that are mirrored.

▫ Use the OOPS command to restore entities erased from the display when they are copied into a block definition.

Warning(s)

■ Blocks created with multiple layers may give unexpected results when you turn layers off or freeze them.

■ You can redefine blocks by creating a block with the same name as one that already exists in the drawing. You will receive the following message:

```
Block (block name) already exists.
Redefine it? <N>:
```

If you answer Yes, any existing blocks in the drawing will globally update to the new block definition.

- When redefining blocks in your drawing, you'll need to regenerate to show the modifications.

See also: ATTDEF, EXPLODE, INSERT, REGEN, REGENAUTO, RENAME, Wild-Card Characters, WBLOCK, XREF

Example

```
Command: BLOCK
Block name (or ?): PUMP
Insertion base point:          Pick insertion point ①.
Select objects:                Select the pump entities.
```

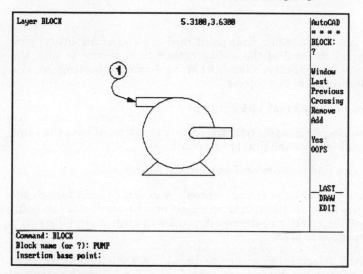

BLOCK Example

BREAK

```
Screen [EDIT] [BREAK:]
Pull down [Modify] [Break]
```

BREAK erases portions of lines, arcs, circles, 2D polylines, and traces. When you select an object to break, the default assumes your pick point is also your first break point.

Prompts

```
Select object:
Enter second point (or F for first point):
```

Options

Select object:	The pick point of your object selection is assumed to be the first break point unless you enter F for first point.
First	If you enter F, you are prompted for first and second break points. (See example.)

Tips

□ To break between a first point and the end of an entity, pick beyond the end of the entity rather than trying to pick the endpoint exactly. Use TRIM to break, starting at the intersection of two objects.

□ You can only break one entity at a time.

□ Entering @ (last point) for the second break point uses the same coordinates as the first break point.

□ Circles and arcs are broken counterclockwise.

□ Once you pick the entity to break, you don't need to touch the entity to show the actual break points. Instead, you can point near the entity and the coordinates will project onto the entity you chose to break.

□ When selecting an entity to break by a method other than picking (Window, Last, etc.), the first break point is automatically prompted for, otherwise, it is assumed to be the pick point. If more than one entity is included in the selection set, the last entity drawn is selected.

Warning(s)

■ 3D break points are projected to the X,Y plane of the current UCS. AutoCAD warns you that this may produce unexpected results. Change the UCS to the X,Y plane of the entity before executing the BREAK command.

■ You may get unexpected results when breaking closed polylines. Use the Open option of the PEDIT command.

- If you break a polyline defined with the Fit or Spline curve options of PEDIT, you cannot decurve the resulting entities.

- You can't break borders of VPORT entities.

See also: PEDIT, TRIM

Example

```
Command: BREAK
Select object:                                        Pick point ①.
Enter second point (or F for first point): F
Enter first point:                                    Pick point ②.
Enter second point:                                   Pick point ③.
Command: BREAK

Select object:                                        Pick point ④.
Enter second point (or F for first point):            Pick point ⑤.
```

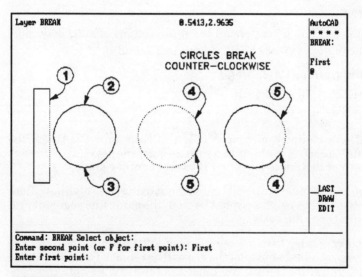

BREAK Examples

CHAMFER

Screen [EDIT] [CHAMFER:]
Pull down [Modify] [Chamfer]

CHAMFER lets you create a beveled edge for intersecting lines and contiguous segments of a 2D polyline. CHAMFER trims or extends two lines at a distance from their intersection point and creates a new line to connect the trimmed ends. It requires two distance values. The first distance value is applied to the first selected line, the second to the second line. The default for distances is 0.

Prompts

Polyline/Distances/<Select first line>:

Options

Polyline	Chamfers all the intersections of a 2D polyline.
Distance	Sets chamfer distances A and B.

Related System Variable(s)

CHAMFERA, CHAMFERB

Tips

▫ Set the chamfer distances (CHAMFERA and CHAMFERB) equal to each other to end up with a 45-degree bevel; set different chamfer distances for A and B to create other angles.

▫ You can chamfer a 2D polyline without using the Polyline option. However, the polylines must be from the same line segment and share the same vertex.

▫ If you chamfer two line segments of a 2D polyline, with an arc in between the segments, the arc will be replaced by the chamfer line. To get this effect, you must use the Polyline option.

▫ The chamfered edge resides on the layer of the picked entities as long as they share the same layer; if the two entities are on different layers, the chamfered edge is placed on the current layer. The same rules apply to color and linetype.

□   You can establish default settings by selecting [Options] - [Chamfer Distances] from the pull-down menu.

□   If you need the endpoints of two lines to meet, set the chamfer distance to 0. You can achieve the same result with the FILLET command.

Warning(s)

■   You cannot chamfer parallel lines.

■   You cannot chamfer borders of viewport entities.

■   Chamfering in plan view is more reliable than chamfering with a viewing direction oblique to the X,Y plane of the current UCS.

■   Chamfering a polyline with chamfer distances of different lengths is based on the direction the polyline was drawn.

■   Chamfering will not work if LIMITS is on and the intersection point is outside the limits.

See also: EXTEND, FILLET, PLINE, TRIM

Example

```
Command: CHAMFER
Polyline/Distances/<Select first line>: D
Enter first chamfer distance <0.0000>: .625
Enter second chamfer distance <0.0000>: .625
```

```
Command: CHAMFER
Polyline/Distances/<Select first line>:          Pick line ①.
Select second line:                              Pick line ②.
```

```
Command: CHAMFER
Polyline/Distances/<Select first line>: P
Select 2D Polyline:                              Pick polyline ③.
4 lines were chamfered
```

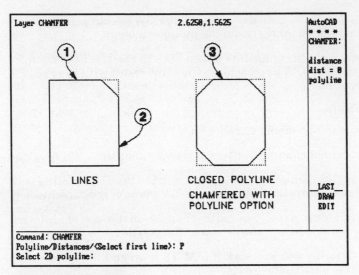

CHAMFER Examples

CHANGE

Screen [EDIT] [CHANGE:]

CHANGE lets you modify existing entities and their properties. The default is <Change point>. Once you have issued the CHANGE command, you may have to regenerate the screen to see the revisions. The CHPROP command contains the Properties option of the CHANGE command.

Prompts

```
Select objects:
Properties/<Change point>:
```

Options

Change point   Lets you redefine the location (or size) of the following entities:

Lines   Relocates the endpoints of the lines closest to the new point you specify. Having ORTHO on forces the lines horizontal or vertical to the current UCS or snap rotation.

Circle	Lets you modify the radius by picking a point to show the new circumference.
Block	Lets you relocate the block insertion point or determine a new rotation angle.
Text	Lets you relocate the text to the change point. In addition, if you type a <RETURN> at the change point prompt, you can redefine the text style, height, rotation angle, and text string.
Attribute Definition	Same as Text option, but you can also change the attribute tag, prompt, and default value.
Properties	Lets you redefine any or all of the following properties: Color, LAyer, LType, and Thickness.

Tips

□ Using CHANGE to change properties has restrictions in 2D. The CHPROP command is recommended to change properties, including 3D entities. See CHPROP for a description of these properties.

□ Change an entity's 3D elevation by MOVing the entity along the Z axis.

□ Change point is similar to TRIM and EXTEND, but it doesn't require a boundary edge and you can change the endpoints of more than one line at a time.

□ If you choose to lengthen (or shorten) a group of parallel lines, make sure ORTHO is on unless you want the lines to converge at the designated change point.

□ When using Change point, you will get unexpected results if you specify a distance and angle.

□ If you want to provide a thickness to text, created with the TEXT, DTEXT, or ATTDEF commands, you must use the CHANGE command.

□ It is easier and faster to use the DDEDIT command to modify attributes and text strings.

Warning(s)

■ Assigning a thickness to the following entities will have no effect: 3D faces, 3D polylines, polygon meshes, and dimensions.

- If you modify an attribute definition, existing attributes will not inherit the changes.

See also: CHPROP, COLOR, DDEDIT, DTEXT, EXPLODE, EXTEND, LAYER, LINETYPE, REGEN, REGENAUTO, STYLE, TEXT, THICKNESS, TRIM

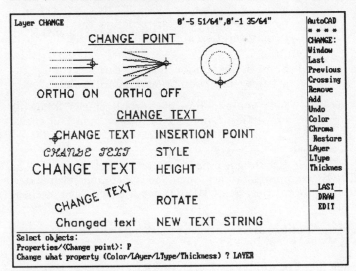

CHANGE Examples

CHPROP

Screen **[EDIT] [CHPROP:]**

You use CHPROP to redefine properties associated with existing entities. CHPROP does not include the Change point and text modification options of the CHANGE command. We recommend using CHPROP instead of CHANGE to change entity properties.

Prompts

```
Select objects:
Change what property (Color/LAyer/LType/Thickness) ?
```

Options

Color   Assigns a color to an entity regardless of the layer it resides on.

LType   Assigns a linetype to an entity regardless of the layer it resides on.

LAyer   Moves an entity from one layer to another.

Thickness   Assigns an extrusion thickness to an entity.

Tips

□ If you need to enter entities on a different layer from the one you're drawing on, you may find it quicker to stay on your current layer and use CHPROP to change the entities later. This also applies to redefining color and linetype.

See also: CHANGE

CIRCLE

Screen **[DRAW] [CIRCLE]**
Pull down **[Draw] [Circle >]**

The CIRCLE command is used to draw circles. The default settings are <Center point> and <Radius>. If DRAGMODE is on or set to AUTO, you can pick the size of the circle by dragging it on the screen.

Prompts

3P/2P/TTR/<Center point>:
Diameter/<Radius>:

Options

Center point   Specify the center point.

Diameter   Specify the diameter by inputting a value or picking two points.

Radius   Specify the radius by inputting a value or picking two points.

3P   Specify three points on the circumference.

2P   Specify two points to indicate the diameter.

TTR   Specify two points (on a line, circle, or arc) that will be tangent to the circle, then specify a radius.

Tips

□ Circles that are offset share the same center point, but the radius is changed based on the offset distance.

□ To create a solid filled circle, use the DONUT command and set the inside radius to 0.

□ To draw circles in an isometric plane, use the ELLIPSE Isocircle option.

□ You can modify the size of an existing circle with the CHANGE or SCALE commands.

□ Circles are treated as a solid face by the HIDE command when you create 3D displays.

□ If your circles look like polygons, it may be caused by setting VIEWRES to a low number.

Warning(s)

■ When using the BREAK command, the deleted portion of a circle is determined by the order of your pick points. Circles break in a counterclockwise direction.

See also: DONUT, ELLIPSE, VIEWRES

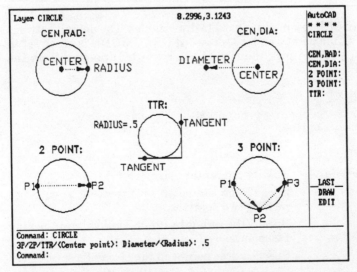

CIRCLE Option Examples

COLOR

The COLOR command controls the color of new entities, overriding the default layer color. The default is <BYLAYER>. To change the color of existing entities, use the CHPROP command. To control layer colors, use the LAYER command. To set a new color, respond with a color number or name. You also can set your entity color using the 'DDEMODES dialogue box. (See example.)

Prompt

New entity color <BYLAYER>:

Options

BYLAYER   New entities inherit the color assigned to the layer upon which they reside.

BYBLOCK   New entities are drawn in white until they are saved as a block. When the block is inserted, it inherits the color value set by the color command.

Color number or name

New entities are assigned a specific color when you enter the color's name or the corresponding number at the prompt. Each color has a standard number assignment:

1 = Red	5 = Blue
2 = Yellow	6 = Magenta
3 = Green	7 = White
4 = Cyan	

You can have up to 255 color assignments depending on your graphics card.

Related System Variable(s)

CECOLOR

Tips

▫ To access colors from 8 to 255, you must refer to the number assignment and not the color name. If you are using the dialogue box, enter the color number in the color code box.

▫ You can obtain multiple line weights, linetypes, and color plots by assigning colors from your drawing to different pens on your output device. Even if you use a monochrome monitor, you won't see the colors, but the plotter will acknowledge the color assignment.

Warning(s)

■ Mixing colors on a single layer can become confusing. Using the layer command to control color and leaving the color command set to BYLAYER helps you identify the layer an entity is on and makes changing entity color a simple process of redefining the color with the LAYER command.

See also: CHANGE, CHPROP, 'DDEMODES, LAYER, PLOT

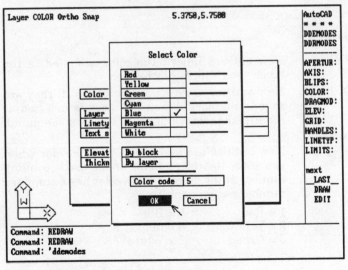

Using 'DDEMODES to Set Color

Coordinate Entry   See Point Entry

COPY

Screen **[EDIT] [COPY:]**
Pull down **[Modify] [Copy]**

COPY creates a replica of an entity. The command uses standard object selection. The original entity or selection set remains unchanged.

Prompts

```
Select objects:
<Base point or displacement>/Multiple:
Second point of displacement:
```

Options

Base point   Determines a point of reference. Think in terms of "From Where." After you locate your reference point, you can drag your object(s) to the new location at the Second point prompt.

Displacement   Enter the distance for X,Y,Z and enter a <RETURN> at the Second point prompt.

Multiple   Copy an entity more than one time by giving a designated reference point and responding to the Second point prompts. Enter a <RETURN> to end. (See example.)

Tips

▫ To copy in 3D space, use X,Y,Z points or displacement.

▫ Use osnaps on intersections, center points, or other logical locations to set the base point.

▫ Your base and second point do not need to be on or near the selection set.

▫ Use array for multiple copies of equally spaced entities.

▫ For multiple copies of complex entities, first block the selection set, then insert and copy. This reduces the drawing size and gives greater flexibility for future global revisions.

Warning(s)

- You cannot change the size or rotation angle of the copy.

- If you accidentally press <RETURN> at the Second point prompt, your copy may end up out in space. This happens because it is using the X,Y,Z base point as the displacement.

See also: ARRAY, BLOCK, MINSERT, MOVE, OFFSET, SELECTION SETS

Example

```
Command: COPY
Select objects:                              Select entities to copy.
Base point or displacement/Multiple: M
Multiple Base point:                         Pick point ①.
Second point of displacement: @2<90
Second point of displacement: @2<0
Second point of displacement: @2,2
Second point of displacement:
```

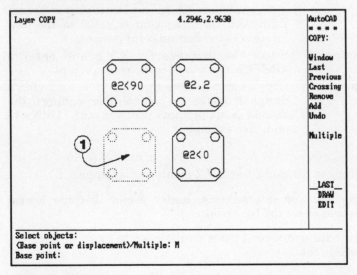

COPY Examples

DBLIST   See LIST   D

DDATTE

Screen **[EDIT]** **[DDATTE:]**

DDATTE (Dynamic Dialogue ATTribute Edit) lets you edit attribute string values with a dialogue box. You can only edit one block at a time.

Related System Variable(s)

ATTDIA

Tips

◻ Enter MULTIPLE DDATTE if you wish to edit more than one block containing attribute information. Use cancel to end the command.

◻ ATTDIA lets you use the dialogue box at the point of insertion if ATTDIA is set to 1.

◻ To globally edit attribute values, use ATTEDIT to change position, height, angle, style, layer, and color.

Warning(s)

■ Not all graphic card drivers have the ability to display dialogue boxes.

See also: ATTEDIT, DIALOGUE BOXES, MULTIPLE

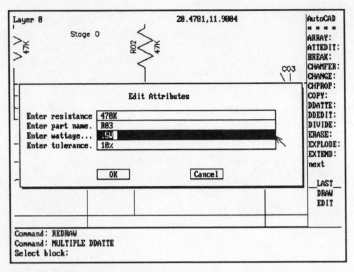

DDATTE Dialogue Box Example

DDEDIT

Screen **[EDIT] [DDEDIT:]**

The DDEDIT (Dynamic Dialogue EDIT) command (Release 11 only) lets you edit text strings and attribute definitions. This only works for displays that support the Advanced User Interface (AUI). The command repeats until you press <^C> (the control key and C) or the <Cancel> or <Return> key one extra time.

Prompt

<Select a TEXT or ATTDEF object>/Undo:

Options

Select a TEXT or ATTDEF object

Selecting text lets you edit the text string; selecting an attribute definition lets you modify the tag, prompt, and default values.

Undo   At the Select a TEXT or ATTDEF object prompt, you can undo the last modified text string and return to the previous value. Once you end the command, the Undo will undo every modification within the command.

Tips

▫ In addition to picking a text string or attribute definition, you can also use the selection set option, Last.

▫ Use DDATTE to edit attribute values in a block.

See also: CHANGE, DIALOGUE BOXES

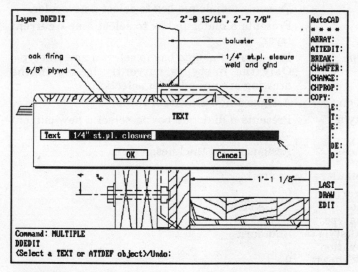

DDEDIT Dialogue Box Example

DDEMODES

Screen **[SETTINGS] [DDEMODES]**
Pull down **[Options] [Entity Creation...]**

The DDEMODES (Dynamic Dialogue Entity creation MODES) dialogue box shows the current settings for Layer, Color, Linetype, Text style, Elevation, and Thickness. You can change any of these variables. Layer, Color, Linetype, and Text style present another dialogue box when selected.

Options

Color	Presents a dialogue box to select a new color.
Layer	Presents a dialogue box to select a new current layer.
Linetype	Presents a dialogue box to select a new linetype. Only the linetypes currently loaded in the drawing are provided for selection.
Elevation	Assigns a new elevation value.
Text style	Presents a dialogue box to select a new current text style.
Thickness	Assigns a new thickness value.

The default settings are:

Layer	0
Color	BYLAYER
Linetype	BYLAYER
Text style	Standard
Elevation	0
Thickness	0

Related System Variable(s)

CECOLOR, CELTYPE, CLAYER, TEXTSTYLE, ELEVATION, THICKNESS

Tips

▫ If you need to enter entities on another layer or change the color, linetype, text style, elevation, or thickness, you may find it quicker to stay on your current layer and edit the entities using CHANGE or CHPROP.

□ DDEMODES can be extended transparently by entering 'DDEMODES within another command.

Warning(s)

■ If you activate the dialogue box while in another command, the changes will take place once you complete the initial command.

■ Only linetypes that have previously been loaded can be accessed through the dialogue boxes.

■ Not all graphic card drivers have the ability to display dialogue boxes.

See also: COLOR, DIALOGUE BOXES, ELEVATION, LAYER, LINETYPE, STYLE, THICKNESS, Transparent Commands

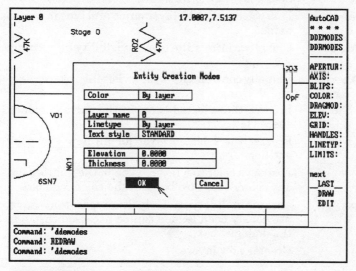

DDEMODES Dialogue Box Example

DDLMODES

Screen **[LAYER:]** **[DDLMODES]**
Pull down **[Settings]** **[Layer Control...]**

DDLMODES (Dynamic Dialogue Layer MODES) presents a dialogue box to control layer options. The options allow you to set the current layer, create new layers, rename layers, and modify layer properties.

Options

Current	Sets a layer as the default.
Rename	Lets you highlight a layer name and type in a new name.
GLOBAL ON	Globally controls the layer's visibility by turning it on and off.
GLOBAL Frz	Globally controls the layer's visibility by freezing and thawing.
VP Frz Cur	Freezes the selected layer in the current model space viewport.
VP Frz New	Freezes the selected layer for all new viewport entities.
Color	Assigns a color to a layer. Type in the number for any colors over number 7 in the color code box.
Linetype	Assigns a linetype. Only linetypes that have previously been loaded can be accessed through the dialogue box.
New layer	Creates new layers.

The default settings are:

Layer	0
Color	White
Linetype	Continuous
On	
Thaw	

Related System Variable(s)

CECOLOR, CELTYPE, CLAYER, TILEMODE

Tips

▫ The LAYER options from the screen menu offer a greater amount of flexibility than the dialogue box.

▫ DDLMODES can be executed transparently by entering 'DDLMODES within another command.

Warning(s)

▪ If you activate the dialogue box while in another command, the changes will not take place until you complete the initial command.

▪ Only linetypes that have previously been loaded can be accessed through the dialogue box.

▪ Not all graphic card drivers have the ability to display dialogue boxes.

▪ Viewport Freeze Current and Viewport Freeze New only work if TILEMODE is off.

See also: COLOR, DIALOGUE BOXES, LAYER, LINETYPE, RENAME, Transparent Commands, VPLAYER

```
Layer OBJECT                          0.0113,0.0152              |AutoCAD

                              Layer Control

                        Global  VP Frz
          Current  Layer name  On Frz  Cur New    Color      Linetype
                   0              ✓               7 white    CONTINUOUS    △
                   CENTERLINE     ✓               3 green    CENTER
                   DIMENSION      ✓               2 yellow   CONTINUOUS
                   HIDDEN         ✓               1 red      HIDDEN
          ✓        OBJECT         ✓               5 blue     CONTINUOUS
                                                                          S

                                                                          S

                                                                          ▽
              New layer  TEXT                          Cancel  OK

                    OK                         Cancel


'ddlmodes
Command: REDRAW
Command: 'ddlmodes
```

DDLMODES Dialogue Box Example

DDRMODES

Screen **[SETTINGS] [DDRMODES]**
Pull down **[Settings] [Drawing Tools...]**

DDRMODES (Dynamic Dialogue Drawing MODES) controls the settings of drawing aids such as Snap, Grid, Axis, and Isometric mode.

Options

The default settings are:

Snap	OFF	1.0
Snap Angle	0	
Grid	OFF	0
Axis	OFF	0
Ortho	OFF	
Blips	OFF	
Isoplane	LEFT	
Isometric	OFF	

Related System Variable(s)

AXISMODE, AXISUNIT, BLIPMODE, COORDS, GRIDMODE, GRIDUNIT, ORTHOMODE, SNAPANG, SNAPISOPAIR, SNAPBASE, SNAPMODE, SNAPSTYL, SNAPUNIT

Tips

◻ When setting the X value for Snap, Grid, and Axis, the Y defaults to the X value. To create a different Y value or aspect, set the X value and then set the Y. This is the same as using the Aspect option.

◻ It is faster to use control keys and function keys to toggle settings on and off and change isoplanes.

◻ DDRMODES can be executed transparently by entering 'DDRMODES within another command.

Warning(s)

■ If you activate the dialogue box while in another command, some changes will not take place until you complete the initial command.

- Not all graphic card drivers have the ability to display dialogue boxes.

See also: AXIS, BLIPMODE, DIALOGUE BOXES, GRID, ORTHO, SNAP, Transparent Commands

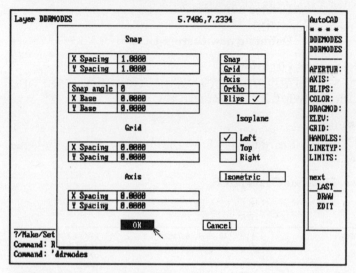

'DDRMODES Dialogue Box Example

DDUCS

Screen **[UCS:]** **[DDUCS:]**
Pull down **[Settings]** **[UCS Control...]**

DDUCS (Dynamic Dialogue User Coordinate System) displays dialogue boxes to create, modify, and control user coordinate systems. The default UCS is the *WORLD* UCS.

Options

Current	Sets the UCS to be currently in effect.
UCS Name	Lets you rename an existing UCS by typing over an existing UCS name.
WORLD	Sets to the World Coordinate System (WCS).

PREVIOUS   Returns to the previous coordinate system.

NO NAME   Displays if the current UCS is unnamed.

List   Displays the UCS's origin and the direction of its X,Y,Z axes.

Delete   Deletes named UCS.

Define new current UCS
      Defines a new current UCS.

Related System Variable(s)

UCSFOLLOW, UCSICON, UCSNAME, UCSORG, UCSXDIR, UCSYDIR, VIEWMODE, WORLDUCS

Warning(s)

- Not all graphic card drivers have the ability to display dialogue boxes.

See also: Dialogue Boxes, UCS

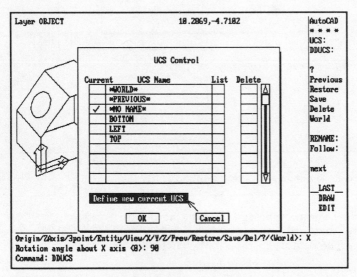

DDUCS Dialogue Box Example 1

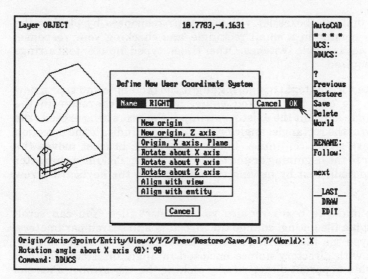

DDUOS Dialogue Box Example 2

DELAY   See SCRIPT

Dialogue Boxes

Dialogue boxes are an enhancement to the keyboard, tablet, pull-down, and screen menus. They provide alternative methods for editing and managing your drawing. All the commands that initiate a dialogue box begin with DD (Dynamic Dialogue). Dialogue boxes are only available on displays supporting the Advanced User Interface (AUI).

When working with dialogue boxes, the screen cursor turns into an arrow pointing up and to the left. Pressing <RETURN> has the same effect as picking the OK box. Pressing <^C> or the <Escape> key has the same effect as picking the Cancel box.

Some dialogue boxes have scroll or slider bars. These let you scroll through lists of items, usually file names. You can move the arrow cursor to scroll one line at a time, one page at a time, or you can dynamically drag the slider box. You can tell whether you are near the beginning, middle, or end of scrolling by the relative location of the slider box.

Most dialogue boxes let you pick your responses by placing the arrow pointer in a small rectangle and checking your response; these act as toggle switches. Other times, typed input or text strings are required.

To enter or edit text strings, highlight the rectangle and type a new value. To edit the existing value, point to a character in the rectangle and edit the existing string. If the text string exceeds the length of the rectangle, angle brackets (< or >) indicate the direction the text string continues. Picking the angle bracket moves the cursor to the beginning or end of the text string. Picking a character lets you edit text by moving the cursor with the keyboard arrow keys.

Some dialogue boxes require you to select files. You can scroll through a file listing, change the directory and search parameters, and type the file name. File lists are displayed in alphanumeric order with directory names enclosed in angle brackets. You can backstep to parent directories by picking the <..> symbol. Pick the Type it button when you want to manually enter the file name. Use the Default button to return to the original dialogue box selection. You can pick the OK button or press <RETURN> to exit the command, or pick the Cancel button or press <^C> to cancel.

Commands that request file names include: ATTEXT, DXBIN, DXFIN, DXFOUT, FILMROLL, IGESIN, IGESOUT, LINETYPE, LOAD, MENU, MSLIDE, SAVE, SCRIPT, STYLE, VSLIDE, and WBLOCK.

You can disable file dialogue boxes by setting the system variable FILEDIA to 0. Commands will then accept file names entered on the command line. You can selectively enable a dialogue box by entering the tilde character (~) when prompted for a file name.

Options

DDATTE	(Dynamic Dialogue ATTribute Edit) lets you edit attributes.
DDEDIT	(Dynamic Dialogue EDIT) edits attribute definitions and text strings.
DDEMODES	(Dynamic Dialogue Entity MODES) sets properties for layer, color, linetype, text style, elevation, and thickness.
DDLMODES	(Dynamic Dialogue Layer MODES) creates and modifies layers.

DDRMODES   (Dynamic Dialogue dRawing MODES) controls drawing aids.

DDUCS   (Dynamic Dialogue User Coordinate System) creates and modifies UCS settings.

Related System Variable(s)

ATTDIA, FILEDIA, MAXSORT

Warnings

- AutoCAD interprets all the changes made while a dialogue box is active as one command. Therefore, if you use UNDO, you will lose any changes that were made while in the dialogue box.

See also: DDEMODES, DDLMODES, DDRMODES, DDATTE, DDUCS, DDEDIT.

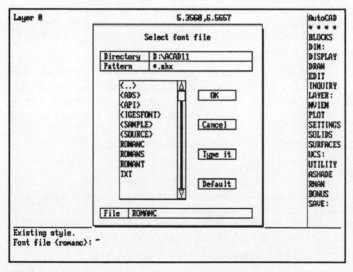

Dialogue Box Example

DIM / DIM1

Screen **[DIM:]**
Pull down **[Draw] [Dim...]**

The DIM command activates the dimensioning mode. The command prompt changes to DIM:, and only the commands associated with dimensioning mode are active. DIM1 activates dimensioning mode for a single command and returns you to the regular command prompt.

Dimensioning commands automatically construct the appropriate dimension lines, arrow or tick marks, extension lines, and dimension text to dimension drawings.

Prompts

DIM: *or* DIM1:

Dimensioning Commands

Dimensioning commands are grouped into four major categories: construction, edit, style (Release 11 only), and utility. These categories are supported by 42 dimension variables whose values you can set to control dimension appearance. You can save groups of variable settings for different dimension style with unique names. You retrieve these variable settings with the DIM: RESTore command.

The following is a breakdown of the four dimensioning command categories. In dimensioning mode, as in the regular command mode, you can abbreviate each command to one, two, or three characters (the fewest characters that are unique to that command). The individual entries in the following pages capitalize the letters you need to type to invoke the dimensioning commands.

Construction	ANgular; Leader; linear (ALigned, Baseline, COntinue, HORizontal, ROtated, VErtical); ORdinate; radial (CEnter, Diameter, RAdius)
Edit	HOMetext, Newtext, OBlique, TEdit, TRotate, UPdate
Style	OVerride, REStore, SAve, VAriables, ?
Utility	dimension variables, Exit, REDraw, STAtus, STYle, Undo

Dimensioning Command Prompts

The typical prompts and options associated with dimensioning commands are described below.

First extension line origin or RETURN to select:
>You can dimension a distance either manually by picking points, or automatically by selecting an object. If you pick a point, it will be used as the origin for the first extension line and you will be prompted for the second extension's origin point. If you press <RETURN>, a new prompt will appear.

Select line, arc, or circle:
>Selecting the appropriate entity will automatically generate extension lines.

Dimension line location:
>Allows you to specify a dimension line location by picking a point for the dimension line to pass through.

Dimension text <value>
>The correct measured dimension text is shown as the default at the text prompt. You accept the automatic dimension text in brackets by pressing <RETURN>, or you can type in another value. If you want to leave the dimension text blank, press the space bar and then <RETURN>.
>
>If you wish to enter text in addition to the default value, enter the text and include brackets at the appropriate location, for example:
>
><> YOUR TEXT or YOUR TEXT <> MORE TEXT

Related System Variable(s)

See Dimension Variables.

Tips

▫ If you select a polyline for linear dimensioning, AutoCAD will treat the polyline segment as if it were a line entity.

▫ A polyline with a width will be dimensioned from its centerline.

▫ Dimension text is based on the current UNITS setting and the current text style.

▫ If the dimension line and text don't fit inside the extension lines (based on AutoCAD's internal programming parameters), dimension lines and text will be placed on the outside of the extension lines. The dimension text placement is based on the second extension line pick point. If you select an object to dimension, the placement is to the side farthest from the pick point.

▫ Dimensioning in model space gives you greater flexibility than dimensioning in paper space. Dimensions in paper space are not associative to entities created in model space.

Warning(s)

■ Verify the dimension variables (especially DIMASO) before dimensioning your drawing. You can do this by using the STAtus command at the DIM: prompt.

■ Dimension text will not work properly if your current text STYLE is set to a vertical orientation.

■ Dimension text height is determined by the variable DIMTXT. However, if your current text STYLE has a preset height, this will override the DIMTXT setting.

See also: Dimension Variables

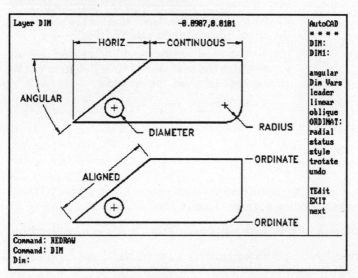

Dimension Category Examples

DIM ALigned

Screen **[DIM:] [linear] [aligned]**
Pull down **[Draw] [Dim...] [Linear] [Aligned]**

ALigned is an option of LINEAR dimensioning. It draws the dimension line parallel to the extension line origin points or to a selected entity.

Prompt

First extension line origin or RETURN to select:

Pick the first and second extension line origins, or press <RETURN> and pick a line, polyline, circle or arc to dimension.

Example

Dim: **AL**
First extension line origin or RETURN to select: ◢
Select line, arc, or circle: Point ①.
Dimension line location: Point ②.
Dimension text <2.0156>: ◢

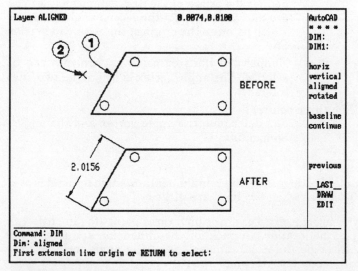

DIM ALigned Example

DIM ANgular

Screen [DIM:] [angular]
Pull down [Draw] [Dim...] [Angular]

ANgular dimensions angles. There are three ways to show angular
dimensions: pick two nonparallel lines; pick an arc or circle and
another point; or pick three points.

Prompt

Select arc, circle, line, or RETURN:

Options

arc
: The center of the arc is considered the angle
vertex, and the endpoints become the origin
points for the extension lines. You determine the
location for the dimension arc and the dimension
text.

circle
: The center of the circle is considered the vertex
of the angle. The point used to pick the circle
defines the origin of the first extension line. You
are then prompted for the second angle endpoint,
which becomes the origin of the second extension
line.

line
: Nonparallel lines or polyline segments can be
selected. The angle vertex is where the two lines
intersect.

RETURN (three points)
: You determine the angle vertex and the angle's
endpoints.

Tips

▢   AutoCAD dimensions the complementary angle for angles over
180 degrees when two lines are picked.

▢   If you select a circle or arc or pick three points to dimension an
angle, the location you pick for the dimension arc determines
which angle AutoCAD dimensions — the angle including the
location point, or its complement.

◻ If you press <RETURN> at the text location prompt, the dimension text is automatically centered within the dimension arc. If you pick a point and want to place it in the center later, use the HOMetext command.

Example

```
Dim: AN
Select first line:                      Point①.
Second line:                            Point②.
Enter dimension line arc location:      Point③.
Dimension text <54>: ↵
Enter text location: ↵
```

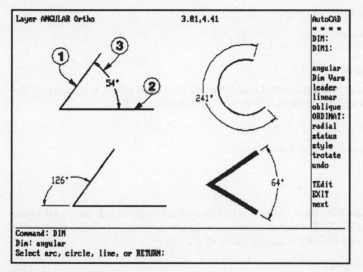

DIM ANgular Example

DIM Baseline

Screen **[DIM:]** **[linear]** **[baseline]**
Pull down **[Draw]** **[Dim...]** **[Linear]** **[Baseline]**

Baseline dimensions multiple distances measured from a common reference point. Once you have created the first linear dimension, select the Baseline command to dimension the rest of the distances. Each dimension will be offset from the last using the same first extension line. You provide the second extension line origin point.

Prompts

```
Second extension line origin:
Dimension text <4.1250>:
```

Options

The Baseline command can be used in conjunction with any of the following linear dimensioning commands:

```
ALigned, HORizontal, ROtated, VErtical
```

Related System Variable(s)

DIMDLI

Tips

▢   Once you have selected the Baseline command, you can press <RETURN> to pick successive second extension line origins and accept default dimension text values.

Warning(s)

▪   The UPdate command will not modify existing baseline dimension offsets if DIMDLI is changed.

See also: DIM: COntinue

Example

Draw a linear dimension.

```
Dim: B
Second extension line origin:          Point ①.
Dimension text <4.1250>: ↵
Dim: ↵
BASE
Second extension line origin:          Point ②.
Dimension text <5.7500>: ↵
```

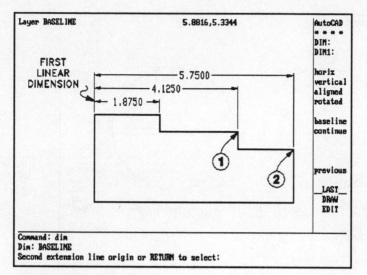

DIM Baseline Example

DIM CEnter

Screen **[DIM:] [radial] [center]**
Pull down **[Draw] [Dim...]**
Click center mark icon

The CEnter command constructs a dimensioning center mark or center lines for circles and arcs.

Related System Variable(s)
DIMCEN

Tips

□   The Diameter and RAdius commands will automatically draw center marks if DIMCEN has a value other than 0.

□   DIMCEN will construct tick marks inside circles and arcs if set to a positive value; a negative value will construct center lines that extend outside the diameter; and 0 will omit any marks.

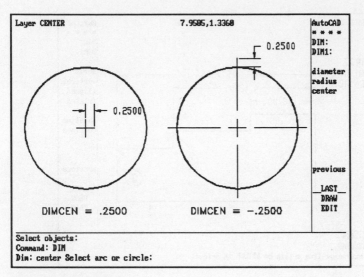

DIM CEnter Example

DIM COntinue

Screen **[DIM:] [linear] [continue]**
Pull down **[Draw] [Dim...] [Linear] [Continue]**

Continuous dimensioning refers to dimensions measured from the last extension line origin of the previous linear dimension. Once you have created the first linear dimension, select the COntinue option to dimension from. Each dimension line will be drawn aligned with the last. If the dimension text does not fit, the dimension line will be placed outside the dimension. All you provide is the second extension point.

Prompts

```
Second extension line origin:
Dimension text <2.2500>:
```

Options

Continuous dimensioning is used in conjunction with any of the linear dimensioning commands:

```
ALigned, HORizontal, ROtated, VErtical
```

Related System Variable(s)

DIMDLI

Tips

□ Once you have selected the COntinue option, you can press <RETURN> to repeat the command.

Warning(s)

■ The UPdate command will not modify existing continuous dimensions if the DIMDLI value is changed.

See also: DIM: Baseline

Example

Draw a linear dimension.

```
Dim: CO
Second extension line origin:          Point ①.
Dimension text <2.2500>: ↵
Dim: ↵
Second extension line origin:          Point ②.
Dimension text <1.6250>: ↵
```

```
Layer CONTINUO              5.5999,5.3143        AutoCAD
                                                 * * * *
                                                 DIM:
                                                 DIM1:
    FIRST
    LINEAR                                       horiz
    DIMENSION                                    vertical
          ┌─  1.8750 ─┼─  2.2500 ─┼─ 1.6250 ─┤   aligned
                                                 rotated

                                                 baseline
                                                 continue


                         ①
                                                 previous
                              ②
                                                 _LAST_
                                                 DRAW
                                                 EDIT

Command: dim
Dim: CONTINUE
Second extension line origin or RETURN to select:
```

DIM COntinue Example

DIM Diameter

Screen [DIM:] [radial] [diameter]
Pull down [Draw] [Dim...] [Diameter]

Diameter dimensions circles and arcs. By changing the values of the dimension variables DIMTIX, DIMTOFL, and DIMCEN, you can portray different dimensioning styles.

Prompt

Select arc or circle:

Related System Variable(s)

DIMCEN

Tips

▫ The pick point for entity selection determines the beginning of the dimension line or leader line.

▫ Leader lines are always at least the length of two arrowheads. If the angle of the leader line is greater than 15 degrees from the horizontal and the text is drawn horizontally, a short horizontal leader extension line (the length of an arrowhead) is drawn next to the dimension text.

▫ DIMCEN will construct tick marks inside circles and arcs, if set to a positive value ; a negative value will construct center lines that extend outside the diameter; and 0 will omit any marks. This variable is active only if the dimension line is placed outside the arc or circle.

▫ If DIMTIX is off, the dimension text is drawn outside the arc or circle with a leader.

▫ If DIMTOFL is on, a dimension line is drawn between the extension lines.

Example

Dim: **D**
Select arc or circle: Point ①.
Dimension text <2.000>: ↵

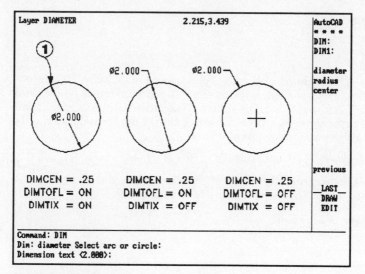

DIM Diameter Example

DIM Exit

Screen **[DIM:]** **[EXIT]**
Pull down Any **[Exit]** *label*

Exit will return you from dimensioning mode to the command prompt (or you can press <^C> to cancel).

DIM HOMetext

Screen **[DIM:]** **[next]** **[HOMETEXT]**
Pull down **[Draw]** **[Dim...]** **[Edit Dim...]** **[Home]**

HOMetext moves associative dimension text to its original location if you have used TEdit or changed dimension variables and updated dimensions.

Prompt

```
Select objects:
```

Tips

▫ The TEdit Home option is the same as using the HOMetext option. Both of these options place the dimension at its original rotation angle. The HOMetext option can manipulate more than one dimension at a time, whereas the TEdit Home option only modifies one dimension at a time.

Warning(s)

■ This command only works if the dimension you are editing is associative (DIMASO on) and is not exploded.

See also: DIM: TEdit

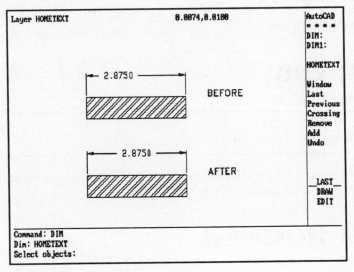

DIM HOMetext Example

DIM HORizontal

Screen [DIM:] [linear] [horiz]
Pull down [Draw] [Dim...] [Linear] [Horizontal]

HORizontal is an option of LINEAR dimensioning. It draws the dimension line horizontally. You can pick the first and second extension line origins, or you can press <RETURN> and then pick the entity to dimension.

Prompt

First extension line origin or RETURN to select:

Tips

▫ If you use a circle, the diameter is dimensioned. The quadrants at 0 and 180 degrees are considered the two endpoints for the extension lines. Other entities are dimensioned between their endpoints.

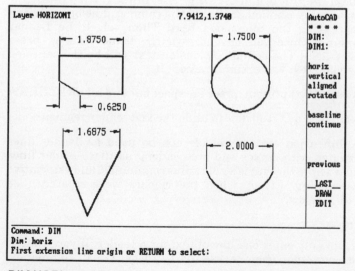

DIM HORizontal Example

DIM LEAder

Screen [DIM:] [leader]
Pull down [Draw] [Dim...] [Leader]

Leader, made up of an arrowhead, lines, and text, is used to dimension complex areas or add reference notes. Leaders are drawn from the point of the arrowhead to where you want the dimension text or notes to be placed.

Prompts

Leader start:
To point:
Dimension text <1.3750>:

Tips

□ Leader uses the latest dimension text value as its default value. To dimension an object but place the dimension text with a leader, begin dimensioning the object with another dimensioning command. Cancel the command before entering or accepting the dimension text. Then select the Leader command. Once you have drawn the leader line(s), press <RETURN>. The default dimension text will be the canceled dimension text value; simply accept it.

□ To have no text present, press the space bar and hit <RETURN>.

□ You can use a U response to undo the last leader segment.

□ The dimension edit commands can be used for leader lines associated with circles and arcs as long as those leader lines resulted from the diameter or radius commands, and associative dimensioning was on when the leaders were created. (See warning below.)

Warning(s)

■ You can only enter one line of text for a leader. If you want to enter more than one line, use the TEXT or DTEXT command.

■ If the leader length for the first segment is less than two arrow lengths long, the arrowhead will not be drawn.

■ Dimension edit commands do not work for any dimensions entered by the Leader command.

Example

Create a diameter dimension on a circle and cancel after the dimension text prompt.

Dim: **L**	
Leader start:	Point ①.
To point:	Point ②.
To point: ↵	
Dimension text <1.3750>: ↵	Accept the value from the diameter dimension.

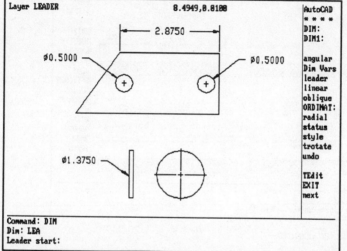

DIM LEAder Example

DIM Newtext

Screen **[DIM:] [next] [NEWTEXT]**
Pull down **[Draw] [Dim...] [Edit Dim...] [Text]**

Newtext lets you revise associative dimension text. Pressing <RETURN> will return dimension text to its default value. If you wish to enter text in addition to the measured value, enter the text and include <> brackets at the appropriate location to represent the default dimension text.

Prompt

Enter new dimension text:

Warning(s)

■ This feature only works if the dimension you are editing is associative (DIMASO on) and was not exploded.

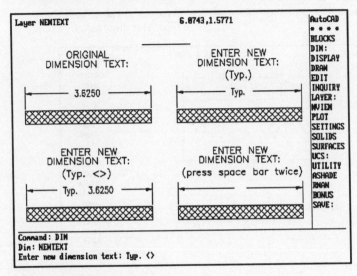

DIM Newtext Example

DIM OBlique

Screen **[DIM:] [oblique]**
Pull down **[Draw] [Dim...] [Edit Dim...] [OBLIQUE]**

OBlique lets you redefine the angle of existing dimension extension lines without altering the dimension value. If you enter a <RETURN> without specifying an angle, the extension lines return to their original angle.

Prompts

```
Select objects:
Enter obliquing angle (RETURN for none):
```

Tips

▫ Use to reposition dimensions that interfere with other entities.

Warning(s)

▪ OBlique only works if the dimension you are editing is associative (DIMASO on) and was not exploded.

DIM ORdinate

```
Screen [DIM:] [ORDINAT:] [Xdatum] or [Ydatum]
Pull down [Draw] [Dim...] [Ordinate] [Xdatum],
[YDATUM], or [Automatic]
```

ORdinate (datum) dimensioning (Release 11 only) lets you dimension individual X and Y distances from a common origin 0,0. The dimension text is automatically aligned with the leader line. Once you pick the feature to dimension, either point in the X or Y direction indicating the type of dimension, or select Xdatum or Ydatum.

Prompts

```
Select Feature:
Leader endpoint (Xdatum/Ydatum):
```

Options

Leader endpoint When picking a point, the difference between the feature location and the leader endpoint is used to determine whether it is an X or Y dimension. If the difference in the Y axis is greatest, the dimension measures the Y coordinate; if not, it measures the X.

Xdatum Creates the X datum regardless of the length and location of the leader line.

Ydatum Creates the Y datum regardless of the length and location of the leader line.

Tips

▫ Keep ORTHO on for greater control of the leader line location.

▫ You can change the location of 0,0 by redefining the UCS.

Warning(s)

▪ Datum dimensions are relative to 0,0 at the time of creation. If you change the current UCS and dimension more points, they will not be accurate relative to any dimension made while in the previous UCS.

▪ This command only works if the dimension you are editing is associative (DIMASO on) and was not exploded.

See also: UCS

Example

```
Dim: OR
Select Feature: CENTER of                      Point ①.
Leader endpoint (Xdatum/Ydatum): Ydatum
Leader endpoint:                               Point ②.
Dimension text <1.4500>: ↵
Dim:
```

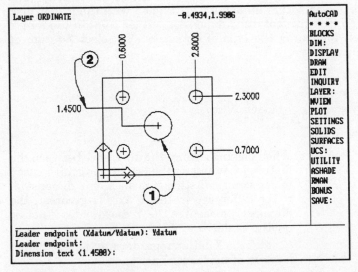

DIM ORdinate Example

DIM OVerride

Screen [DIM:] [next] [Override]
Pull down [Settings] [Set Dim Vars...] [Dim Style]
[Override]

DIM OVerride (Release 11 only) lets you override the dimension variables used to create individual dimensions without changing the variables' current values. If a selected dimension uses a named dimension style, the style definition can be updated to use the new variable value, and all other dimensions that use that style will also be updated.

Prompts

```
Dimension variable to override:
Current value <default> New value:
Dimension variable to override:
Select objects
```

Tips

▫ You can pick several dimensions assigned to different DIMSTYLEs. You are asked if you want to modify the variables for each style that is represented.

Warning(s)

▪ OVerride only works if the dimension you are editing is associative (DIMASO on) and was not exploded.

See also: DIM: REStore, DIM SAve

DIM RAdius

Screen [DIM:] [radial] [radius]
Pull down [Draw] [Dim...] [Radius]

RAdius dimensions circles and arcs. By changing the values of the dimension variables DIMTIX, DIMTOFL, and DIMCEN, you can portray different dimensioning styles.

Options

The pick point for entity selection determines the location of the arrowhead and the start of the dimension line.

Related System Variable(s)

DIMCEN, DIMTIX, DIMTOFL

Tips

□ The leader line location is determined by the pick point used during entity selection.

□ DIMTIX, if set OFF, forces the text outside a circle or arc at the end of an extension line.

□ DIMTOFL, if set ON, draws a dimension line between the extension lines.

□ If set to a positive value, DIMCEN will create center marks inside circles and arcs. A negative value will construct center lines that extend outside the diameter. A setting of 0 will omit any marks. This variable is active only if the dimension line is placed outside the arc or circle.

□ Leader lines are always at least the length of two arrowheads. If the angle of the leader line is greater than 15 degrees from the horizontal and the text is drawn horizontally, a short horizontal extension line (the length of an arrowhead) is drawn next to the dimension text.

Example

```
Dim: RA
Select arc or circle:          Point ①.
Dimension text <.875>: ↵
```

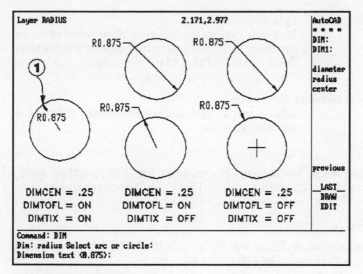

DIM RAdius Example

DIM REStore

Screen **[DIM:] [next] [Restore]**
Pull down **[Settings] [Set Dim Vars...] [Dim Style...]
[Restore]**

Restores an existing dimstyle as the current dimension style
(Release 11 only).

Prompts

```
Current dimension style: default
?/Enter dimension style name or RETURN to select
dimension:
```

Options

?   Allows you to review named dimension styles
saved in the drawing. Responding with an
asterisk (*) gives a sorted listing of all named
styles. You can use any of the wild-card options
to create a more specific list.

Enter dimension style name
>Lets you restore an existing dimension style as the default. If you enter the name of a style that does not exist, the message Unknown dimension style appears.

RETURN to select dimension
>Allows you to pick a dimension that references the desired style.

Tips

▫ If you want to compare the current style to another style, precede the style name with a tilde (~). Only those variables that are different are listed.

Warning(s)

▪ Creating a new dimension style with the DIM: SAve command makes that style the default to restore.

▪ This command only works if the dimension you are editing is associative (DIMASO on) and was not exploded.

See also: DIM: SAve, Wild-Card Characters

DIM ROtated

Select **[DIM:]** **[linear]** **[rotated]**
Pull down **[Draw]** **[Dim...]** **[Linear]** **[Rotated]**

ROtated is an option of LINEAR dimensioning. It draws the dimension line at any angle that you specify while it keeps the extension lines perpendicular.

Prompt

Dimension line angle <0>:

Specify the dimension line angle. The default is always 0. You can type in a new angle or pick two points to indicate the angle.

Tips

▫ HORizontal, VErtical, and ALigned are similar to the ROtated
dimension command. The dimension line for HORizontal is
rotated at an angle of 0; the dimension line for VErtical is rotated
at an angle of 90; and the dimension line for ALigned is based
on the angle of the entity or extension line origins.

Example

```
Dim: RO
Dimension line angle <0>: 45
First extension line origin or RETURN to select:  ↵
Select line, arc, or circle:       Point ①.
Dimension line location:           Point ②.
Dimension text <1.2374>:  ↵
```

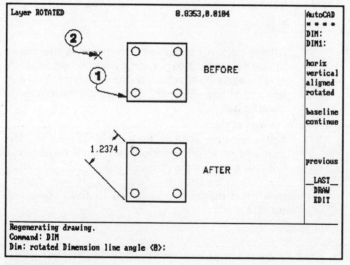

DIM ROtated Example

DIM SAve

Screen [DIM:] [next] [Save]
Pull down [Settings] [Set Dim Vars...] [Dim Style...]
[Save NEW]

DIM: SAve (Release 11 only) lets you save multiple dimension variable settings under one dimstyle name. You can retrieve dimstyles with the DIM: REStore command. You can modify saved dimstyles with the DIM: OVerride command or by reissuing the DIM: SAve command after making dimension variable changes.

Prompts

?/Name for new dimension style:

Options

?   Allows reviewing named dimension styles saved in the drawing. Responding with an asterisk (*) gives a sorted listing of all named styles. You can use any of the wild-card options to create a more specific list.

Name for new dimension style:
           Enter a name for the new style. If you use the name of an existing dimstyle, you'll receive the following message: That name is already in use, redefine it? <N>. If you answer yes, all dimensions assigned to that style will update.

Tips

◻ If you want to compare the current style to another style, precede the style name with a tilde (~). Only those variables that are different are listed.

Warning(s)

■ DIMASO and DIMSHO are never saved by DIM: SAve.

See also: DIM: OVerride, DIM: REStore, STYLE, Wild-Card Characters

DIM STAtus

Screen [DIM:] [status]
Pull down [Settings] [Set Dim Vars...] [Dim Globals...]
[Status]

STAtus lists the current settings of all dimension variables.

Tips

◻ To modify dimension variables, enter the name of the variable at the DIM: prompt or use the SETVAR command.

Warning(s)

▪ Make sure you are at the DIM: prompt before entering the STAtus command. If you are at the command prompt, you will get the more generalized status report of your drawing file.

DIM STYle

Screen [DIM:] [style]

STYle lets you select a predefined text style for your default dimensioning text.

Prompt

New text style <*default*>:
                    The default setting is the current text style.

Warning(s)

▪ You can only select existing styles. If you need to create styles, use the STYLE command.

▪ If you choose a style with a height set to 0, the dimension text height is determined by the DIMTXT and DIMSCALE settings. If your current text height is defined by a style with a preset height, the DIMTXT and DIMSCALE settings are ignored.

See also: Dimension Variables

DIM TEdit

Screen **[DIM:]** **[TEdit]**
Pull down **[Draw]** **[Dim:]** **[Edit Dim...]** **[Move]**

Text Edit (Release 11 only) lets you change the location of dimension text. The default lets you dynamically drag the dimension text with your pointing device.

Prompts
```
Select dimension:
Enter text location (Left/Right/Home/Angle):
```

Options

Left	Place dimension text as far to the left of the dimension line as possible and still maintain a two-arrowhead-length dimension line on the left side.
Right	Place dimension text as far to the right of the dimension line as possible and still maintain a two-arrowhead-length dimension line on the right side.
Home	Place dimension text back to its original location.
Angle	Give a new rotation angle for dimension text.

Related System Variable(s)
DIMSHO, DIMTAD, DIMTVP

Tips

▫ TEdit only works if the dimension you are editing is associative (DIMASO on) and was not exploded.

▫ The left and right options only work with linear, radius, and diameter dimensions.

▫ The position of the dimension text depends on the settings of DIMTAD and DIMTVP variables.

▫ The TEdit Home option is the same as using the HOMetext option. Both of these options place the dimension at its original location and rotation angle. The HOMetext option can manipulate more than one dimension at a time, whereas the TEdit Home option only modifies one dimension at a time.

◻ The TEdit Angle option is the same as using the TRotate option. The TRotate option can manipulate more than one dimension at a time, whereas the TEdit Angle option only modifies one dimension at a time.

Warning(s)

■ Even though you can use any of the selection set options, you can only edit one dimension at a time.

See also: DIM: HOMetext, DIM: TRotate

DIM TRotate

Screen **[DIM:] [trotate]**
Pull down **[Draw] [Dim...] [Edit Dim...] [Rotate]**

Dimension Text Rotate lets you rotate existing dimension text (Release 11 only).

Prompts

Enter new text angle:
Select objects:

Tips

◻ TRotate only works if the dimension you are editing is associative (DIMASO on) and was not exploded.

◻ TRotate is the same as using the TEdit angle option. TRotate can manipulate more than one dimension at a time, whereas the TEdit Angle only modifies one dimension at a time.

See also: DIM: TEdit

DIM Undo

Screen [DIM:] [undo]

Undo, while in the dimensioning mode, voids the latest dimensioning operation. You can undo one step at a time until you reach the beginning of the current dimensioning session.

Warning(s)

■ An UNDO executed during the DIM: prompt will not recognize the REDO command.

■ If you issue an UNDO at the command prompt, everything that was accomplished during a dimensioning session will be undone. Issuing a REDO will restore the dimensioning session.

See also: UNDO

DIM UPdate

Screen [DIM:] [next] [UPDATE]
Pull down [Draw] [Dim:] [Edit Dim...] [UPDATE]

UPdate modifies associative dimension entities. The dimension entities are regenerated to match the current UNITS, text STYLE, dimension variables, and DIMSTYLE.

Related System Variable(s)

DIMASO

Warning(s)

■ UPdate only works if the dimension you are editing is associative (DIMASO on) and was not exploded.

■ Changing the dimension variable DIMDLI (Dimension Line Increment for continuous or baseline dimensions) will not affect any existing dimensions created with the Baseline or COntinue dimension options.

- HOMetext also will UPdate dimension entities.

See also: Dimension Variables

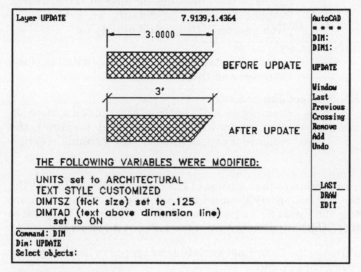

DIM UPdate Example

DIM VAriables

Screen [DIM:] [next] [Variabls]
Pull down [Settings] [Set Dim Vars...] [Dim Style...]
[List Variables]

DIM: VAriables (Release 11 only) lets you review individual dimstyle variable settings. You can compare dimstyles and get a listing of just those variables that are different.

Prompts

Current dimension style:
?/Enter dimension style name or RETURN to select dimension:

Options

?   Activates the wild-card options for listing the
                         names of the dimstyles defined in the drawing.
                         Responding with the default, an asterisk (*),
                         gives a sorted listing of all dimstyles.
Enter dimension style name
                         Enter a dimstyle name and receive a listing of the
                         variables and their settings.

RETURN to select dimension
                         Pressing a <RETURN> lets you pick a dimension
                         in your drawing. AutoCAD determines the
                         assigned dimstyle and lists the variable settings.

Tips

▫   You can compare the settings of the different dimstyles. At the
    Enter dimension style name prompt, type a tilde (~) before
    typing the dimstyle name. You receive a listing of only those
    settings that are different from the current dimstyle.

▫   You change the individual variables by typing in their names at
    the command prompt.

See also: DIM: OVerride, DIM: REStore, DIM VAriables,
Dimension Variables

Dimension Variables

Screen **[DIM:] [Dim Vars]**
Pull down **[Settings] [Set Dim Vars...] [Dim Globals...]**

Dimension variables (not to be confused with the DIM: VAriables
command above) control the appearance of your dimensions.
Dimension variables control features such as arrowhead or tick
mark size, text location, and size. Some of the variables contain
values, while others act as on and off switches. (See the list below.)

You change the different variable settings by entering the
individual variable names at the command prompt (Release 11
only) or the DIM: prompt.

Use the DIM: UPdate and DIM: OVerride command if you change
variables after entities are dimensioned.

DIMASO

DIMASO is the variable that controls associative dimensioning. DIMASO controls whether dimension entities (lines, arcs, arrows, and text) are grouped together to act as one entity or are independent of each other. DIMASO affects linear, angular, diameter, ordinate, and radius dimensioning. In addition, the dimension becomes directly associated with the dimensioned entity and will automatically reflect size changes if the entity is edited. If DIMASO is on when an entity is dimensioned, you can use the dimension edit commands. The default setting is ON.

Options

ON   Dimension entities act as one.

OFF   Dimension entities act individually and are not directly associated to the entities that are dimensioned.

Other Dimension Variables

Following is a list of dimension variables and their defaults. (See Appendix B for a complete list of all system variables.)

Dimension Variable	Default	Purpose
DIMALT	Off	Alternate units selection
DIMALTD	2	Alternate unit decimal places
DIMALTF	25.4000	Alternate unit scale factor
DIMAPOST		Default suffix for alternate text
DIMASO	On	Create associative dimensions
DIMASZ	0.1800	Arrow size
DIMBLK		Arrow block name
DIMBLK1		First arrow block name
DIMBLK2		Second arrow block name
DIMCEN	0.0900	Center mark size
DIMCLRD	BYBLOCK	Dimension line color
DIMCLRE	BYBLOCK	Extension line and leader line color
DIMCLRT	BYBLOCK	Dimension text color
DIMDLE	0.0000	Dimension line extension
DIMDLI	0.3800	Dimension line increment for continuation
DIMEXE	0.1800	Extension above dimension line
DIMEXO	0.0625	Extension line origin offset
DIMGAP	0.0900	Gap from dimension line to text
DIMLFAC	1.0000	Linear unit scale factor

Dimension Variable	Default	Purpose
DIMLIM	Off	Generate dimension limits
DIMPOST		Default suffix for dimension text
DIMRND	0.0000	Rounding value
DIMSAH	Off	Separate arrow blocks
DIMSCALE	1.0000	Overall scale factor
DIMSE1	Off	Suppress the first extension line
DIMSE2	Off	Suppress the second extension line
DIMSHO	Off	Update dimensions while dragging
DIMSOXD	Off	Suppress outside extension dimension
DIMSTYLE	*UNNAMED	Current dimension style
DIMTAD	Off	Place text above the dimension line
DIMTFAC	1.0000	Tolerance text height scaling factor
DIMTIH	On	Text inside extensions is horizontal
DIMTIX	Off	Place text inside extensions
DIMTM	0.0000	Minus tolerance
DIMTOFL	Off	Force line inside extension lines
DIMTOH	On	Text outside extensions is horizontal
DIMTOL	Off	Generate dimension tolerances
DIMTP	0.0000	Plus tolerance
DIMTSZ	0.0000	Tick size
DIMTVP	0.0000	Text vertical position
DIMTXT	0.1800	Text height
DIMZIN	0	Zero suppression

Tips

▫ The following edit commands affect associative dimensions when used on dimensions and dimensioned entitles: TRIM (only with linear dimensions), EXTEND (only with linear dimensions), STRETCH (only with linear and angular dimensions), ARRAY (only with rotated polar arrays), MIRROR, ROTATE, and SCALE.

▫ Placing your first associative dimension creates a layer named DEFPOINTS. DEFPOINTS (definition points) are points that link the dimension to the entity being dimensioned. Entities residing on the DEFPOINTS layer are never plotted. If you want to plot entities on this layer, you must first rename the layer. You can osnap to defpoints with the NODe option.

Warning(s)

■ If you explode an associative dimension, you can no longer use the dimension editing commands.

DIM VErtical

Screen [DIM:] [linear] [vertical]
Pull down [Draw] [Dim...] [Linear] [Vertical]

VErtical is an option of LINEAR dimensioning. It draws the dimension line vertically. You can either pick the first and second extension line origins, or you can press <RETURN> and then pick the entity to dimension.

Prompt

First extension line origin or RETURN to select:

Tips

▫ If you select a circle, the diameter is dimensioned. The quadrants at 90 and 270 degrees are considered the two endpoints.

See also: DIM: DIMASO

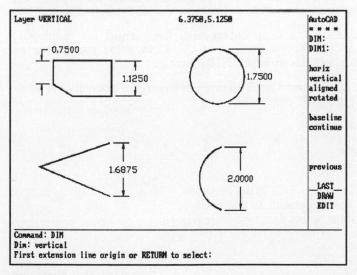

DIM VERtical Example

DIST

Screen [INQUIRY] [DIST:]
Pull down [Utility] [Distance]

DISTANCE is an inquiry command that determines the direct distance between two points, the angle they form in the X,Y plane, the angle from the X,Y plane, and the distance between them along the X, Y, and Z axes.

Prompts

First point:
Second point:

Related System Variable(s)

DISTANCE

Tips

□ The order in which you pick points determines the angle in the X,Y plane and positive or negative values for deltas X, Y, Z.

□ The UNITS setting determines the format for displaying distance. Enter a number at the First point prompt for an example of the current UNITS format.

□ You can determine the distance between the endpoints of a line with the LIST command.

See also: LIST

Example

```
Command: DIST
First point:                    Point ①.
Second point:                   Point ②.
Distance = 3.1869,
Angle in X-Y Plane = 48,  Angle from X-Y Plane = 0
Delta X = 2.1250,  Delta Y = 2.3750,   Delta Z = 0.0000

Command: DIST
First point:                    Point ①.
Second point:                   Point ③.
Distance = 7.0000,
Angle in X-Y Plane = 0,  Angle from X-Y Plane = 0
Delta X = 7.0000,  Delta Y = 0.0000,   Delta Z = 0.0000
```

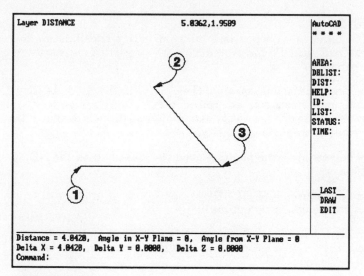

```
Layer DISTANCE                    5.0362,1.9589        AutoCAD
                                                       * * *

                                                       AREA:
                      ②                                DBLIST:
                                                       DIST:
                       ↑                               HELP:
                                                       ID:
                                                       LIST:
                                         ③             STATUS:
                                          ↓            TIME:



                    ↓                                 _LAST_
                ①   ────────────────→               DRAW
                                                     EDIT


Distance = 4.0420,  Angle in X-Y Plane = 0,  Angle from X-Y Plane = 0
Delta X = 4.0420,  Delta Y = 0.0000,   Delta Z = 0.0000
Command:
```

DIST Examples

DIVIDE

Screen **[EDIT] [DIVIDE:]**
Pull down **[Modify] [Divide]**

DIVIDE marks an entity at equal-length segments according to a quantity you specify. The divided entity isn't physically separated; rather, points or blocks are placed as markers at each division point. You can divide lines, circles, arcs, and polylines.

Prompts

```
Select object to divide:
<Number of segments>/Block:
```

Options

Number of segments
> Enter the number of segments for division.

Block
> Divides an entity with a block currently defined in the drawing. After providing the block name, you are prompted for the number of segments.

Tips

▫ If you cannot see the points dividing an entity, try adjusting the PDMODE and PDSIZE system variables and then regenerating the screen.

▫ The Block option lets you align the block with the divided entity. An aligned block is rotated around its insertion point and drawn parallel to the divided entity. An unaligned block is drawn with a 0 rotation angle to the entity.

▫ You can osnap to the points placed by DIVIDE with the NODe option.

▫ You can manipulate DIVIDE's markers as a group with the Previous selection set option.

▫ Establish default settings for the DIVIDE command by selecting [Options] - [Divide Units] and [D/M Block Name] from the pull-down menu.

Warning(s)

▪ You can divide only one entity at a time.

▪ When dividing an entity with a block, make sure the block definition is within the current drawing.

▪ You cannot change the XYZ scale factor of a block used for entity division.

▪ When using the Block option, only those attributes defined as Constant are brought into the drawing. If you try editing the attribute, the message `Block has no attributes` appears.

▪ Divide markers are placed in the UCS of the entity being divided. They are always placed on the entity regardless of the current elevation setting.

See also: MEASURE, NODE, POINT

Example

```
Command: DIVIDE
Select object to divide:            Pick polyline ①.
<Number of segments>/Block: 5
Command: DIVIDE
Select object to divide:            Pick line ②.
<Number of segments>/Block: B
Block name to insert: ANGLE
```

Align block with object? <Y> ↵
Number of segments: **5**

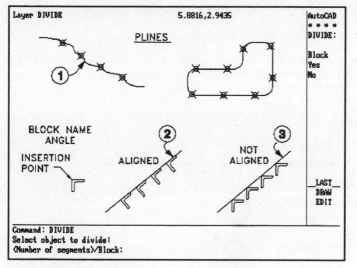

DIVIDE Examples

DONUT / DOUGHNUT

Screen **[DRAW] [DONUT:]**
Pull down **[Draw] [Donut]**

The DONUT command draws solid-filled rings and circles. DONUT entities are constructed from closed wide polyarc segments. You provide an inside diameter value (or two points) and an outside diameter (or two points). The default settings are <0.5000> inside diameter and <1.0000> outside diameter.

Prompts

```
Inside diameter <0.5000>:
Outside diameter <1.0000>:
Center of doughnut:
```

Tips

◻ Extrude donuts into cylinders by assigning thickness.

◻ Construct a solid filled circle by setting a donut's inside diameter to 0.

◻ You can edit donuts with PEDIT because they are polyarcs.

◻ Donuts are only solid if FILL is on.

◻ You can establish default settings by selecting [Options] - [Donut Diameters] from the pull-down menu.

Warning(s)

■ If you explode a donut, you end up with two arcs with no width.

See also: FILL, PLINE, PEDIT

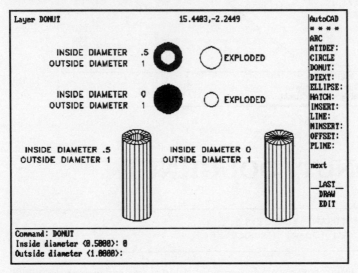

DONUT Example

DRAG / DRAGMODE

Screen [SETTINGS] [DRAGMOD:]

DRAGMODE gives you the ability to draw and edit entities, like circles, arcs, polylines, and blocks, by dynamically dragging the image into position in the drawing. The default setting is <Auto>. It enables drag for any command that supports dragging.

Prompt

ON/OFF/Auto <Auto>:

Options

ON	Enabled when requested. You type DRAG at the command prompt when you want to drag.
OFF	Ignores all requests to drag.
Auto	Automatically enables drag for those commands that can use it.

Related System Variables

DRAGMODE, DRAGP1, DRAGP2

Tips

▫ You can dynamically drag the size and shape of the following entities during their construction: arcs, blocks, circles, lines, polylines, donuts, polygons, ellipses, and shapes.

▫ You can dynamically drag entities during the following editing commands: CHANGE, COPY, DVIEW, INSERT, MIRROR, MOVE, ROTATE, SCALE, and STRETCH.

▫ When using multiple viewports, you can see the entities drag only in the current viewport. If you pick entities in other viewports, you can watch them drag in the viewport from which they were chosen.

DTEXT

Screen **[DRAW] [DTEXT:]**
Pull down **[Draw] [Dtext]**

The DTEXT (Dynamic TEXT) command lets you enter text in your drawing with more control than the TEXT command. Although the end results of DTEXT and TEXT are similar, there are a few differences:

In DTEXT, you can watch the text appear on the screen as you are typing at the keyboard.

In DTEXT, you can move the cursor to different parts of the drawing and enter more text without exiting the command.

In DTEXT, you press the <RETURN> key once to enter a second line of text; in TEXT you must press the <RETURN> key twice.

Prompts

```
Justify/Style/<Start point>:
Height <default>:
Rotation angle <default>:
Text:
```

Options

Start point	Text justification is at the bottom left of the first character for each line of text.
Justify	Specify the text justification:
Align	Specify the beginning and ending point of a line of text. The text height is adjusted to fit between these points.
Fit	Specify the beginning and ending point of a line of text. You determine the height. The width is controlled by the two endpoints and the text is adjusted to fit.
Center	Specify the center of the text horizontally and the base of the text vertically.
Middle	Specify the middle of the text horizontally and vertically.
Right	Text justification is at the bottom right of the last character for each line of text.
TL	Text justification is at the top left of the tallest character (Release 11 only).
TC	Text justification is at the top center of the tallest character (Release 11 only).
TR	Text justification is at the top right of the tallest character (Release 11 only).
ML	Text justification is at the middle left, between the top of the tallest character and the bottom of the lowest descender (Release 11 only).
MC	Text justification is at the middle center, between the top of the tallest character and the bottom of the lowest descender (Release 11 only).
MR	Text justification is at the middle right, between

	the top of the tallest character and the bottom of the lowest descender (Release 11 only).
BL	Text justification is at the bottom left of the lowest descender (Release 11 only).
BC	Text justification is at the bottom center of the lowest descender (Release 11 only) .
BR	Text justification is at the bottom right of the lowest descender (Release 11 only) .
Style	Change the current style default. The style must have been created with the STYLE command.
↵	If you press <RETURN>, the last text entered is highlighted. You are then prompted for a new text string. The new text is placed directly below the highlighted text with the same style, height, and rotation as the highlighted text.
Height	Assign a text height. You are not prompted for this when using Align or a text style with a predefined height.
Rotation angle	Specify the text angle.
Text	Supply the text string.

The default settings are:

Start point	Left justified
Height	0.2000
Rotation angle	0

Special Character Codes

You can enter codes in your text string to obtain the following special characters:

%%o	Toggle overscore mode on/off
%%u	Toggle underscore mode on/off
%%d	Draw degrees symbol
%%p	Draw plus/minus tolerance symbol
%%c	Draw diameter symbol
%%%	Draw a single percent symbol

When you are entering text, the control characters appear in the drawing. Once you end the command, the appropriate characters replace the control codes.

Related System Variable(s)

TEXTSIZE, TEXTSTYLE

Tips

◻ You can preset the font, alignment, height, and rotation of text by selecting [Options] - [Dtext Options >] from the pull-down menu. These preset variables are automatically activated when you pick [Draw] - [Dtext] from the pull-down menus. When you are using the screen menus, the text variables are based on the last text inserted during the drawing session. The next drawing session defaults to the preset height and font; however, you must redefine the rotation angle and text justification.

◻ When using the same block of text for multiple drawings, save time by wblocking the text. You can also import ASCII text from a separate file on disk with the ASCTEXT.LSP program from the AutoCAD BONUS disk. If installed, you can select it with [BONUS] - [ASCTEXT] from the screen menu, or [File] - [EXCHANGE >] - [Import Text] on the pull-down menus.

◻ You can assign a thickness to text, but only after the text is inserted. You do this by using the CHANGE or CHPROP command.

◻ DTEXT text always appears to the right of the insertion point. Once you press <RETURN> to end the command, the text adjusts itself to the correct justification.

◻ Osnap INSert locates the insertion point of text.

◻ Edit text strings with the DDEDIT (Release 11 only) or CHANGE commands.

◻ The spacing between multiple lines of text is determined by the individual text font definition files.

Warning(s)

■ During the DTEXT command, the tablet is inactive.

■ Base your text height on the scale you plan to plot the drawing. The text height you specify in AutoCAD should be the height of plotted text multiplied by the plot scale factor.

■ You cannot use the Fit option for text styles assigned a vertical orientation.

See also: CHANGE, DDEDIT, QTEXT, STYLE, TEXT

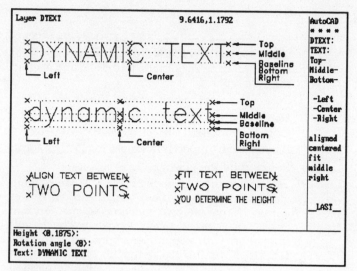

DTEXT Examples

DVIEW

Screen **[DISPLAY] [DVIEW:]**
Pull down **[Display] [Dview Options...]**

DVIEW (Dynamic VIEW) is a tool for viewing 3D models. DVIEW is similar to the VPOINT command. However, in DVIEW you can dynamically drag and rotate all or part of a 3D model with the aid of slider bars. You can display a perspective view of the model and toggle back and forth between parallel and perspective views. The DVIEW command is similar to the concept of using a camera to view a target. You can set a camera point, target point, lens length, and position front and back clipping planes. The default setting is for parallel (not perspective) projection.

Prompts

```
Select objects:
CAmera/TArget/Distance/POints/PAn/Zoom/TWist/CLip/
Hide/Off/Undo/<eXit>:
```

Options

CAmera	Pick a camera angle relative to the target. This is similar to the VPOINT rotate option. You can move your camera point up and down and around the target point.
TArget	Rotate the target point around the camera.
Distance	Determine the distance from the camera to the target. This option turns perspective viewing on.
POints	Prompts you to specify a camera and target point.
PAn	Pan around the view.
Zoom	When perspective viewing is off, you can zoom in and out of the view based on the zoom center option. If perspective viewing is on, you can change the lens length of the camera. The default is a camera with a 50mm lens. Increasing the lens length is similar to using a telephoto lens; decreasing the lens length is similar to using a wide angle lens.
TWist	Determine the view twist angle. Rotate the camera around the line of sight to the target point.
CLip	Specify the front and back clipping planes. A clipping plane is perpendicular to the line of sight between the camera and target.
Hide	Performs a hidden line removal on the current DVIEW selection set.
Off	Turns perspective viewing off.
Undo	Reverses the last DVIEW option.
eXit	Exits the command and regenerates the drawing to reflect any changes.

Related System Variable(s)

BACKZ, FRONTZ, LENSLENGTH, TARGET, VIEWCTR, VIEWDIR, VIEWMODE, VIEWSIZE, VIEWTWIST, WORLD-VIEW

Tips

□ During object selection, you can specify the entities by their assigned layers with the Bylayer option from the screen menu.

□ During object selection, pick only key entities to display and drag on the screen. Once you establish a view point in DVIEW, exit and the rest of the drawing entities are displayed from that viewpoint.

□ At the Select objects prompt, you can press <RETURN> without picking entities. A block, called Dviewblock, appears and you can pick viewpoints by watching this block rotate. Once you have chosen a viewpoint, exit DVIEW and your drawing is displayed with the new settings.

□ You can customize the Dviewblock by creating your own 3D drawing with this name. Keep the geometry simple, but make sure the different sides are unique to observe the dynamic movement of the symbol.

□ During perspective viewing, the UCSICON is replaced by a special icon resembling a cube drawn in perspective. This is a reminder that perspective viewing is on and only a subset of commands will work while perspective is active.

□ The slider bars are helpful in determining an approximate angle and view. If you want a precise angle, type in the angle value.

□ Use the VIEW and VPORTS SAVE options to restore perspective views. Viewports retain all the DVIEW display parameters.

Warning(s)

■ Transparent and editing commands are unavailable during the DVIEW command.

See also: VIEW, VPOINT, VPORTS

Example

```
Command: DVIEW
Select objects:              Select table entities.
CAmera/TArget/Distance/POints/PAn/Zoom/TWist/CLip/
Hide/Off/Undo/<eXit>: CA
Enter angle from X-Y plane <90.00>: 30
Enter angle in the X-Y plane from the X axis <-90.00>:
-135
CAmera/TArget/Distance/POints/PAn/Zoom/TWist/CLip/
Hide/Off/Undo/<eXit>: H
Removing hidden lines: 100
Regenerating drawing.
CAmera/TArget/Distance/POints/PAn/Zoom/TWist/CLip/
Hide/Off/Undo/<eXit>: X
Regenerating drawing.
```

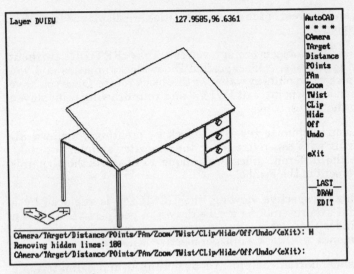

DVIEW Example

DXBIN

Screen [UTILITY]   [DXF/DXB]   [DXBIN:]
Pull down [File]   [EXCHANGE >]   [DXB In]

DXB, or Drawing Interchange Binary, is a binary drawing exchange file format. You can import DXB files with the DXBIN command. Even though there is no direct AutoCAD command to write a DXB file, you do have the capability. Configure AutoCAD for an ADI plotter, select the DXB file output option, and plot to a file. DXB files have the file extension .DXB.

Prompt

DXB file:

Tips

▫   Creating a DXB plot file converts a 3D drawing into 2D. Set the viewpoint with VPOINT or DVIEW before plotting to a file. Once the plot is complete, you can import the file with the DXBIN command. The drawing will consist entirely of line segments, including arcs, circles, curves, and text. This process is useful in producing a 2D perspective drawing.

DXFIN / DXFOUT

Screen **[UTILITY]** **[DXF/DXB]** **[DXFIN:]** or **[DXFOUT:]**
Pull down **[File]** **[EXCHANGE >]** **[DXF In]** or **[DXF Out]**

DXF, or Drawing Interchange File, format is a standard ASCII text file for exchanging AutoCAD drawings with other CAD packages or specialized analysis programs. DXFIN loads a drawing interchange file. DXFOUT writes a drawing interchange file. DXF files have the file extension .DXF.

Prompts

File name <default>:
Enter decimal places of accuracy (0 to 16)/Entities/
Binary <6>:

Options

Decimal places of accuracy
> Determines the accuracy of floating point numbers. The default value is 6.

Entities   Outputs selected entities to the DXF file.

Binary   Writes a binary drawing interchange file.

Tips

▫ A complete DXF file only loads into a new drawing file. When entering a new drawing name at the main menu, enter an equal sign (=) after the name to use AutoCAD's original defaults.

▫ You can load the DXF entities section into an existing drawing. Information such as block definitions and layering information is not included.

▫ Use the AUDIT command to check for corrupt data after importing a DXF file with the DXFIN command. You can activate the AUDIT command from the main menu or at the command prompt.

See also: AMELITE

EDGESURF

Screen **[DRAW] [next] [3D Surfs] [EDGSURF:]**
Screen **[SURFACES] [EDGSURF:]**
Pull down **[Draw] [Surfaces...] [EDGE]**

EDGESURF is a command that generates a 3D polygon mesh by approximating a Coons surface patch from four adjoining edges. The edges can be made up of lines, arcs, or open polylines anywhere in 3D space. The endpoints of each entity must intersect to form a closed path. You can pick the edges in any order. The first edge or entity selected defines the M direction of the mesh. The two edges that intersect the M edge determine the N direction for the mesh. (See 3D MESH for M and N directions.)

Prompts

```
Select edge 1:
Select edge 2:
Select edge 3:
Select edge 4:
```

Related System Variable(s)

SURFTAB1, SURFTAB2

Tips

□ You can edit an edgesurf entity with the PEDIT command.

□ You can also smooth an edgesurf entity with the PEDIT command.

□ Exploding an edgesurf mesh results in individual 3D faces.

See also: 3DMESH, 3DFACE

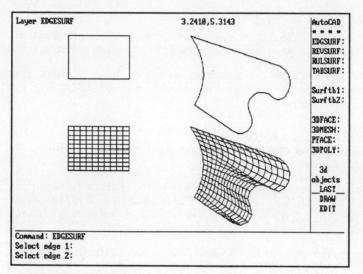

EDGESURF Examples

ELEV

Screen [SETTINGS] [ELEV:]

The ELEVation command sets the elevation and extrusion thickness of entities you draw. The elevation is the entity's location along the Z axis. The extrusion thickness (negative or positive) is its height above (or below) the Z elevation. The elevation setting only affects those entities whose Z value is not otherwise specified. You can also set the elevation and thickness with the DDEMODES dialogue box.

Prompts

```
New current elevation <0.0000>:
New current thickness <0.0000>:
```

Related System Variable(s)

ELEVATION, THICKNESS

Tips

▫ The current UCS determines an entity's Z location or elevation. Any elevation other than 0 is applied during entity construction.

▫ You can provide an elevation and thickness to text and attributes once they are inserted. Use the CHANGE or CHPROP command.

Warning(s)

▪ You cannot assign a thickness to 3D faces, 3D polylines, 3D polygon meshes, or dimensions.

▪ The ELEV command may be dropped in a future release. Use the UCS, DDUCS, or DDEMODES command as a replacement for elevation control. Use the THICKNESS system variable for extrusion thickness.

▪ The combination of ELEV and UCS can be confusing. It is best to use UCS and not change the elevation setting.

See also: CHANGE, 'DDEMODES

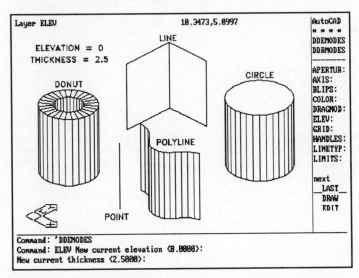

Entities Drawn With Thickness

ELLIPSE

Screen [DRAW] [ELLIPSE:]
Pull down [Draw] [Ellipse]

The ELLIPSE command gives you several methods for constructing ellipses. The default method uses major and minor axes specified by endpoints. (See example.)

Prompts

<Axis endpoint 1>/Center:
Axis endpoint 2:
<Other axis distance>/Rotation:

Options

Center	Specify a center point and one endpoint of each axis.
Rotation	Specify the rotation around the major axis. The rotation angle is between 0 and 89.4 degrees.
Isocircle	If you enable Isometric mode, the ELLIPSE prompt will include an Isocircle option. Isometric circles will be drawn in the current isoplane. You provide the center point and radius or diameter.

Tips

▫ Ellipses are closed polylines made up of short arc segments. You can use all the commands that edit polylines.

▫ To construct an elliptical arc, draw an ellipse and use the BREAK or TRIM edit commands.

▫ You can create your own ellipse by saving a circle as a block and inserting it with different X and Y values.

See also: EXPLODE, ISOPLANE, PLINE, PEDIT

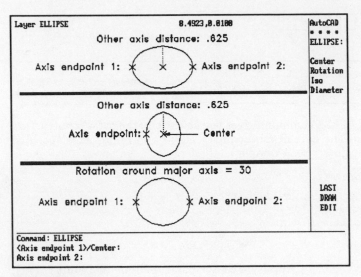

Ellipse Examples

END

Screen **[UTILITY] [END:]**
Pull down **[File] [End]**

The END command saves the drawing file and exits to AutoCAD's main menu. The old drawing file becomes the new .BAK file.

See also: QUIT, SAVE

ERASE

Screen **[EDIT] [ERASE:]**
Pull down **[Modify] [Erase]**

ERASE deletes entities from the drawing.

Prompt

Select objects:

Tips

◻ Use the U, UNDO, or OOPS command to restore the last group of erased entities. If you executed commands after erasing entities, use the OOPS command.

◻ You can delete part of an entity with the TRIM, BREAK, STRETCH, or CHANGE command.

See also: OOPS, UNDO

EXPLODE

Screen [EDIT] [EXPLODE:]

EXPLODE converts blocks, polylines, dimensions, hatches, and meshes into their component entities.

Prompt

Select block reference, polyline, dimension, or mesh:

Tips

◻ Exploding some entities may result in a change in their color and linetype as they return to their original layer, color, and linetype.

◻ Exploded polylines become lines and arcs, and 3D meshes become 3D faces.

◻ Pre-explode blocks, hatch patterns, and drawing files by inserting them with an asterisk (*) preceding their insertion name. Pre-explode dimensions by turning DIMASO off.

Warning(s)

▪ An exploded polyline loses its tangent and width characteristics.

▪ Exploding a block containing attributes will replace the attribute value with the attribute definition tag name.

▪ You cannot explode a block with unequal X, Y, and Z scale

factors, a mirrored block, a minserted block, or Xrefs and their dependent blocks.

■ Exploding hatches or dimensions places all their entities on layer 0.

See also: DIMENSION, BLOCK, HATCH, PLINE, 3D MESH

EXTEND

Screen **[EDIT] [EXTEND:]**
Pull down **[Modify] [Extend]**

EXTEND lengthens a line, open polyline, or arc to a boundary edge. Boundary edges include lines, circles, arcs, polylines, and viewport borders (paper space). You can have more than one boundary edge, and an entity can be both a boundary edge and an entity to extend.

Prompts

```
Select boundary edge(s) ...
Select objects:
<Select object to extend>/Undo:
```

Options

Undo   Undoes the last entity extended without exiting
                the command.

Tips

□ The extrusion direction of entities that are boundary edges and the entities to extend must be parallel to the Z axis of the current UCS.

□ Extending entities from another viewpoint (other than the plan viewpoint) to entities in the current viewport can produce unwanted results because boundary edges are projected to the current viewpoint. For best results, view the extending entities from their plan view.

□ You can select more than one boundary edge. The entities you are extending end at the first boundary. Pick the entity again, and it will extend to the next boundary edge.

□ You can extend only one entity at a time.

▫ Extending a linear associative dimension automatically updates the dimension.

▫ If an entity won't extend, pick a new point on the entity closer to the endpoint you are extending.

Warning(s)

▪ Blocks, text, and traces cannot be boundary edges or objects to extend.

▪ Entities extend to the center of wide polylines.

▪ Ends of wide polylines are always square. Extending a wide polyline to an angled boundary results in a portion of the polyline extending past the boundary edge.

See also: CHANGE, STRETCH, TRIM

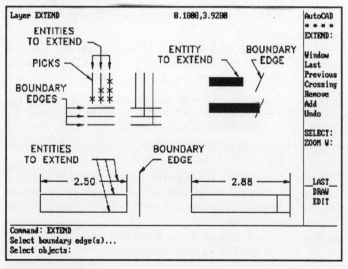

EXTEND Examples

FILES

FILES displays the File Utility menu. It provides an alternative to
DOS (or your operating system) for managing your files. These file
utilities can also be accessed from the main menu.

Options

0. Exit File Utility Menu
> Return to the main menu or return to your
> drawing.

1. List Drawing files
> Lists AutoCAD drawing files. This is equivalent
> to the DOS command DIR *.DWG /W /P.

2. List user specified files
> Lists files based on your specifications. You can
> use the wild-card options * and ? for DOS systems
> and *, ?, [ ] and - on UNIX systems.

3. Delete files Specify each file to delete individually or use the
> wild-card options * and ?. You are prompted for
> a N(o) or Y(es) before each file is actually deleted.

4. Rename files Rename a file and place the file in a different
> directory at the same time.

5. Copy file Copy a file from a drive and directory (source)
> into another drive and directory (destination). In
> addition, you can specify a different name for the
> copied file.

6. Unlock file Unlock one or more files (Release 11 only). You
> can use the wild-card options.

Tips

□ When you refer to a file name, don't forget to include the
extension (.DWG for drawing files). AutoCAD will not
acknowledge a drawing file unless it has the .DWG extension.
If you copy a file and forget to include the extension, you must
use the RENAME command to supply the extension.

□   Rename (option 4) will copy a file from one directory to another
     (you can keep the same file name) and delete the original file.

□   You can copy (option 5) a file from one drive and directory to
     another and rename the file at the same time. This will not
     delete the original file.

□   Selecting the word File from the pull-down menu lets you use
     other functions such as SAVE, END, and QUIT.

Warning(s)

■   AutoCAD's File Utility options will not give you information
     about file size, date, and time the file was last opened. Use DOS
     or a file utility program if you want this information.

■   If you enter the File Utility menu from within a drawing file, do
     not delete the active drawing file, temporary files, or lock files.
     Temporary files have the extensions .AC, AC, or .$A; lock files
     have the extension .??K.

FILL

Screen **[DRAW]** **[PLINE:]** *or* **[SOLID:]** *or* **[TRACE:]**
then **[FILL ON]** *or* **[FILL OFF]**

FILL, a toggle command, controls whether polylines, solids, and
traces are displayed and plotted as filled, or just the outline is
displayed and plotted. The default setting is <On>.

Prompt

ON/OFF <On>:

Options

ON   Polylines, solids, and traces are displayed and
               plotted as filled.

OFF   Only the outlines of polylines, solids, and traces
               are displayed and plotted.

Related System Variable(s)

FILLMODE

Tips

▫ If the entity's extrusion direction is parallel to the viewing direction and the Hide option has not been used, you can display and plot entities with FILL on.

▫ You can save REGEN and REDRAW time if you keep FILL off.

▫ You may find it faster to plot broad lines with a wider plotter pen tip rather than have the plotter try to fill in drawing entities.

▫ The SHADE command will fill in regardless of the Fillmode setting.

Warning(s)

■ When you change the FILL setting, you won't see the change until the drawing is regenerated.

See also: PLINE, REGEN, SOLID, TRACE

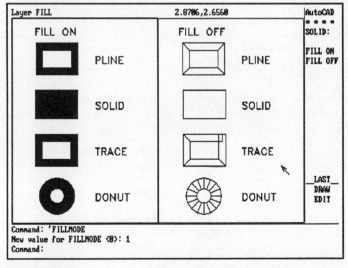

FILL Examples

FILLET

Screen [EDIT] [next] [FILLET:]
Pull down [**Modify**] [**Fillet**]

FILLET lets you create an arc with a predefined radius between any two lines, polylines, circles, and arcs. If your selected entities do not meet, or they extend past an intersecting point, FILLET will extend or trim the entities until they intersect. The fillet arc is inserted based on the fillet radius. The default fillet radius is <0>.

Prompt

Polyline/Radius/<Select two objects>:

Options

Polyline	Fillets all the intersections of a 2D polyline. The intersections must be contiguous segments.
Radius	Sets the fillet radius. Once you have set a radius, you press <RETURN> or reselect the fillet command to execute the command.

Related System Variable(s)

FILLETRAD

Tips

□ You can establish a default setting by selecting [Options] - [Fillet Radius] from the pull-down menu.

□ Filleting in plan view is more reliable than filleting when your viewing direction is oblique to the X,Y plane of the current UCS.

□ Fillets are determined by the pick location of the entity. Select the end point or side of the object you want the fillet applied to.

□ You can fillet a 2D polyline without using the polyline option. However, the polylines must be from the same line segment, share the same vertex, or be separated by one other segment. If you fillet two polylines separated by one other segment, the segment will be replaced with the results of the fillet command.

□ The fillet arc resides on the layer of the picked entities as long as they share the same layer; if the two entities are on different layers, the fillet is placed on the current layer. The same rules apply to color and linetype.

Warning(s)

- You cannot fillet two parallel lines.

- Fillet will not work if LIMITS is on and the fillet intersection point is outside the limits.

- If a portion of a line must be trimmed, it will be the shorter end.

- You cannot fillet borders of viewport entities.

See also: CHAMFER, EXTEND, PLINE, TRIM

Example

```
Command: FILLET
Polyline/Radius/<Select two objects>: R
Enter fillet radius <0.00>: .5

Command: FILLET
Polyline/Radius/<Select two objects>:        Pick lines ① & ②.

Command: FILLET
Polyline/Radius/<Select two objects>: P
Select 2D polyline:                           Pick polyline ③.
4 lines were filleted
```

FILLET Examples

FILMROLL

G

Screen **[ASHADE] [ACTION] [FLMROLL:]**
Pull down **[Utility] [AutoShade...] [FILMROLL]**

FILMROLL produces a file containing a description of the entities that can be processed into a fully shaded AutoShade rendering. The filmroll file also contains camera, lighting, and scene descriptions that are created in the drawing from tools provided in the AutoShade program. AutoShade is a separate program. For more information, see the AutoShade User Guide.

Prompt

Enter the filmroll file name *<dwg-name>*:

GRAPHSCR / TEXTSCR

Type: **GRAPHSCR** *or* **TEXTSCR**

These two commands flip your screen between graphics mode and text mode. GRAPHSCR flips the screen to the graphics screen; TEXTSCR flips the screen to the text screen. On a DOS-based system, the <F1> key toggles between these two screens. They may also be used transparently.

Tips

▢ Commands such as HELP, STATUS, TIME, and LIST flip your screen into text mode.

▢ You can review your last few prompts and responses by flipping to the TEXTSCR mode.

▢ These commands are primarily used in scripts and menus to toggle the screen.

▢ These commands have no effect on a dual-screen system.

GRID

Screen [SETTINGS] [GRID:]
Pull down [Settings] [Grid On/Off   ^G]

GRID displays reference dots at any user-defined increment. It helps you get a perspective of the space you are working in and the size of your drawing entities. GRID is dynamic. You can modify the increment value and turn the setting on or off. <^G> (or the <F7> function key on DOS-based systems) is a toggle switch to turn the grid on and off. The defaults are <0.0000> spacing and OFF. You can also set grid with the DDRMODES dialogue box.

Prompt

Grid spacing(X) or ON/OFF/Snap/Aspect <0.0000>:

Options

Grid spacing(X)	Set the X and Y grid increments. If an X is placed after the number, it makes the grid a multiple of the current snap value.
ON	Grid is visible.
OFF	Grid is invisible.
Snap	Grid increment equals the current snap increment. This works the same as if you set the grid equal to 0.
Aspect	Set individual horizontal and vertical grid increments.

Related System Variable(s)

GRIDMODE, GRIDUNIT

Tips

▫ Each viewport retains its own grid setting.

▫ If you are working in the WCS or a UCS that is the same as the WCS, the grid is displayed to the drawing limits. If you are working in a UCS different from the WCS, the grid will extend to the edges of your viewport.

□   If the grid is set to an increment that is too small to be shown on the screen, the message `Grid too dense to display` appears at the command prompt. Once you zoom into a portion of the drawing, you will be able to see the grid. If the grid is too dense, you can press <^C> to cancel the grid regeneration.

□   To use the aspect option while in the pull-down menu, you must first set the X spacing and then the Y spacing.

□   When you are editing a drawing, some of the grid dots may disappear when entities under them are moved or erased. Any display command will cause the grid dots to reappear.

Warning(s)

■   Grid is a visual aid and will not plot.

■   Regardless of the grid setting, it is the snap setting that helps you input accurate points.

See also: 'DDRMODES, SNAP

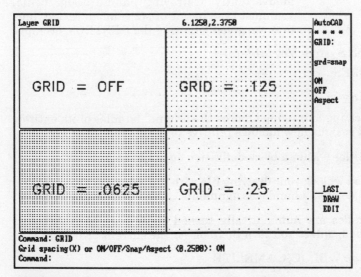

GRID Examples

HANDLES

Screen **[SETTINGS] [HANDLES:]**

The HANDLES command assigns a unique label to every drawing entity. This label, in hexadecimal format, is permanently stored in the drawing (unless you destroy it) and is used to access entities. Handles can be used by AutoLISP programs, or to link entities to external programs like databases. The default setting is OFF.

Prompt

Handles are disabled.
ON/DESTROY:

Options

ON   Assign a handle to every entity.

DESTROY   Delete all handles within a drawing. To prevent inadvertently destroying handle assignments, you must type in one of six random text strings that are given following the DESTROY prompt.

Related System Variable(s)

HANDLES

Warning(s)

■ Inserting a drawing ignores the original handles of its entities and assigns new handles relative to the current drawing.

■ Entities within a block definition do not have handles.

■ If you wblock your drawing file with the asterisk (*) option, you will delete all handle assignments.

■ Handles are automatically turned on as long as AMElite is loaded, unless you turn them off for the current drawing.

See also: WBLOCK, AMELITE

HATCH

Screen **[DRAW] [HATCH:]**
Pull down **[Draw] [Hatch]**

The HATCH command cross-hatches or pattern-fills an area enclosed by existing entities. It creates an unnamed block with the specified pattern. Hatch patterns are stored in a file named ACAD.PAT.

Prompt

Pattern (? or name/U,style):

Options

Pattern	Enter a hatch pattern name. Once a name is given, you must enter the scale and angle for the pattern. When typing the hatch pattern, include an asterisk (*) before the name if you want the hatch block pre-exploded.
? or name	Lists one or all the hatch pattern names including a short description. You can use wild-card characters to produce a specific list.
U	User-defined; you provide the pattern. You are prompted for the spacing and angle for straight lines. You can also "double hatch" an area or create a perpendicular cross-hatch.
style	You can specify the hatch style by appending a style code to the hatch pattern name separated by a comma. Your choices are:
N	Normal; hatch every other boundary.
O	Outermost; hatch only outermost boundary.
I	Ignore; hatch everything inside outermost boundary.

Related System Variable(s)

SNAPBASE, SNAPANG

Tips

□ Hatch lines are projected to the current construction plane defined by the USC.

□ If the area to be hatched is very complex, you may find it easier to draw a polyline around the perimeter and hatch the polyline. You also may want to save the polyline on a frozen layer for future reference.

□ If you need precise hatch pattern placement, set the system variable SNAPBASE to a point where you want the hatch pattern to originate. Be sure to reset it after hatching, because SNAP and GRID use it also.

□ If you explode a hatch pattern, you may consider regrouping those entities into a block. It will take up less drawing space and will be easier to manipulate.

□ You can establish hatch defaults for the current editing session by selecting [Options] - [HATCH OPTIONS >] from the pull-down menu. The settings are only activated when you select [Draw] - [Hatch] from the pull-down menu.

□ If you hatch an area containing text, attributes, traces, solids or shapes, you can have the hatch draw around the entity as long as you include the entity during your object selection.

□ If you find the hatch pattern is too big or too small while it is generating, halt the process by typing <^C>. You can then issue the UNDO or ERASE Last commands and re-enter the pattern.

□ You can hatch a block. Blocks are processed as individual drawing entities. During object selection, you just need to pick the block you want to hatch.

□ You can explode a hatch pattern and turn it back into individual drawing entities. The entities default to layer 0, and the color and linetype are set to bylayer.

□ To speed up your drawing regeneration and redraw time, keep hatching on its own layer, and freeze the layer until you are ready to plot.

□ In paper space, you can use viewport edges as hatch boundaries.

Warning(s)

- We recommend you hatch areas enclosed by a boundary whose endpoints all intersect precisely. If there is an opening in the boundary, the hatch pattern may go beyond the boundary.

- When you list a hatch block, the hatch name, scale, and rotation angle are not given.

- Exploding a hatch places all the entities on layer 0.

See also: BLOCK, EXPLODE, SNAP

Some Hatch Pattern Examples

HELP / ?

Screen [**Inquiry** [**HELP:**]
Screen [*** * * ***] [**HELP**]
Pull down [**Assist**] [**Help!**]

HELP provides information on commands and how they function, including cross references to the AutoCAD Reference Manual. If you use 'HELP or '? while in another command, you will receive information on that particular command. The ' (apostrophe) executes the HELP command transparently, and you can continue with your initial command after reading the help information. Otherwise, HELP lists every AutoCAD command and gives you general help. If you want to find out about an individual command, type in the command name.

Prompt

Command name (RETURN for list):

See also: Transparent Commands

HIDE

Screen **[DISPLAY] [HIDE:]**
Pull down **[Display] [Hide]**
Pull down **[Display] [Vpoint 3D...] [HIDE]**

Normally, AutoCAD displays the edges of all entities. The HIDE command calculates solid areas defined by those edges. It determines what should be hidden from your viewpoint and temporarily removes those edges and entities from sight. HIDE only evaluates circles, polylines (assigned a width), solids, traces, 3D faces, meshes, and extruded edges of entities assigned a thickness as opaque surfaces. In addition, extruded circles, polylines (assigned a width), solids, and traces are considered solid entities, having top and bottom faces.

Tips

◻ Only the current viewport will perform the HIDE.

◻ A regeneration will cause entities to be displayed normally. We recommend turning REGENAUTO off to suppress regenerations after using the HIDE command.

◻ Once you have hidden lines suppressed, you may want to create a slide file for future reference.

□ You can have hidden lines visible on the screen and displayed as different colors by creating additional layer names identical to the existing names, but containing the prefix HIDDEN (Release 11 only). Every time you issue the HIDE command, the hidden lines will be visible and will take on the color of the hidden layer name. The linetype will default to the linetype definition of the entity.

□ If you want hidden lines suppressed during plotting, you must answer Yes to the Remove hidden lines prompt of the PLOT or PRPLOT command.

Warning(s)

■ HIDE evaluates entities residing on a layer turned off during the hide process. However, if the layer is frozen, HIDE will not evaluate the entities on that layer.

■ You may get unexpected results for objects that intersect.

See also: DVIEW, SLIDE, VIEW, VPOINT

HIDE Example

ID

Screen [INQUIRY] [ID:]
Pull down [Utility] [ID Point]

ID identifies the absolute X,Y,Z coordinates of any selected point. The point is identified graphically with a blip mark if BLIPMODE is on.

Prompt

Point:

Related System Variable(s)

LASTPOINT

Tips

▫ Use the ID command to establish a point for relative or polar coordinate input.

▫ ID point coordinates are stored in the LASTPOINT until another command is issued updating this variable.

Example

```
Command: ID
Point:                                    Select any point.
Point:  X = 8.0827     Y = 5.7762     Z = 0.0000
```

IGESIN / IGESOUT

Screen [UTILITY] [IGES] [IGESIN:] *or* [IGESOUT:]
Pull down [File] [EXCHANGE >] [IGES In] *or* [IGES Out]

IGES (Initial Graphics Exchange Standard) is a drawing exchange file format that is supported by many other CAD programs. IGESIN lets you import an IGES file into a new AutoCAD drawing. IGESOUT lets you generate an IGES file from your current AutoCAD drawing. The file extension is .IGS.

I

Prompt

```
File name:
```

Related System Variable(s)

FILEDIA

Warning(s)

- Use IGESIN only in a new drawing file before drawing any entities.

- Because there are different types of IGES translation programs, some entities and data may not translate properly. Be sure to compare the translated drawing with the original.

See also: The IGES Interface Specifications document that came with your AutoCAD package.

INSERT

```
Screen [BLOCKS] [INSERT:]
Screen [DRAW] [INSERT:]
Pull down [Draw] [Insert]
```

INSERT merges a block or drawing file into the current drawing. Once you pick an insertion point, you can then specify X,Y,Z scale values and the rotation angle. The insertion point in the drawing corresponds to the block insertion base point or a drawing's base point. The default settings are: the X scale factor = 1, the Y scale factor = X, and the rotation angle is 0.

Prompts

```
Block name (or ?) <default>:
Insertion point:
X scale factor <1> / Corner / XYZ:
Y scale factor (default = X):
Rotation angle <0>:
```

Options

Block name   Specify the block or drawing name. Using an asterisk (*) before the name inserts a block or drawing as individual entities. If you insert a

	block with an asterisk, you can only give one scale factor for X, Y, and Z, and it can't be negative.
?	Activate wild-card options for reviewing the names of blocks defined in the current drawing. The default, an asterisk, displays a sorted listing of all named blocks. You can use any of the wild-card options to create a more specific list.
~	Display the File dialogue box for easy selection.
X scale factor	Enter the X scale.
Corner	The Corner option can be selected at the X scale factor prompt. You specify a scale via two points that form a rubber-band box. The first point is the insertion point and the second point becomes the other corner. The X and Y dimensions of the box become the X and Y scale factors for the block.
XYZ	Initiates prompting for XYZ scale factors.

Preset Features

Preset options provide a way to establish scale and rotation prior to picking the insert point. These options are used primarily in menu macros to enable dragging of blocks at a preset scale during insertion. The five options can be used in two ways. The first is to preset the values by entering one of the options preceded by a P at the insertion point prompt. However, if you prefix the option with a P, the values are temporary and you are again prompted for the values after the insertion point has been established. To have preset options applied after the insertion point is picked, enter the preset options without the P prefix.

Scale	Preset an XYZ scale factor.
Xscale	Preset an X scale factor.
Yscale	Preset a Y scale factor.
Zscale	Preset a Z scale factor.
Rotate	Preset a rotation angle.

Related System Variable(s)

ATTDIA, ATTDISP, ATTREQ, EXPERT

Tips

▫ Once you insert a block, you can edit it with editing commands, such as MOVE, COPY, ARRAY, and MIRROR. The components of block entities cannot be edited individually.

▫ If you respond with negative values for the scale factor prompts, the block will insert mirrored.

▫ Inserting a block by preceding its name with the asterisk is almost the same as exploding a block once it has been inserted. The only difference is that the BLOCK ? or INSERT ? options won't list the block name.

▫ A 1 x 1-unit block can be sized dynamically to fill a variety of box drawing needs. Every time you insert it, you can give the actual size of the desired box. The X scale factor will become the width, and the Y scale factor will become the height. If you are working in 3D, you can make a 3D box with a 1-unit Z value.

▫ You can update a drawing file with a revised block definition by inserting a new block definition. Type the block name and include an = sign immediately after the last character. This tells AutoCAD to ignore the existing block definition and to use the new definition. All existing blocks will be redefined to the new block.

▫ You can rename a block with the RENAME command.

▫ You can insert a block or drawing file and assign it a different name in your current drawing. At the Block name prompt, type in the block name, include an =, and enter the new block name.

▫ Inserted blocks reside on the layer that was current when they were inserted. Entities brought in with an asterisk reside on the layers from which they were created. Exploding blocks return entities to their original layer.

▫ Entering a P before Scale (PS), Xscale (PX), Yscale (PY), Zscale (PZ) or Rotate (PR) at the Insertion point prompt lets you temporarily preview how the block will look while it is dragged in the drawing. You cannot preview or preset values if you are inserting with the asterisk option.

▫ Only entities created in model space can be inserted into another drawing. You can include paper space entities by blocking those objects. They can then be used in model or paper space.

□ You can establish default settings for the current drawing session by selecting [Options] - [INSERT OPTIONS >] from the pull-down menu. The default settings are only activated when you select [Draw] - [INSERT] from the pull-down menu.

□ The system variable ATTREQ, if set to 0, lets you insert attributes without prompting and applies the attribute's default values. For normal prompting, the variable is set to 1.

□ The system variable ATTDIA, if set to 1, will cause a dialogue box (DDATTE) to appear when you insert blocks with attributes. The box displays the prompt and default value, which you can edit freely. A value of 0 causes normal attribute prompting.

Warning(s)

■ If you redefine a block, you must regenerate the drawing to see the changes.

■ If you modify a block containing attribute definitions and insert the modified block into a drawing containing old attributes, any constant attributes are replaced by new constant attributes. If an attribute definition is removed, attributes will be removed from existing blocks. Variable attributes remain unchanged even if their definition is omitted in the new block. New variable attributes will be included in all new insertions, but will not appear in previous block insertions.

■ If you want existing attributes to be completely updated, you must replace the old blocks with new ones.

See also: ATTDEF, ATTDIA, ATTDISP, ATTEDIT, ATTREQ, BASE, BLOCK, DDATTE, DRAGMODE, MINSERT, RENAME, WBLOCK, Wild-Card Characters

Example

```
Command: INSERT
Block name (or ?): PUMP
Insertion point:                        Pick point ①.
X scale factor <1> / Corner / XYZ: 2
Y scale factor (default=X): 1
Rotation angle <0>: ↵
```

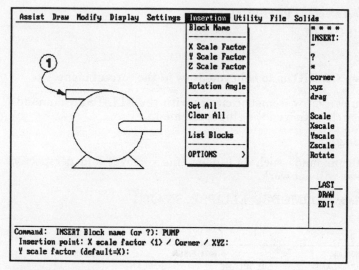

INSERT Example

ISOPLANE

Screen **[SETTINGS] [next] [SNAP] [Style] [Iso]**
Pull down **[Settings] [Drawing Tools...] [Isometric]**

The ISOPLANE command lets you draw in isometric mode with the grid and crosshairs displayed isometrically. Pressing <^E> toggles to the next isoplane. The default is the left plane. You also can set the Isoplane with the DDRMODES dialogue box.

Prompt

Left/Top/Right/<Toggle>:

Options

Left	Left isoplane is active in the 90-degree and 150-degree axis pair.
Top	Top isoplane is active in the 30-degree and 150-degree axis pair.
Right	Right isoplane is active in the 90-degree and 30-degree axis pair.

Related System Variable(s)

SNAPISOPAIR

Tips

▫ Keep ORTHO on to help you draw in the correct plane.

▫ You can draw isometric circles with the ELLIPSE command's Isocircle option on the ellipse submenu.

Warning(s)

■ 3D commands such as hidden line removal and perspective views will not work.

See also: 'DDRMODES, ELLIPSE, SNAP

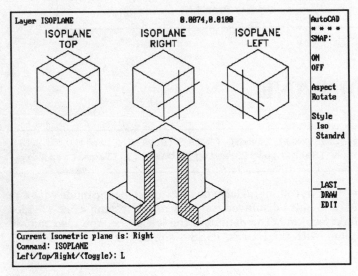

Isoplane Examples

Keys / Toggles

K

The following key combinations act as control keys or toggles (the ^ represents the CTRL key):

Control Keys

<^B>	Snap on/off
<^C>	Cancel
<^D>	Coordinate display on/off
<^E>	Isoplane left/top/right
<^G>	Grid on/off
<^H>	Backspace
<^O>	Ortho on/off
<^S>	Stop the text screen from scrolling
<^T>	Tablet on/off
<^V>	Change the active viewport (model space)
<^X>	Delete the entire line of input

Function Keys

These are the function key assignments for various AutoCAD platforms:

	DOS	Sun	OS/2	Xenix
Flip Screen	F1	F1	F2	F1
Coordinate display on/off	F6	F2	F3	F6
Grid on/off	F7	F3	F4	F7
Ortho on/off	F8	F4	F5	F8
Snap on/off	F9	F5	F6	F9
Tablet on/off	F10	F6	F7	F10
Toggle Isoplane	—	F7	F8	—

LAYER

Screen [LAYER:]
Pull down [Settings] [Layer Control...]

AutoCAD layers act as transparent drawing overlays. The LAYER command is used to control layer visibility, status, color, and linetype. You draw on the current layer. When you name a layer, the name can be up to 31 characters. The default is Layer 0 with Color = White, Linetype = Continuous, On, and Thawed. You also can control layers with the DDLMODES dialogue box.

Prompts

?/Make/Set/New/ON/OFF/Color/Ltype/Freeze/Thaw:

Options

?	Allows you to review the names of layers defined in the drawing. The default, an asterisk (*), displays a sorted listing of the named layers. You can use any of the wild-card options to create a more specific list.
Make	Create a new layer and make it current.
Set	Make the layer current.
New	Create new layer(s).
ON	Turn layer(s) on.
OFF	Turn layer(s) off.
Color	Assign a color to layer(s).
Ltype	Assign a linetype to layer(s).
Freeze	Make the layer invisible and prevents the layer from regenerating.
Thaw	Unfreeze a layer.

Related System Variable(s)

CLAYER, TILEMODE

Tips

□ You can't delete, purge, or rename layer 0. However, you can change its color and linetype assignment, including its On/Off Freeze/Thaw state.

□ When you create new layers, you can type more than one layer name at a time as long as they are separated by commas. The same applies to setting color and linetype.

□ If you set color and linetype bylayer, any entities you draw default to the color and linetype of the current layer.

□ You can pick linetype options from the screen menu. If you use the pull-down menus, you need to load the linetype first.

□ If you draw an entity on the wrong layer, you can use the CHANGE or CHPROP command to reassign the entity to a different layer.

□ Blocks containing entities drawn on layer 0 adopt the current layer's properties upon insertion.

□ Turning TILEMODE off (0) lets you determine a layer's visibility by viewport.

□ You control viewport layer visibility with the VPLAYER command (Release 11 only).

Warning(s)

■ You can make a layer current that is turned off, but you can't make a frozen layer current.

■ Associative dimensioning creates a layer called DEFPOINTS (definition points). The dots are visible even though the layer is turned off. The dots will not plot unless you rename the layer.

■ Activating AMElite creates a layer named AME_PRZ. Do not edit entities on this layer if you plan to create, edit, or analyze AME solids.

See also: CHANGE, CHPROP, COLOR, BLOCK, 'DDEMODES, 'DDLMODES, LINETYPE, LTSCALE, PURGE, RENAME, VPLAYER, Wild-Card Characters

Example

```
Command: LAYER
?/Make/Set/New/ON/OFF/Color/Ltype/Freeze/Thaw: N
New layer name(s):
2-TEXT,2-WALLS,2-FURNITURE,2-DIMENSION
?/Make/Set/New/ON/OFF/Color/Ltype/Freeze/Thaw: C
Color: blue
Layer name(s) for color 5 (blue) : 2-DIMENSION,2-TEXT
?/Make/Set/New/ON/OFF/Color/Ltype/Freeze/Thaw: S
New current layer : 1-WALLS
```

?/Make/Set/New/ON/OFF/Color/Ltype/Freeze/Thaw: **F**
Layer name(s) to Freeze: **?-TEXT,?-DIMENSION**
?/Make/Set/New/ON/OFF/Color/Ltype/Freeze/Thaw: ⏎

LIMITS

Screen **[SETTINGS] [LIMITS:]**
Pull down **[Utility] [Limits]**

LIMITS defines your active drawing area. This area is defined by the absolute coordinates of the lower left and upper right corners. The LIMITS command lets you modify these points and turn limits checking on and off.

Prompts

```
Reset Model space limits:
ON/OFF/<Lower left corner> <0.0000,0.0000>:
Upper right corner <12.0000,9.0000>:
```

Options

ON   Turns limits checking on; you cannot pick a point outside the limits.

OFF   Turns limits checking off (default); you can pick a point outside the limits.

Lower left corner
               Changes the lower left corner coordinates.

Upper right corner
               Changes the upper right corner coordinates.

Related System Variable(s)

LIMCHECK, LIMMIN, LIMMAX, TILEMODE

Tips

□ Set your limits to represent the full size of what you plan to draw or a little larger.

□ If you enlarge the limits, you must use ZOOM All to display the lower left and upper right corners. If you have entities outside the limits, the display will include those entities as well. ZOOM All shows you the current limits or drawing extents, whichever is greater.

□ There are no limits in the Z direction.

□ If grid is on and you are in the WCS, grid dots are displayed to the drawing limits.

□ Model space and paper space each have their own limits.

□ You can PLOT and PRPLOT to the drawing limits.

Warning(s)

■ If limits checking is enabled and you pick a point outside the limits, you will get the message **Outside limits, and your command may not complete.

See also: PLOT, STATUS, ZOOM

LINE

Screen **[DRAW] [LINE:]**
Pull down **[Draw] [Line]**

LINE lets you draw straight line segments. You can enter 2D or 3D points at the From point and To point prompts.

Prompts

From point:
To point:
To point:
To point:

Options

Continue   At the From point prompt, you can begin a line at the endpoint of the most recently drawn line or arc by selecting Continue or pressing <RETURN>.

Close   Entering C (Close) at the To point prompt closes the line segments created during the command, connecting the last endpoint to the original start point.

Undo   Entering U (Undo) at the To point prompt undoes the last line and returns you to the previous point.

Tips

□ If you turn ORTHO on, you can draw orthogonal lines.

□ You can save time and draw lines more accurately by using snap and osnap.

□ If you want to draw lines with different line weights, use polylines or traces, or assign colors to the lines and plot with different pens.

□ If an arc is the last entity drawn, you can draw a line tangent to the arc endpoint by using the Continue option and specifying only the line length. The direction is determined by the endpoint of the arc.

Warning(s)

■ Using the Undo option while in the LINE command is different from issuing an UNDO at a command prompt. Undo during the LINE command releases you to the previous point and lets you continue drawing lines. Using the UNDO at the command prompt backsteps to the previous command.

See also: PLINE, TRACE

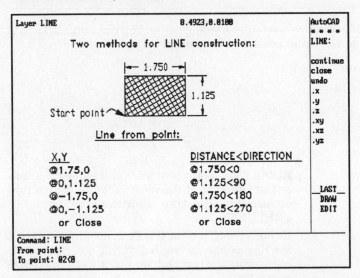

LINE Example

LINETYPE

Screen **[SETTINGS] [LINETYP:]**
Pull down **[Utility] [Load LTypes]**
Pull down **[Options] [Entity Creation...]**
Pull down **[Settings] [Layer Control...]**

LINETYPE assigns a linetype for new entities, loads linetype definitions stored in library files, and creates new linetype definitions. Linetypes are made up of dashes, dots, and spaces.

Standard linetypes include continuous, border, center, dash-dot, dashed, divide, dot, hidden, and phantom. Each linetype also has two predefined variations with twice and half the scale of the standard linetypes.

You can control the linetype of new entities individually or by their layer assignment. The default is BYLAYER. You can also set linetypes with DDEMODES and DDLMODES.

Prompts

?/Create/Load/Set:

Options

?	Display a sorted listing of the named linetype libraries. You can use any of the wild-card options to create a more specific list. If FILEDIA is set to 1, the ? displays the File dialogue box. The linetype library file extensions are .LIN.
Create	Create new linetypes.
Load	Load linetypes defined in existing library files. You can use any of the wild-card options to load linetypes.
Set	Set a linetype for new entities.

In addition to standard linetype names such as HIDDEN and DASHED, you can specify BYBLOCK and BYLAYER.

BYLAYER	New entities receive the linetype of the layers on which they reside.
BYBLOCK	New entities are drawn with the continuous linetype until they are saved as a block. When the

block is inserted, it inherits the linetype set by the LINETYPE command.

Related System Variable(s)

CELTYPE, BYLAYER, FILEDIA

Tips

▫ Only lines, circles, arcs, and 2D polylines can display broken linetypes.

▫ You can control the scale of linetypes with the LTSCALE command or by creating new linetypes.

▫ If you decide to use multiple linetypes on a single layer, it may be faster and easier to create new entities with the linetype bylayer and change the linetype for any exceptions.

▫ You can delete or rename all linetypes (except continuous) with the PURGE and RENAME commands.

▫ Using non-continuous linetypes can slow down redraws and regenerations. You can use the continuous linetype until you are ready to plot, then use the CHANGE or CHPROP command, or respecify a layer linetype for plotting.

▫ Some plotters can produce their own linetypes. To take advantage of these hardware linetypes and maximize display speed, use only the continuous linetype and key linetypes to different entity colors.

Warning(s)

■ Mixing linetypes on a single layer can become confusing. Using the LAYER command to control linetype and leaving LINETYPE set bylayer helps you identify the layer an entity is on, and makes changing linetypes a simple process of respecifying the linetype with the LAYER command.

■ Some plotters don't support hardware linetypes based on an entity's color assignment. To use AutoCAD's linetypes, set your plotter to plot continuous lines at all times.

■ Linetypes must be loaded before they can be assigned or set.

■ If you change an entity's linetype, you must regenerate the screen to see the revisions.

See also: CHANGE, CHPROP, 'DDEMODES, 'DDLMODES, LAYER, LTSCALE, PLOT, RENAME

```
Layer LINETYPE                    9.1858,0.0107              AutoCAD
                   CONTINUOUS                                * * * *
    — — — — —  BORDER        — · — — · — · —  DIVIDE         LINETYP:
                                                             ?
  — — — — — — — —  BORDER2   — · · — · — · — · — ·  DIVIDE2
                                                             Create
    — —  · — —  BORDERX2     — · · — · · — · · —  DIVIDEX2   Load
                                                             Set
    — · — — · —  CENTER       · · · · · · · · · · ·  DOT
                                                             Yes
  — — — — · — — · —  CENTER2   · · · · · · · · · · · · ·  DOT2   No
    — —  — —  CENTERX2       · · · · · · · · ·  DOTX2
  — · — · — — · —  DASHDOT    — — — — — — — — —  HIDDEN
  — · — — · — — · —  DASHDOT2  — — — — — — — —  HIDDEN2
    — · — — · — — · —  DASHDOTX2  — — — — — — —  HIDDENX2
    — — — — — — —  DASHED     — — · · — — · · —  PHANTOM      LAST
                                                             DRAW
  — — — — — — — —  DASHED2    — — · · — — · · — ·  PHANTOM2    EDIT
    — —  — —  — —  DASHEDX2   — —  — —  — —  PHANTOMX2
Command: LINETYPE
?/Create/Load/Set: Load
Linetype(s) to load:
```

Listing of Standard Linetypes

LIST / DBLIST

Screen **[INQUIRY] [LIST:]** *or* **[DBLIST:]**
Pull down **[Utility] [List]**

The LIST command provides detailed information on selected entities within a drawing. The DBLIST (Data Base) command provides information on all entities within a drawing. These commands provide various information depending on the entity. If the list is long and begins to scroll off the screen, you can press <^S> or PAUSE to halt the scroll. Depressing any key will continue the listing process. Pressing <^C> will cancel the list. If you have a printer, you can toggle on <^Q> before issuing the command and send the data directly to the printer.

Prompts

Select objects:

Tips

◻ It is faster to determine the length of a line with the LIST command than with the DISTANCE command.

◻ If HANDLES are enabled, the handle number in hexadecimal notation is provided.

Warning(s)

■ If you pick too many entities to list, it is hard to tell which descriptions fit which entities.

■ LIST for hatch patterns will always show the scale factors as 1 and the rotation angle as 0.

See also: AREA, DIST

LOAD   See SHAPE

LTSCALE

Screen **[SETTINGS] [next] [LTSCALE:]**
Pull down **[Options] [Linetype Scale]**

LTSCALE (LineType SCALE) assigns a global scale multiplier for all linetypes. The default is <1.0000>.

Prompt

New scale factor <1.0000>:

Related System Variable(s)

LTSCALE

Tips

◻ A rule of thumb for determining a drawing's proper linetype scale is to multiply the drawing's scale factor by .375. Once you have plotted the drawing, you can fine tune the linetype scale value.

▫ To decrease redraw and regen time, set your linetype scale to a large value and change the value just before you plot the drawing. Setting all your linetypes to continuous bylayer is even faster. When you are ready to plot, change linetypes with the LAYER command.

Warning(s)

■ If you change your drawing's linetype scale, you won't see a change until the drawing regenerates.

See also: LINETYPE, REGEN

LTSCALE Examples

LTYPE   See LAYER and LINETYPE

MEASURE

MEASURE marks an entity at equal segment lengths that you specify. The entity isn't physically separated; rather, points or blocks are placed as markers at each segment end point. You can measure lines, circles, arcs, and polylines.

Prompts

```
Select object to measure:
<Segment length>/Block:
```

Options

Segment length   Enter the desired segment length. Segments are measured starting with the endpoint of the entity closest to the pick point you use to select an object.

Block   Measure the entity with a block currently defined in the drawing. After providing the block name, you are prompted for the segment length.

Tips

▫ If you can't see points measuring an entity, try adjusting the PDMODE and PDSIZE system variables and issuing a REGEN.

▫ You can osnap to the points with the NODe option.

▫ When you are using the Block option, you are asked if you want to align the block with the entity to measure. If you answer Yes, the block is rotated around its insertion point so that it is drawn parallel to the entity being measured. If you answer No, the block is drawn with a 0 rotation angle relative to the entity.

▫ You can manipulate the markers as a group by using the Previous selection set option.

▫ You can establish default settings by selecting [Options] - [Measure Distance] and [D/M Block Name] from the pull-down menu.

Warning(s)

- You can measure only one entity at a time.

- You cannot change the X,Y,Z scale factor of a block used to measure an entity.

- If you want to measure an entity with a block, make sure the block has been defined within the current drawing. You can check by typing a ? after the BLOCK or INSERT command. If the block name does not appear, insert the block but cancel before picking an insertion point; then issue the MEASURE command.

- When you are using the Block option, only those attributes defined as constant will be inserted into the drawing. If you try editing an attribute, the message `Block has no attributes` appears.

- Markers are placed in the UCS of the entity being measured. They are always placed on the entity regardless of the current elevation setting.

See also: DIVIDE, NODE, POINT

Example

```
Command: MEASURE
Select object to measure:          Pick polyline ①.
<Segment length>/Block: .5

Command: MEASURE
Select object to measure:          Pick polyline ②.
<Segment length>/Block: B
Block name to insert: BEAM
Align block with object? <Y> ↵
Segment length: .5
```

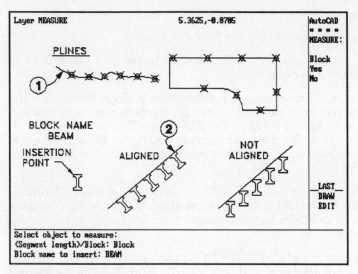

MEASURE Examples

MENU

Screen [UTILITY] [MENU:]

MENU loads and displays a menu file for the current drawing. This file defines the screen, pull-down, and tablet menus, including the pick buttons if you're using a pointing device with buttons. The uncompiled source file is an ASCII text file with the extension .MNU. AutoCAD compiles the menu and forms a file with the extension .MNX, which it actually loads. The default menu is ACAD.

Prompts

Menu file name or . for none <acad>:

Options

Menu file name   Enter the name of a menu file, excluding the extension .MNU or .MNX.

. (period)   Disables all menus. You can access the commands by typing them at the command prompt.

Related System Variable(s)

MENUNAME, MENUECHO

Tips

▫ All menu files have an extension of .MNU. These files are compiled for speed, and a new menu file is created with the extension .MNX. If an .MNU file is updated, AutoCAD recognizes the file date and time and automatically recompiles and loads the new .MNX file when you first start it.

Warning(s)

■ The name of the last menu file used is stored in the drawing file. If you enter an existing drawing and receive the message, `Enter another menu file name (or RETURN for none):`, it only means that the last menu file used for that drawing could not be located. You can type ACAD and use the menu that comes with AutoCAD. This assumes that ACAD.MNU or ACAD.MNX is located in a directory recognized by AutoCAD.

■ MENUECHO always defaults to 0 when you end a drawing session, regardless of the setting.

See also: TABLET

MINSERT

```
Screen [BLOCKS] [MINSERT:]
Screen [DRAW] [MINSERT:]
```

The MINSERT (Multiple INSERT) command is a combination of the INSERT and ARRAY (rectangular) commands. MINSERT lets you insert multiple copies of a block in a rectangular pattern. It has the same prompts as the INSERT command for insertion point, X,Y scaling, and rotation angle.

Prompts

```
Block name (or ?):
```

Options

?   Allows you to review the names of blocks defined in the current drawing. The default, an asterisk, displays a sorted listing of all named blocks. You can use any of the wild-card options to create a more specific list.

After you enter a block name, you will see the standard INSERT prompts for insertion point and scaling. MINSERT then prompts for the rectangular array:

```
Number of rows (---):
Number of columns (|||):
Unit cell or distance between rows (---):
Distance between columns (|||):
```

You provide the number of rows and columns, and the distance between rows and columns.

Tips

▫ Responding with a tilde (~) when prompted for a block name activates the File dialogue box.

▫ MINSERT uses less memory than inserting and arraying a block.

▫ You can array at an angle with the MINSERT command, just like the ARRAY command. You must change your snap rotation angle, define a UCS at the desired angle, or use the ROTATE command once the blocks have been inserted.

Warning(s)

■ All the blocks making up a MINSERT array must remain intact. You can't explode the array, nor can you minsert the block with an asterisk preceding the block name.

See also: ARRAY, BLOCK, INSERT

MIRROR

Screen **[EDIT] [next] [MIRROR:]**
Pull down **[Modify] [Mirror]**

The MIRROR command creates a mirrored replica of a selected group of entities. You can keep the original group of entities or have them deleted. The default is to not delete them.

Prompts

```
Select objects:
First point of mirror line:
Second point:
Delete old objects? <N>
```

Options

First point of mirror line
> Designates the first point on an axis about which the entities are mirrored.

Second point   Designates the second point on an axis about which the entities are mirrored.

Delete old objects? <N>
> A Yes response erases the entities to be mirrored.

Related System Variable(s)

MIRRTEXT

Tips

□ If MIRRTEXT is set to 0, text and variable attributes are not mirrored. However, text and constant attributes assigned to a block that is mirrored will be mirrored regardless of the MIRRTEXT setting.

□ You can also mirror a block by inserting it with negative X and Y values.

□ Mirroring viewport entities in paper space has no effect on model space views or entities.

Warning(s)

■ You cannot explode a mirrored block.

■ Associate dimension text is not mirrored regardless of the MIRRTEXT setting.

See also: INSERT

Example

```
Command: MIRROR                        Select entities.
Select objects:                        Point ①.
First point of mirror line:            Point ②.
Second point:
Delete old objects? <N> ↵
```

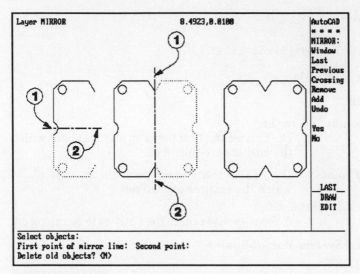

MIRROR Example

MODEL SPACE   See MSPACE

MOVE

Screen **[EDIT] [next] [MOVE:]**
Pull down **[Modify] [Move]**

MOVE relocates entities anywhere in 3D space.

Prompts

```
Select objects:
Base point or displacement:
Second point of displacement:
```

Options

Base point   Enter a point of reference to apply the
               displacement distance (below), or by which to
               drag the selected entity.

Displacement   Enter the distance for X,Y,Z, or drag the entity
                to specify the displacement.

Tips

◻ If you want to move entities to another layer, you must use the
  CHANGE or CHPROP commands.

Warning(s)

▪ If you accidentally press <RETURN> at the Second point
  prompt, your entities could end up out of view. This happens
  because MOVE uses the X,Y,Z base point coordinates as
  displacement distances.

See also: COPY

Example

```
Command: MOVE
Select objects:                          Select dotted circle.
Base point or displacement:              Point ①.
Second point of displacement:            Point ②.
```

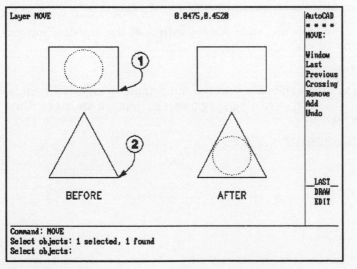

MOVE Example

MSLIDE

Screen [UTILITY] [SLIDES] [MSLIDE:]

MSLIDE (Make SLIDE) creates a snapshot of your current screen display in a file with the extension .SLD. The slide is of the current viewport and is independent of the drawing file from which it was created. The screen is redrawn as the slide is made. The default name for the slide is the current drawing file name. Use the VSLIDE command to view slides.

Prompt

Slide file <default>:

Tips

▢ Since slide files do not contain any entity data, viewing slides occurs at redraw speed.

▢ Slide files are convenient to use as references.

▢ You can view any slide file regardless of the drawing you are currently editing.

Warning(s)

▪ If you save a slide file with the same name as an existing slide, you will not receive a warning message that you are overwriting the file.

See also: SCRIPT, VSLIDE

MSPACE

Pull down **[Display] [Mview >] [Mspace]**

MSPACE (Model SPACE) (Release 11 only) switches from paper space to model space. Paper space is used to annotate, dimension, compose, and plot 2D or 3D drawings created in model space.

The system variable TILEMODE is also used to switch between paper space and model space. The default is on. If you turn TILEMODE off (paper space current), you must create at least one viewport with the MVIEW command before you can work in model space.

Related System Variable(s)

TILEMODE

Tips

▫ Model space and paper space retain their own limits.

▫ Plotting in model space only plots the current viewport.

See also: MVIEW, PSPACE, TILEMODE, VPLAYER

MULTIPLE

Type **MULTIPLE**

MULTIPLE is a command modifier that causes any command to repeat. Type the word MULTIPLE before a command. To end the command, press <^C> to cancel. No command prompt is issued if you enter MULTIPLE alone.

Tips

▫ MULTIPLE saves time when editing many attributes (MULTIPLE DDATTE) and when inserting blocks (MULTIPLE INSERT).

Warning(s)

- MULTIPLE remembers and repeats the main command, but it does not retain command parameters or options.

- You can't use MULTIPLE with PLOT or PRPLOT.

MVIEW

Screen **[DRAW] [MVIEW]**
Pull down **[Display] [Mview >]**
[Mview *option*]

MVIEW (Make VIEW) (Release 11 only) creates and restores viewports, controls viewport visibility, and performs hidden line removal during paper space plots.

Prompt

ON/OFF/Hideplot/Fit/2/3/4/Restore/<First Point>:

Options

First point	Create a viewport by picking two diagonal points. This new viewport becomes the current viewport.
ON	All entities in the selected viewports are visible.
OFF	All entities in the selected viewports are invisible.
Hideplot	Select viewports for hidden line removal during plotting.
Fit	Create a viewport the size of your graphics screen.
2/3/4	Create viewport configurations of two, three, or four viewports.
Restore	Restore viewport configurations saved with the VPORTS command.

Related System Variable(s)

MAXACTVP, TILEMODE

Warning(s)

■ The number of viewports turned on cannot exceed the maximum allowable number of active viewports (MAXACTVP).

See also: MSPACE, PSPACE, TILEMODE, VPLAYER, VPORTS

Object Snaps   See OSNAPS

OFFSET

Screen **[DRAW] [OFFSET:]**
Screen **[EDIT] [next] [OFFSET:]**
Pull down **[Modify [Offset]**

OFFSET lets you copy a line, arc, circle, or polyline parallel to itself by an offset distance or through a point. The default is <Through>.

Prompts

Offset distance or Through <Through>:
Select object to offset:

Options

Offset distance   Enter the offset distance by typing a value or picking two points. Pick the side to offset at the Side to offset prompt.

Through   Pick a point to offset through.

The command repeats until you press <^C> to cancel.

Tips

□ The entity you pick to offset must have its extrusion direction parallel to the Z axis of the current UCS. You may find the results more predictable if you offset while in the plan view of the current UCS.

□ If you desire to offset entities at equal distances, it may be faster to use the ARRAY command.

□ You can establish a default by selecting [Options] - [Offset Distance] from the pull-down menu. This default is only for the current drawing session and is activated only when selecting [Modify] - [Offset] from the pull-down menu.

Warning(s)

- You can only offset one entity at a time.

- You cannot use the object selections Window, Crossing, or Last with OFFSET.

See also: ARRAY, COPY, UCS

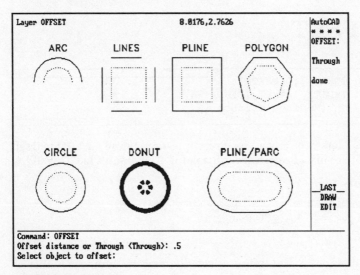

OFFSET Examples

OOPS

Screen **[BLOCKS] [BLOCK:] [OOPS]**
Screen **[EDIT] [ERASE:] [OOPS]**
Pull down **[Modify] [Oops!]**

OOPS restores the last entity, or group of entities, that were deleted by the most recent ERASE command in the current drawing session.

Tips

▫ You can issue the OOPS command after creating a BLOCK or WBLOCK to restore those entities.

Warning(s)

▪ OOPS will not restore entities erased before the PLOT or PRPLOT commands.

See also: BLOCK, UNDO, WBLOCK

ORTHO

```
Command: ORTHO
Pull down [Settings] [Ortho On/Off   ^O]
```

ORTHO constrains lines, polylines, and traces to horizontal and vertical. ORTHO mode also controls the angle at which you pick the second point in many other drawing and editing commands. ORTHO is a toggle, and the default is <Off>. You can also set ORTHO with the DDRMODES dialogue box.

Prompts

ON/OFF <Off>:

Options

ON   Enables ORTHO mode.
OFF   Disables ORTHO mode.

Related System Variable(s)

ORTHOMODE

Tips

▫ If ORTHO is on, your second pick point can be either horizontal or vertical depending on how far your crosshairs are from the first point. The larger of these distances determines the direction.

▫ ORTHO angle is based on the snap rotation angle and current UCS.

- Keyboard coordinate entry and OSNAP override ORTHO.

- Keep ORTHO on when working in isometric mode.

Warning(s)

- ORTHO mode is inactive during perspective views.

See also: 'DDRMODES

OSNAP

Screen **[SETTINGS] [next] [OSNAP:]**
Pull down **[Assist] [OSNAP: <mode>]** *or specific mode*

OSNAP (Object SNAP) lets you apply one or more object snap modes to point selection. These object snap modes calculate the coordinates of geometric points on selected entities. Think of OSNAPs as snapping to attachment points on your drawing entities. When you enable an OSNAP, the cursor displays an aperture box, which must cross the entity to be snapped to. There are 12 different OSNAP modes. The default is Off or NONe.

You use the OSNAP command to set a "running" mode to be in effect for all subsequent point selections.

You can preset more than one OSNAP mode by entering a comma between each OSNAP mode without using any spaces. You can override a running mode by typing an OSNAP mode when a point is requested, or by using the pull-down menus or screen menu overrides. The screen menu overrides are displayed by the * * * * menu item on the root screen menu. The STATUS command displays the current OSNAP mode(s).

Prompt

Object snap modes:

Options

CENter, ENDpoint, INSertion, INTersection, MIDpoint, NEArest, NODe, NONe, PERpendicular, QUAdrant, QUIck, TANgent.

Related System Variable(s)

OSMODE

Tips

▢ Keep your aperture and pickbox different sizes to distinguish between them.

Warning(s)

■ Running OSNAPs are inactive during entity selection (Release 11 only). To apply an OSNAP, select the desired OSNAP override. Release 10 may produce unexpected results, such as selecting a circle while CENter osnap mode is active.

See also: APERTURE

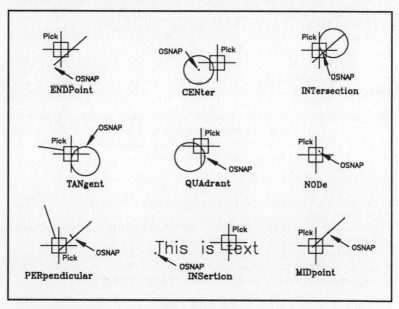

OSNAP Examples

PAN

Screen [DISPLAY] [PAN:]
Pull down [Display] [Pan]

PAN lets you scroll around your drawing without altering the current zoom ratio. It is similar to repositioning paper on a drafting board for easier access to another part of a drawing. You do not physically move entities or change your drawing limits; you move your display window across your drawing. PAN is also a transparent command. The default is to provide a displacement in relative coordinates.

Prompts
Displacement:
Second point:

Options

Displacement   Enter a relative X,Y distance and at the Second point prompt, press <RETURN> or enter a pair of coordinates for the Displacement and the Second point prompts.

Tips

▫ You can pan independently within each viewport.

▫ You can pick two points to show the From and To points representing the distance and angle.

▫ ZOOM Dynamic produces the same results as the PAN command, but it can pan further in one command.

▫ Pans become part of the ZOOM Previous queue.

Warning(s)

■ You cannot perform a transparent pan while in the VPOINT, DVIEW, ZOOM, VIEW, or PAN commands, or while you are in paper space.

See also: Transparent Commands

Example

```
Command: 'PAN
Displacement:              Point ①.
Second point:              Point ②.
```

Left viewport shows drawing before PAN, right viewport after.

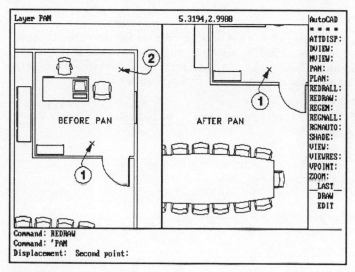

PAN Example

PAPER SPACE   See PSPACE

PEDIT

Screen **[EDIT] [next] [PEDIT:]**
Pull down **[Modify] [PolyEdit]**

PEDIT edits 2D or 3D polylines and 3D polygon meshes. The editing options are based on the type of polyline you chose to edit. There are two basic sets of editing functions. The first set operates on the entire polyline; the second set lets you edit individual vertexes. The default is eXit or <X> to exit the command. The default for the vertex editing options is <N> for Next vertex.

Prompts

```
Select polyline:
Close/Join/Width/Edit vertex/Fit curve/Spline curve/
Decurve/Undo/eXit <X>:
Next/Previous/Break/Insert/Move/Regen/Straighten/
Tangent/Width/eXit <N>:
```

Options

The following table shows the editing options for the three types of polyline entities. PEDIT automatically identifies the type of polyline that is being edited and adjusts its prompts accordingly. See the explanations below for individual options.

	2D Polylines	3D Polylines	Polygon Meshes
Close/Open	X	X	
Join	X		
Width	X		
Edit vertex	X	X	X
Next	X	X	X
Previous	X	X	X
Break	X	X	
Insert	X	X	
Move	X	X	X
Regen	X	X	X
Straighten	X	X	
Tangent	X		
Width	X		
eXit	X	X	X
Left			X
Right			X
Up			X
Down			X
Fit curve	X		
Spline Curve	X	X	
Decurve	X	X	
Undo	X	X	X
eXit	X	X	X
Smooth surface			X
Desmooth			X
Mclose/Mopen		X	
Nclose/Nopen		X	

PEDIT assumes you want to use more than one editing option. The command will repeat itself until you choose eXit (the default) or press <^C> to cancel. (See descriptions of each PEDIT option.)

Tips

- Before you select the PEDIT option, you must first pick a polyline to edit.

- A 2D polyline can be edited in any UCS as long as its extrusion direction is parallel to the Z axis.

- Edit polyface meshes with the PFACE command.

- To convert lines and arcs into polylines, use the join option.

- To convert polylines into lines and arcs, use the EXPLODE command.

See also: EXPLODE, PLINE, POLYLINE, 3DMESH, 3DPOLY

PEDIT Close / Open

The method you use to construct polylines determines whether the polyline is considered open or closed.

An open polyline occurs when you enter the last point by typing in the coordinates, or you pick the last point on the drawing.

The system automatically closes the polyline from the starting to ending point when you select the Close option from the screen menu or enter C.

Close closes an open polyline by drawing a polyline segment from the first point of the first polyline segment to the endpoint of the last polyline segment.

Open removes the closing segment of a closed polyline.

PEDIT Join

Join takes individual 2D polylines, lines, and arcs and combines them into one 2D polyline. Select the PEDIT command and at the Select polyline prompt, pick the entity to convert. If the entity is not a polyline, you'll receive the message: Entity selected is not a polyline. Do you want to turn it into one?

Tips

□ In order to join entities, they must be contiguous. That is, their endpoints must meet at the same coordinates.

□ When using the Join option, you can use the Window or Crossing selection methods to pick the items to join. Your selection may include entities you don't want included in the selection set. As long as these entities aren't contiguous with another entity, they will not join.

Warning(s)

▪ You cannot join to a closed polyline.

▪ If the endpoints don't match, the entities will not join.

Example

```
Command: PEDIT
Select objects:                          Pick line ①.
Entity selected is not a polyline
Do you want to turn it into one? <Y> ↵
Close/Join/Width/Edit vertex/Fit curve/Spline
curve/Decurve/Undo/eXit <X>: J
Select objects:                          Select remaining entities.
3 segments added to polyline
Open/Join/Width/Edit vertex/Fit curve/Spline curve/
Decurve/Undo/eXit <X>: ↵
```

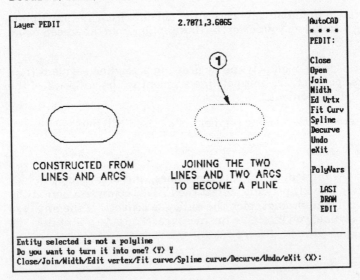

PEDIT Join Example

PEDIT Width

Width redefines the width of an entire 2D polyline.

Tips

▫ You cannot specify tapers with this option — you can only give one width to the entire polyline segment. If you want different widths between vertexes, use the Width option of Edit vertex.

PEDIT Edit vertex

Edit vertex lets you individually edit the vertexes that make up a polyline segment. An X appears at the first vertex for editing. If any of the segments were drawn with a specified tangent direction, an arrow is drawn in that direction.

Prompts

2D Polyline:
```
Next/Previous/Break/Insert/Move/Regen/Straighten/
Tangent/Width/eXit <N>:
```

3D Polyline:
```
Next/Previous/Break/Insert/Move/Regen/Straighten/eXit
<N>:
```

Polyline Mesh:
```
Vertex (0,0). Next/Previous/Left/Right/Up/Down/Move/
REgen/eXit <N>:
```

Options

Next	Next moves the X or arrow marker to the next vertex. The order is based on the initial construction of the polyline.
Previous	Previous moves the X or arrow marker to the previous vertex. The order is based on the initial construction of the polyline.
Break	Break a polyline between two vertexes. Position the X on a vertex and select Break. Position the X on any other vertex and select Go. When you break a closed polyline segment it becomes open, and the closing segment is removed. If you leave the X on the same vertex for Break and Go, it is equivalent to using the @ last point option with the BREAK command.
Insert	Inserts a new vertex. The vertex is added ahead of the X marker.

Move	Moves the vertex marked with an X to a new location.
Regen	Regenerates the polyline.
Straighten	Straighten creates a single segment between two vertexes. Any vertexes that are between the two you pick are deleted.
Tangent	Attaches a tangent direction for curve fitting to the vertex marked with the X.
Width	Edits the width between two vertexes. You can specify a starting and an ending width. The current polyline segment is considered to be between the X marker and the vertex found with the Next option. The polyline must be regenerated before you will see the results.
eXit	Exits the Edit vertex submenu and returns you to the PEDIT prompt. You can also use eXit to cancel the Break and Straighten routines.
Undo	Undoes, one step at a time, the most recent Edit vertex commands.
Go	Used during the Break and Straighten options to tell the system you are ready to break or straighten the segments between two vertexes.
Left	For 3D mesh, move left to a previous vertex in the N direction.
Right	For 3D mesh, move right to the next vertex in the N direction.
Up	For 3D mesh, move up to the next vertex in the M direction.
Down	For 3D mesh, move down to the previous vertex in the M direction.

PEDIT Fit Curve

Regenerates the current polyline, placing arc segments between the vertexes.

Tips

▫ You can decurve a Fit curve.

Warning(s)

▪ If you edit a Fit curve polyline with BREAK, EXPLODE, or TRIM, the Decurve option is no longer available.

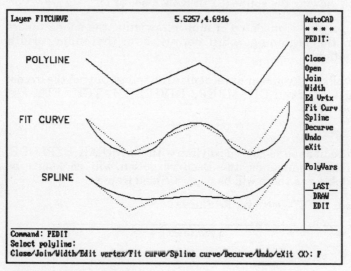

See also: PEDIT Decurve, Spline

PEDIT Fit Curve Examples

PEDIT Spline Curve

Spline curve uses the polyline vertexes as control points for a B-spline curve. The spline passes through the beginning and ending points of the polyline and is pulled towards the other vertexes, but does not pass through them. You can view the frame of the spline by setting the SPLFRAME system variable on.

Related System Variable(s)

SPLINETYPE, SPLINESEGS, SPLFRAME

Tips

▫ You can decurve a spline curve.

▫ If you use the Edit vertex option, the X marker appears on the frame regardless of the current SPLFRAME setting.

▫ The greater the value for SPLINESEGS, the more precise the curve will be, and the closer to the control points. If you enter a negative number, you end up with a smoother curve. Setting SPLINESEGS to a negative number is not allowed for 3D polylines.

□   If the polyline is defined with arcs, the arcs are straightened when viewing the spline (SPLFRAME set to 1).

□   If a polyline is made up of multiple widths, the spline tapers from the beginning width definition to the ending width definition.

□   The following commands recognize the spline, but not the frame: AREA (entity), CHAMFER, DIVIDE, HATCH, FILLET, MEASURE.

Warning(s)

■   If you edit a spline-curved polyline with the BREAK, EXPLODE, or TRIM commands, the Decurve option will no longer be available and there will be no associated frame.

See also: PEDIT Decurve, Fit Curve

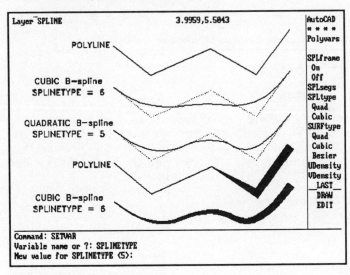

PEDIT Spline Curve Example

PEDIT Decurve

Decurve removes the curves from any polyline that was either Fit curved or Spline curved, and returns it to its original state.

PEDIT Undo

Undo takes you back one PEDIT option at a time. This is different from the UNDO command, which backsteps to the previous command. For example, if you issued four PEDIT options, all four PEDIT options would be reversed or undone by one use of the UNDO command or four uses of the PEDIT Undo option.

See also: UNDO

PEDIT eXit

Use eXit to leave the PEDIT command and return to the command prompt. The PEDIT command default is eXit. You can also press <^C> to cancel.

PEDIT Smooth surface / Desmooth

Smooth replaces a 3D mesh with a smooth surface. Desmooth returns a smooth 3D mesh to its original state.

Related System Variable(s)

SURFTYPE, SPLFRAME

Warning(s)

- Meshes that contain more than 11 vertexes in either the M or N direction cannot be changed into a Bézier surface.

- Cubic B-spline surfaces require a minimum control point mesh size of 4 x 4.

- Quadratic B-spline surfaces require a minimum control point mesh size of 3 x 3.

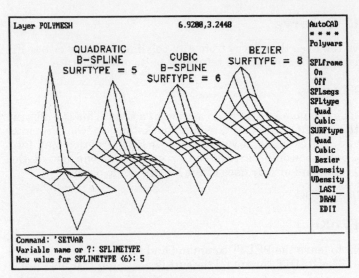

PEDIT Smoothed 3D Mesh Examples

PEDIT Mopen / Mclose Nopen / Nclose

Mopen/Mclose opens or closes a 3D mesh in the M direction. Nopen/Nclose opens or closes a 3D mesh in the N direction.

PFACE

Screen [DRAW] [next] [3D Surfs] [PFACE:]
Screen [SURFACES] [PFACE:]

The PFACE (PolyFACE) (Release 11 only) command creates arbitrary polyface meshes. The mesh is composed of vertexes and faces you specify. It is mainly used for AutoLISP and ADS applications.

Prompts

Vertex 1:
Face 1, vertex 1:

Options

VERTEX   Specify the location for each vertex.

FACE   Specify the vertex numbers that define each face.

Related System Variable(s)

PFACEVMAX

Tips

▫ You can enter the vertexes as 2D and 3D points.

▫ You can make the edges of the polyface mesh invisible by entering a negative vertex number for the beginning vertex of the edge.

▫ You can use the LAYER and COLOR commands when defining faces. Enter L or LAYER and C or COLOR when prompted to define a face. Changing the layer and color doesn't affect any new entities you create for subsequent commands.

▫ Even though you can use osnaps on polyface meshes, you cannot pick the vertexes with the NODe option.

Warning(s)

■ You must keep track of each vertex and its number assignment in order to define the faces.

■ If you press <^C> or cancel before exiting the command, you must start over.

■ You can use the following edit commands on PFACE meshes: ARRAY, CHPROP, CHANGE, ERASE, LIST, MIRROR, MOVE, ROTATE, SCALE, STRETCH, and EXPLODE. However, you cannot use the PEDIT command.

■ The whole mesh becomes invisible even when you assign only part of the mesh to a frozen layer.

■ A PFACE mesh converts into 3DFACES when exploded.

See also: EDGESURF, REVSURF, RULESURF, TABSURF, 3DFACE

Example

```
PFACE
Vertex 1: 3,2
Vertex 2: 9,2
Vertex 3: 9,6
Vertex 4: 3,6
Vertex 5: 6,4,9
Vertex 6: ↵
Face 1, vertex 1: LAYER
New layer <0>: FRONT
Face 1, vertex 1: 1
Face 1, vertex 2: 2
Face 1, vertex 3: 5
Face 1, vertex 4: ↵
Face 2, vertex 1: LAYER
New layer <0>: BACK
Face 2, vertex 1: 3
Face 2, vertex 2: 4
Face 2, vertex 3: 5
Face 2, vertex 4: ↵
Face 2, vertex 3: 5
Face 2, vertex 4: ↵
Face 3, vertex 1: ↵
```

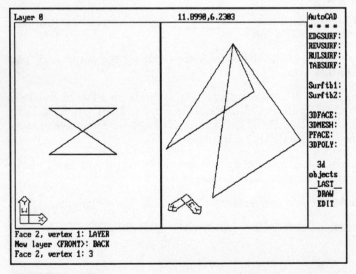

PFACE Example

PLAN

Screen **[DISPLAY] [PLAN:]**
Pull down **[Display] [Plan View (UCS)]** or **[Plan View (World)]**

PLAN displays the plan view of any defined UCS or the WCS. A plan view is defined as having a view point of 0,0,1. The default setting is <Current UCS>.

Prompts

<Current UCS>/UCS/World:

Options

Current UCS	Restore the plan view of the current UCS (the default).
UCS	Restore the plan view of a previously defined UCS.
World	Restore the plan view of the WCS.

Related System Variable(s)

UCSFOLLOW

Tips

◻ PLAN only affects the current viewport.

Warning(s)

■ Issuing the PLAN command turns off perspective and clipping.

■ You cannot use this command while in paper space.

See also: UCS, VPOINT

PLINE

A polyline is a series of line and arc segments that share the same vertexes and are processed as a single entity. The PLINE command draws 2D polylines. It has a line mode and an arc mode, each with different prompts. You start both modes by specifying a From point. To edit polylines, you can use PEDIT and most of the regular edit commands.

Prompts

```
From point:
Current line-width is 0.0000
Arc/Close/Halfwidth/Length/Undo/Width/<Endpoint of
line>:
Angle/CEnter/CLose/Direction/Halfwidth/Line/Radius/
Second pt/Undo/Width/<Endpoint of arc>:
```

Options

Arc	Switches from drawing polylines to polyarcs and activates a submenu for the polyarc options.
Angle	A polyarc option whereby you specify the included angle. Since arcs are drawn counterclockwise, use a negative angle if you want to draw the arc clockwise.
CEnter	Specifies the CEnter of the arc.
Close	Similar to the close option for lines and polylines; however, an arc is used to close the segments.
Direction	Specifies a starting direction.
Line	Switches you back into line mode.
Radius	Specifies the radius of the arc.
Second pt	Allows you to construct a three-point arc.
Close	Closes the polyline segments created during a PLINE command connecting the start point to the end point.

Halfwidth	Specifies the width from the center of a polyline to one of its edges. The number is doubled for the actual width.
Length	Lets you specify the length of a new polyline segment at the same angle as the last polyline segment. If you use this option after constructing a polyarc, the polyline will be tangent to the polyarc.
Undo	Undoes a line segment and returns you to the previous point.
Width	Creates polylines with width and mitered intersections. You can even construct polyline segments with tapers by defining different starting and ending widths. Once you have drawn a tapered line segment, the next segment defaults to the ending width of the previous segment. The default width is zero.

Tips

- DONUTS, ELLIPSES, and POLYGONS are created from 2D polylines.

- CHAMFER and FILLET have special options for polylines.

- You can request the area of a polyline by selecting the Entity option; you will also be given the perimeter or length. The LIST command will give you the same information.

- If you draw polylines with an assigned width just to achieve line weights on the finished plot, you can get the same effect by assigning colors to represent different line weights and plotting with different pen point thicknesses.

- You can establish a default polyline width from the pull-down menu by selecting [Options] - [2D Polyline Width].

- Before you can select any of the options for creating polylines, you must first enter a start point.

See also: AREA, CHAMFER, FILL, FILLET, OFFSET, PEDIT, 3D POLYLINE

PLOT / PRPLOT

Main Menu **Option 3 (Plot a drawing)**
Main Menu **Option 4 (Printer Plot a drawing)**
Screen **[PLOT] [PLOTTER]** *or* **[PRINTER]**
Pull down **[File] [Plot]** *or* **[Print]**

PLOT and PRPLOT (PRinter PLOT) are the two methods you can
use to get output, or hard copy, of your drawing file. PLOT directs
your drawing to a plotter or to a plot file. PRPLOT directs your
drawing to a printer plotter (dot matrix or laser printer) or a
PRPLOT file.

You can plot from the main menu or within the drawing editor. If
you plot from the main menu, you are asked which drawing file you
want to plot. If you plot from within the drawing, it's assumed you
want to plot the current drawing. Only layers that are set to On
and Thawed are plotted.

In model space, the plot depends on the current viewport and the
chosen plotting options. In paper space, the plot depends on how
much of the drawing (including viewports) falls within the chosen
plotting options. Viewports turned off are not plotted.

The initial default settings for plotting are determined when you
configure your plotter and printer plotter. Changes to the default
settings are stored between editing sessions.

Prompts
Specify the part of the drawing to be plotted by
entering:
Display, Extents, Limits, View or Window <D>:

Options

Display   Plot what is visible in the current viewport in
model space and the current view in paper space.
If you are issuing the command from the main
menu, it is the last view or viewport visible when
the drawing was last ended or saved.

Extents   The plot is based on the drawing extents. It takes
into account all drawing entities regardless of the
limits setting.

Limits	The plot is based on the drawing limits. If the current viewport is not a plan view (0,0,1), the plot is then based on ZOOM Extents.
View	Plot a previously saved view.
Window	Plot the area you designate as a Window by picking two diagonal coordinates. You can enter two coordinates with your pointing device, or type in the absolute coordinates. If perspective is on, you can't use this option.

After you have specified the part of the drawing to be plotted, you are shown the current plotting parameters and prompted: Do you want to change anything? <N>. If you answer Yes, you are shown the current pen assignments for each color:

Entity Color	Pen No.	Line Type	Pen Speed	Entity Color	Pen No.	Line Type	Pen Speed
1 (red)	1	0	38	9	1	0	38
2 (yellow)	2	0	38	10	2	0	38
3 (green)	3	0	38	11	3	0	38
4 (cyan)	4	0	38	12	4	0	38
5 (blue)	5	0	38	13	5	0	38
6 (magenta)	6	0	38	14	6	0	38
7 (white)	7	0	38	15	7	0	38
8	8	0	38				

```
Line types  0 = continuous line
            1 = ................
            2 = . . . . . . . .
            3 = ---------------
            4 = - - - - - - - -
```

Enter values, blank=Next value, Cn=Color n, S=Show current values, X=Exit

For each color (Entity Color), you can assign a different plotter pen (Pen No.), linetype, and pen speed depending on the plotter you are configured for.

blank=Next value

Once you have entered the appropriate number, press <RETURN> or the space bar to go to the next parameter. If you keep pressing <RETURN>, you will eventually end up at the beginning, and can begin the process all over again.

Cn=Color n   If you want to jump to the next entity color, type a C. If you want to go directly to a specific entity color, type C and the number assigned to the color. For example, if you want to go directly to Entity Color number 6, type C6.

S=Show current values
Shows the current values of pen number, linetype, and pen speed assignments.

X=Exit   When you have completed pen number, linetype, and pen speed assignments, enter an X to go to the next prompt.

After you have exited from assigning pens, you are prompted to establish the remaining plotting parameters.

Write the plot to a file? <N>

Yes   Creates a plot file. The file extension for a plotter is .PLT and for a printer is .LST.

No   Plots directly to the plotter or printer.

Size units (Inches or Millimeters) <I>:
Establishes the plot size in inches or millimeters.

Plot origin in Inches <0.00,0.00>:
Plot origin is based on the plotter or printer you are configured for. The plot origin for plotters is usually located at the lower left-hand corner of the paper; for printers, the upper left-hand corner. To obtain multiple plots on one sheet of paper, you can change the plotting origin for each plot.

Standard values for plotting size

Size	Width	Height
A	10.50	8.00
B	16.00	10.00
C	21.00	16.00
D	33.00	21.00
E	43.00	33.00
MAX	64.50	36.00

Enter the Size or Width,Height (in Inches) <MAX>:
These values are general in nature and can change depending on the available paper size and

hardware. You can enter your own set of values, which are stored to the name USER.

Rotate plot 0/90/180/270 <0>:

Rotate the drawing on the paper. You can answer No for 0 degrees rotation or Yes for 270 degrees rotation. Rotations of 90 and 180 degrees are available in Release 11 only.

Pen Width in Inches <0.010>:

The pen tip width is requested so AutoCAD can optimize the number of pen strokes to fill in any polylines, solids, and traces.

Adjust area fill boundaries for pen width? <N>

This is used for plotting, not prplots. If you answer Yes, AutoCAD will maintain dimensional accuracy when plotting with wide pens on all boundaries for polylines, solids, and traces.

Remove hidden lines? <N>

Model Space — If your drawing was constructed with 3D entities, you can have hidden edges removed during the plot. You must answer Yes even if you executed the HIDE command before entering the plot command.

Paper Space — Using the MVIEW command's Hideplot option instructs AutoCAD to perform hidden line removal on a viewport's contents during a paper space plot.

Plotted Inches=Drawing Units or Fit or ? <F>:

This is how you specify the scale. We recommend drafting at full scale and scaling the drawing to the paper at plot time or in paper space. At this point you have three choices.

Plotted Inches=Drawing Units

Tells what scale to plot the drawing. You do this by specifying how many plotted inches equal how many drawing units. You can change the plotted scale and/or the paper size with each plot.

Fit
You have AutoCAD determine a plotting scale to fit the selected plot area as large as possible.

?
Displays a help screen describing the plotting scale options.

Position paper in plotter.
Press to continue or S to Stop for hardware setup.

> Some plotters allow you to change other settings such as pen pressure and acceleration. If your plotter has these features, you may want to stop for additional hardware setup.

You can terminate the plot by pressing <^C> to cancel. Since your plotter may have an internal or external buffer, the cancel might not be immediate due to the information already being processed in the buffer.

Tips

▫ If you want to assign the same plotting parameter (pen number, linetype, or pen speed) globally, you can enter an asterisk before the value. This will update the current parameter and any that follow.

▫ You can produce different line weights and multiple color plots even if you use a monochrome monitor, by assigning colors in your drawing to different pen sizes and colors on most output devices. Some plotters even allow you to produce different linetypes by this method.

▫ Plan to spend time testing different plotting media. You may need to try several different combinations of papers, pens, pen speeds, and colors to get good results. In addition, room temperature and humidity will affect plotting quality.

▫ You can create a DXB file by configuring AutoCAD for the ADI plotter driver and selecting the DXB file output option.

▫ Many plotters offer pen plotting parameters that you can use in place of AutoCAD's settings.

Warning(s)

■ You cannot plot a slide file.

■ AutoCAD doesn't retain plot settings for each drawing. It remembers the last plotting parameters, whatever the drawing.

■ If you are using AutoCAD's linetypes, set your plotter to produce continuous lines only or you may get unexpected results.

■ There is always an inaccessible margin along the perimeter of a plotted drawing. The amount of space depends on the make and model of each plotter.

- You cannot use OOPS and UNDO for any commands before a PLOT or PRPLOT.

See also: LIMITS, VIEW, ZOOM

POINT

Screen **[DRAW] [next] [POINT:]**
Pull down **[Draw] [Point]**

The POINT command creates a point entity in X,Y,Z space. Points are often used as reference markers. Use the POINT command to place points in your drawing. Place a point by absolute, relative, or polar coordinates, or pick a point in the drawing with your pointing device. (See Point Entry.) You can osnap to points using the NODe option.

Prompt

Point:

Related System Variable(s)

PDMODE, PDSIZE

Tips

▫ You can change the way points are displayed (shape and size) from the pull-down menu. Select [Options] - [Point Size] and [Point Type...].

▫ You can have only one combination of PDMODE and PDSIZE in a drawing at a time. If you change the settings, the drawing will globally update at the next regeneration.

▫ Points that are placed on the DEFPOINTS layer by associative dimensioning are not affected by PDMODE or PDSIZE.

Warning(s)

- Unlike blips, points are part of the drawing and will plot. If you don't want the points to plot, you can erase them, create them on a layer and turn it off, or set PDMODE to 1.

See also: DIVIDE, MEASURE

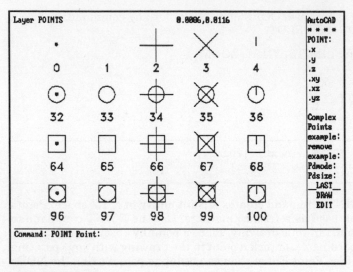

Point Examples

Point Entry

Point entry is based on the Cartesian coordinate system; every point has an X,Y,Z value. The X axis is the horizontal distance; the Y axis is the vertical distance; the Z axis is at right angles to the plane defined by the X and Y axes. If you don't specify a Z value, it defaults to the current elevation.

Options

Pick a point on the screen with your pointing device.

Pick a point on the screen with the keyboard arrow keys.

Specify a point by entering its absolute coordinates. Absolute coordinates are based on the current UCS origin. Examples are: 3,2 or 3,2,0.

Specify a point by entering its relative coordinates. Relative coordinates are relative to the last-entered point and are preceded with the @ symbol. Examples are: @-5,0 or @-5,0,0.

Specify an absolute or relative point by entering polar coordinates. Polar coordinates specify a distance and angle or direction. The format for an absolute polar coordinate is distance<angle; precede

with an @ for a relative polar coordinate. Examples are: 3<90 or @3<90.

Specify a spherical point. This is a 3D variation of the polar format. A point is specified by its distance from the current UCS origin, its angle in the X,Y plane, and its angle up from the X,Y plane. Use the < symbol between each value. The format for an absolute spherical point is distance<direction in the X,Y plane<direction up from X,Y plane; precede with an @ for a relative spherical point. Examples are: 4<90<30 or @4<90<30.

Specify a cylindrical point (Release 11 only). This is another 3D variation of the polar format. A point is specified by its distance from the current UCS origin, its angle in the X,Y plane, and its Z distance. Use the < symbol to separate the distance and angle; use a comma to separate the angle and Z distance. The format for an absolute cylindrical point is distance<direction in the X,Y plane, Z value; precede with an @ for relative cylindrical points. Examples are: 8<22,5 or @8<22,5.

Osnap (object snap) to existing geometric points.

You can use a combination of any of the above methods (and point filters) to locate a point. (See Point Filters below.)

Related System Variable(s)

LASTPOINT, LASTANGLE

Tips

□ Specify the last coordinate by entering an @ symbol.

□ Points are expressed in relation to the current UCS. If you are working in a UCS and want to enter a point based on the WCS, precede the coordinates with an asterisk. This entry can be used for relative as well as polar input. If used for relative points, the format is @*X,Y or @*distance<direction.

□ Using polar coordinate entry (@distance < direction) is easy and fast since you don't have to deal with negative numbers.

□ If Limits checking is on and you enter a point outside the limits, you will receive the message **Outside limits. Either re-enter a point inside the limits, turn Limits checking off, or change the Limits.

See also: OSNAP, POINT, SNAP, UCS, UCSICON, UNITS, WCS

Point Filters

Screen **[DRAW] [LINE:]** or **[DRAW] [next] [POINT:]**
Screen **[SURFACES] [3DFACE:]** or **[3DPOLY:]**
Screen **[INQUIRY] [ID:]**
Pull down **[Assist] [FILTERS >]**

Point filtering lets you use the coordinate components of existing points in your drawing to build a new point. You can use any combination of existing X, Y, and Z values and new values entered by the keyboard.

Options:

.X	Accept the X value of the next point.
.Y	Accept the Y value of the next point.
.Z	Accept the Z value of the next point.
.XY	Accept the XY value of the next point.
.XZ	Accept the XZ value of the next point.
.YZ	Accept the YZ value of the next point.
Default	XYZ

Tips

□   Use filters to easily specify a Z value when working in 3D.

See also: POINT, Point Entry

POLYFACE   See PFACE

POLYGON

Screen **[DRAW] [next] [POLYGON:]**
Pull down **[Draw] [Polygon]**

The POLYGON command draws 2D regular polygons; the number of sides ranges between 3 and 1024. You can draw the polygon by inscribing or circumscribing a circle. Since polygons are closed polylines, you can use the PEDIT command for editing.

Prompts

```
Number of sides:
Edge/<Center of polygon>:
```

Options

Edge   Specify the size by picking the endpoints of one edge.

Center of polygon
                Specify the center point about which the polygon will be drawn. All vertexes are equidistant from the center point.

Inscribed in circle
                The vertexes touch the circumference of an imaginary circle.

Circumscribed about circle
                The midpoint of each edge touches the circumference of an imaginary circle.

Tips

□   When you use the Inscribed option and pick a point to show the radius, that point determines the location for the first vertex as well as the rotation angle.

□   When you use the Circumscribed option and pick a point to show the radius, that point determines the location for the midpoint of the first edge as well as the rotation angle.

□   Polygons are drawn with 0 line width regardless of the default polyline width and contain no tangent information. You can use the PEDIT command and assign a width and tangents once the polygon is created.

□   Polygons are drawn counterclockwise.

□   You can establish a default by selecting [Options] - [Polygon Creation] from the pull-down menus. The defaults are available only in the current drawing session and are activated when you select [Polygon] from the pull-down menu.

See also: PEDIT, POLYLINE

Example

```
Command: POLYGON
Number of sides: 7
Edge/<Center of polygon>: E
First endpoint of edge:          Point ①.
Second endpoint of edge:         Point ②.

Command: POLYGON
Number of sides: 7
Edge/<Center of polygon>:        Pick center point.
Inscribed in circle/Circumscribed about circle (I/C): I
Radius of circle: 1.5
```

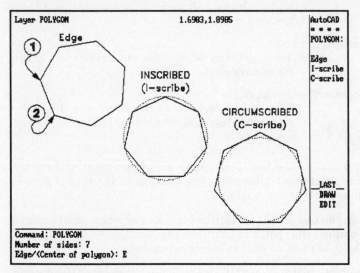

POLYGON Examples

POLYLINE   See PLINE

PSPACE

Pull down [Display] [Mview >} [Pspace]

The PSPACE (Paper SPACE) command (Release 11 only) switches from drawing in model space to paper space. You know you are working in paper space when the letter P appears on the status line and the paper space icon is displayed in the lower left hand-corner of your drawing. UCSICON must be on in paper space to see the icon.

Related System Variable(s)

TILEMODE

Tips

◻ If TILEMODE is not set to 0, you are reminded to set this variable.

◻ You must have at least one viewport created with the MVIEW command. If you do not have a viewport, you are reminded to create one.

◻ Use paper space to compose and plot various views of your model or drawing; use model space to create your 2D and 3D models or drawings.

◻ Dimensioning in model space gives you more flexibility. You can take advantage of associative dimensioning when editing your drawing.

◻ Paper space and model space retain their own limits.

Warning(s)

■ The VPORTS command is disabled when working in paper space. Use the Save and Restore options of the VIEW command.

■ The system variable UCSFOLLOW has no effect in paper space.

See also: MSPACE, MVIEW, TILEMODE, UCSICON, VIEW, VPLAYER, VPORTS

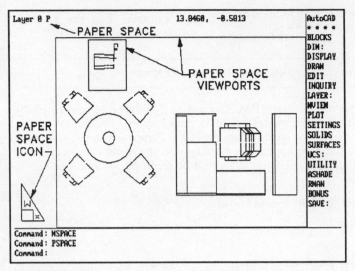

PAPER SPACE

PURGE

Screen **[UTILITY] [PURGE:]**

PURGE will delete or eliminate unused blocks, dimstyles, layers, linetypes, shapes, and text styles. You set up the command by indicating the symbol types that you want to purge. PURGE prompts you for a confirmation before it performs the purge.

Prompts

```
Purge unused Blocks/Dimstyles/LAyers/LTypes/SHapes/
STyles/All:
```

Options

Blocks	Delete unused blocks.
Dimstyles	Delete unused dimension styles.
LAyers	Delete unused layers.
LTypes	Delete unused lineypes.
SHapes	Delete unused shapes.
STyles	Delete unused styles.

All   Delete all unused symbols. You are prompted
                       individually for each item.

Tips

□ Purging is a good way to reduce drawing file size.

□ You cannot purge layer 0, the continuous linetype, or the text
   style STANDARD.

□ The following commands have their own Delete options: VIEW,
   UCS, and VPORT.

Warning(s)

■ You must issue the PURGE command before you alter the
   database during the current editing session.

■ Since blocks can be nested and drawn on multiple layers, you
   can only purge one reference level at a time. Once you've
   completed the PURGE command, you may want to end the
   drawing, reopen the file, and issue PURGE a second time. You
   may have to do this several times to purge all unused items.

QTEXT

Screen **[SETTINGS]** **[next]** **[QTEXT:]**

QTEXT (Quick TEXT) is a mode that displays boxes in place of text
strings (including attributes) to save time redrawing or
regenerating text. The box is the approximate height and length of
the text string.

Prompts

ON/OFF <Off>:

Options

ON   Display text strings as boxes.
OFF   Display text strings normally.

Related System Variable(s)

QTEXTMODE

Tips

□ If QTEXT is on, any new text you enter will display normally until the drawing regenerates.

□ If QTEXT is on and you use the CHANGE or DDEDIT command to edit the text, or the LIST command for database information, the actual text is edited or listed.

Warning(s)

■ Qtext boxes may take up more space than the actual text string.

See also: REGEN

QUIT

```
Screen [UTILITY] [QUIT]
Pull down [File] [Quit]
```

The QUIT command exits the drawing editor without updating the drawing file. The drawing is unmodified from the last SAVE or END command.

Prompts

```
Really want to discard all changes to drawing?
```

Options

Yes   Quit and don't update the drawing since the last END or SAVE was issued. You are returned to the main menu.

No   Don't quit, but stay in the drawing editor.

See also: END, SAVE

REDEFINE / UNDEFINE

R

Type **REDEFINE** *or* **UNDEFINE**

UNDEFINE disables built-in AutoCAD commands so you can replace them with another command of the same name, using AutoLISP or another programming method. REDEFINE restores the original AutoCAD command. To redefine or undefine a command, type the command name in response to the prompt.

Prompt
Command name:

Options

.(period)   Preceding an undefined command name with a period recalls the original AutoCAD command for that single condition.

If you attempt to execute a command that has been undefined, you will get the message Unknown command.

Tips

▫ REDEFINE and UNDEFINE are only valid for the current editing session.

▫ You can only use UNDEFINE and REDEFINE for commands, not for command options. For example, you can undefine the complete layer command, but not the specific layer options.

REDO   See UNDO

REDRAW / REDRAWALL

Screen [DISPLAY] [REDRAW:] *or* [REDRALL:]
Screen [* * * *] [REDRAW]
Pull down [Display] [Redraw]

REDRAW cleans up the current viewport by redrawing the screen. REDRAWALL cleans up all viewports. Blips are removed, and any entities or parts of entities that disappeared, or seemed erased due to editing, are redrawn. Grid dots are redrawn if the grid is on. These can also be executed transparently.

Tips

▫ Some commands, like turning GRID on or off, or turning a LAYER on, execute a redraw.

▫ You can execute a REDRAW while in dimensioning mode.

▫ Entities are redrawn on layers that are turned off even though they are not seen; entities on frozen layers are not redrawn.

▫ Grid density affects redraw speed.

▫ You can stop a redraw by pressing <^C> to cancel.

See also: REGEN, REGENALL, TRANSPARENT, VIEWRES, BLIPMODE

REGEN / REGENALL

Screen [DISPLAY] [REGEN:] *or* [REGNALL:]

REGEN causes the current viewport to be regenerated. REGENALL regenerates all viewports. When a drawing is regenerated, all the data and geometry associated with an entity are recalculated. Changes made to some existing entities require a regeneration before they are made visible. You can stop a regeneration by pressing <^C> to cancel. You can control automatic regenerations with the REGENAUTO command. REGEN and REGENALL cannot be executed transparently.

Tips

▫ ZOOM All and Extents always force a regeneration regardless of the REGENAUTO setting.

▫ ZOOM VMAX never requires a REGEN.

▫ Entities on layers that are turned off are regenerated even though they are not seen; entities on frozen layers are not regenerated.

▫ You can issue a REGEN from within the PEDIT command's Edit vertex mode.

See also: EDIT, REDRAW, REDRAWALL, REGENAUTO, VIEWRES

REGENAUTO

Screen [DISPLAY] [RGNAUTO:]

REGENAUTO lets you suppress some (not all) regenerations. The default setting is <On>.

Prompt
ON/OFF <On>:

Options

ON	Enables all regenerations. Turning it on creates a regeneration.
OFF	Suppresses regenerations.

Related System Variable(s)
REGENMODE, EXPERT

Tips

▫ REGENAUTO OFF can suppress regenerations caused by the following commands: BLOCK, COLOR, FILL, LAYER, LINETYPE, LTSCALE, QTEXT, and STYLE.

▫ ZOOM All and Extents always create a regeneration.

▫ ZOOM VMAX never requires a regeneration.

□ If REGENAUTO is off and AutoCAD wants to regenerate, you will receive the following message About to regen, proceed? <Y>, unless the EXPERT system variable is set greater than 0.

See also: REGEN, REGENALL, VIEWRES

RENAME

Screen [UTILITY] [RENAME:]

RENAME lets you rename blocks, layers, linetypes, styles, UCS, views, and viewport configurations (Release 11 only). Consider using RENAME when you need to change naming standards, or when you encounter typing errors in existing named items.

Prompts

Block/Dimstyle/LAyer/LType/Style/Ucs/VIew/VPort:
Old (object) name:
New (object) name:

Tips

□ To rename a drawing file, use the File Utility menu.

□ You can rename a layer with the DDLMODES command and a UCS with the DDUCS command.

□ If you have to rename the same items for more than one drawing, create a script file and automate the process.

Warning(s)

■ You cannot rename layer 0, external reference layers, the linetype Continuous, and shapes.

■ RENAME only affects the current drawing.

■ You can rename the style STANDARD, but you can't purge that style.

See also: FILES

RESUME   See SCRIPT

REVSURF

Screen [DRAW] [next] [3D Surfs] [REVSURF:]
Screen [SURFACES] [REVSURF:]
Pull down [Draw] [Surfaces...] [REVOLUTION]

REVSURF (SURface of REVolution) is one method of generating a 3D polygon mesh. REVSURF revolves a selected profile or "path curve" around an axis.

The profile or path curve can be made up of a single line, arc, circle, 2D polyline, or 3D polyline. The path curve defines the N direction of the surface polygon mesh. (See 3D MESH.)

The axis can be a line or an open 2D or 3D polyline. If you use a polyline, the revolution axis is considered a line from the first vertex to the last vertex, omitting any other vertexes. The axis defines the M direction of the surface mesh. After you specify the path curve and the revolution axis, you specify a starting angle and an included angle. The default settings are a starting angle of 0 and a 360-degree included angle (full circle).

Prompts
```
Select path curve:
Select axis of revolution:
Start angle <0>:
Included angle (+=ccw, -=cw) <Full circle>:
```

Options

Start angle   Determine the start of the surface of revolution. It can be offset from the path curve.

Included angle   Determine the distance of revolution around the axis.

Related System Variable(s)
SURFTAB1, SURFTAB2

Tips

□ REVSURF creates a single polygon mesh that can be exploded into individual 3D faces.

□ The direction of revolution is determined by the right-hand rule of rotation and the point used to pick the axis of rotation. In the right-hand rule, with only the thumb extended and pointing in the positive axis direction, the fingers curve in the direction of positive rotation.

See also: EXPLODE, PEDIT, 3DMESH

Example

```
Command: REVSURF
Select path curve:                        Point ①.
Select axis of revolution:                Point ②.
Start angle <0>: ↵
Included angle (+=ccw, -=cw) <Full circle>: ↵
```

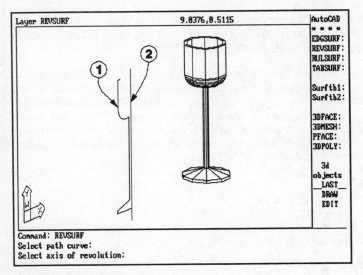

REVSURF Example

ROTATE

Screen **[EDIT] [next] [ROTATE:]**
Pull down **[Modify] [Rotate]**

ROTATE lets you rotate entities around a designated base. After you specify a base point, you specify a relative rotation angle or a reference angle. The default is <Rotation angle>.

Prompts

```
Select objects:
Base point:
<Rotation angle>/Reference:
```

Options

Rotation angle   The amount entities are rotated from their current orientation. A positive number creates a counterclockwise rotation; a negative number creates a clockwise rotation.

Reference   Prompts for the current reference angle and the new reference angle. The selected objects are rotated to the new angle.

Tips

▫ When rotating associative dimension entities, the dimension text is regenerated using the current style and units settings. The dimension text retains its original orientation.

▫ You can rotate text and attdefs with the CHANGE command.

▫ The INSERT command lets you insert blocks rotated.

▫ You can change the rotation angle of blocks with the CHANGE command.

▫ If you move or copy entities and then want to rotate the same entities, select the entities to rotate using the previous selection set.

▫ If you want to rotate your drawing crosshairs and work at a different rotation angle, use the SNAP rotation option or define a UCS.

▫ Rotating a viewport in paper space causes the viewport center point to rotate about the base point while keeping the viewport border parallel to the edges of the graphics display area.

See also: CHANGE, DIM TRotate, INSERT, SNAP, UCS

Example

```
Command: ROTATE
Select objects:                          Select part and dimensions.
Base point:                              Pick ①.
<Rotation angle>/Reference: 25
```

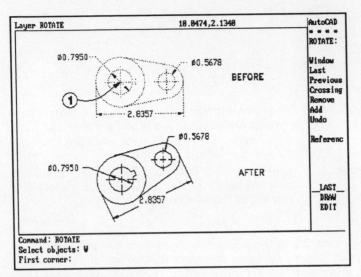

ROTATION Example

RSCRIPT   See SCRIPT

RULESURF

Screen **[DRAW] [next] [3D Surfs] [RULSURF:]**
Screen **[SURFACES] [RULSURF:]**
Pull down **[Draw] [Surfaces...] [RULED Surface]**

RULESURF (RULEd SURFace) generates a 3D polygon mesh depicting the ruled surface between two entities.

The two entities can be points, lines, arcs, circles, 2D polylines, or 3D polylines. If one boundary is a circle or closed polyline, then the other boundary must be closed. A point can be used with any open or closed boundary.

Prompts

```
Select first defining curve:
Select second defining curve:
```

Related System Variable(s)

SURFTAB1

Tips

▫ The ruled surface for a circle starts at the 0 degree quadrant.

▫ The ruled surface for a closed polygon starts at the last vertex and is constructed backwards.

▫ When constructing ruled surfaces for open curves, the endpoints nearest the selection pick points determine the start of the ruled surface.

▫ You can explode a RULESURF into individual 3D faces.

Warning(s)

■ You cannot use a point to define both boundaries.

See also: EXPLODE, PEDIT, 3DMESH

Example

```
Command: RULESURF
Select first defining curve:        Point ①.
Select second defining curve:       Point ②.
```

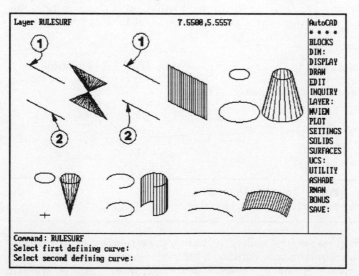

RULESURF Example

SAVE

Screen **[SAVE:]**
Pull down **[File] [Save]**

The SAVE command lets you update your drawing file by saving it to disk without exiting the drawing editor. The current drawing file is the default name. You can specify another directory and/or file name. Each time you save, the previous saved drawing is renamed as the backup (.BAK) drawing.

Prompts

File name <default>:

Related System Variable(s)

FILEDIA

Tips

◻ We recommend periodically saving your drawing during an editing session.

◻ Entering a tilde (~) at the prompt will display the File dialogue box if the system variable FILEDIA is set to 0.

Warning(s)

■ Do not include the drawing extension .DWG. It is assumed.

See also: Dialogue Boxes, END

SCALE

Screen **[EDIT] [next] [SCALE:]**
Pull down **[Modify] [Scale]**

SCALE gives you the ability to change the size of existing entities. You determine the base point by which you want to scale the entities and provide either an overall scale factor or scale a specific dimension to a new distance.

S

Prompts

```
Select objects:
Base point:
<Scale factor>/Reference:
```

Options

Scale factor   Provides a value to multiply the X, Y, and Z dimensions. A value greater than one enlarges the entities; a value between 0 and 1 reduces the size of the entities.

Reference   Specifies an existing dimension and the new length you want the reference length to become.

Tips

▫ Use the SCALE command to resize the entire drawing if your drawing scale or units change.

▫ If you want to scale the size of blocks and text, you can use the CHANGE command.

▫ When scaling associative dimension entities, the dimension text is regenerated using the current style and units settings and the new scale factor.

▫ If you move or copy entities and then want to scale the same entities, you can select the entities to scale using the Previous selection set option.

Warning(s)

■ Drawings are normally drawn full size. When you plot, use the plot routine to scale your drawing output to the plotter.

■ You cannot scale X, Y, or Z values independently.

See also: CHANGE, INSERT, PLOT

Example

```
Command: SCALE
Select objects:                      Select entities.
Base point:                          Point ①.
<Scale factor>/Reference: 1.5
```

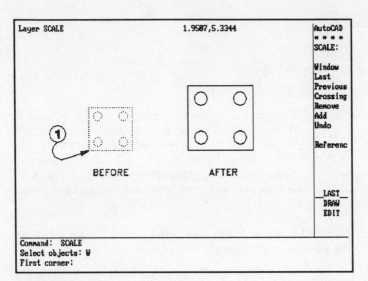

```
Layer SCALE                1.9587,5.3344        AutoCAD
                                                * * * *
                                                SCALE:

                                                Window
                                                Last
                         ○    ○                 Previous
                                                Crossing
                    ○    ○                       Remove
                                                Add
                    ○    ○                       Undo
                         ○    ○
                                                Referenc

                                                _LAST_
                 BEFORE          AFTER          DRAW
                                                EDIT

Command: SCALE
Select objects: W
First corner:
```

SCALE Example

SCRIPT

Screen **[UTILITY] [SCRIPT:]**

SCRIPT files automate routine tasks. A script file is an ASCII text file created with a text editor (such as EDLIN) that contains commands and responses in the exact order of execution. The file has the extension .SCR. The script can be executed with the SCRIPT command to perform the series of commands.

You can execute script files from the operating system prompt by following the program name ACAD with a space and the drawing name, then a space and the script file name without the extension. To execute a script file while in the drawing, use the SCRIPT command. The default script name is the current drawing file name. DELAY, RESUME, and RSCRIPT are commands that control the running of the script.

Prompts

Script file <*default*>:

Options

DELAY   Creates a pause, in milliseconds, between commands. The maximum delay number is 32767, just under 33 seconds depending on the computer.

RESUME   Pressing <^C> or the backspace key will interrupt a script file. To reactivate the script, enter the RESUME command. If the script stopped in the middle of a command, you may need to type the command with a leading apostrophe ('RESUME).

RSCRIPT   RSCRIPT (Repeat SCRIPT) is used mainly to repeat the script file during slide show presentations.

Related System Variable(s)

FILEDIA

Tips

▫ Scripts are often used to display slide shows, plot drawings, and reset system variables. If you change drawing standards and need to update existing drawings, use script files to do the work.

▫ Executing a script file from the operating system prompt bypasses the ACAD.MSG sign-on message.

Warning(s)

■ The UNDO command considers a script sequence as one group. Therefore, you can reverse the effects of a script with a single U command.

See also: Dialogue Boxes, MSLIDE, VSLIDE

SELECT

Screen [EDIT] [next] [SELECT:]

SELECT lets you pick entities to be retained as the next selection set. If you are required to select entities at the next command prompt, you can use the Previous option to recall the selection set.

You create the selection set with the standard object selection options.

Prompts

```
Select objects:
```

Tips

▫   SELECT is often used in macros.

▫   You can't select model space entities when working in paper space and vice versa.

See also: Selection Set

Selection Set

Selection sets are used to group drawing objects for editing. You form a selection set at the Select objects prompt. By default, you add individual objects to the selection set by picking. You can also create or refine selection sets with the options below. As a set is formed, entities in the set are highlighted on-screen. The highlight type varies with your graphic display.

Options

Pick point	Select one entity at a time.
Window	Select entities totally enclosed within a windowed area.
Last	Select the last entity drawn and displayed in the current viewport.
Previous	Select the previous selection set.
Crossing	Select entities crossing or totally enclosed within a windowed area.
BOX	If you move the crosshairs to the right it becomes a window — to the left it becomes a crossing window.
AUto	If the pick fails to select an object, the selection method becomes the BOX option.
SIngle	Ends the selection process after the first object is found.
Multiple	Allows you to pick multiple points before the drawing is searched for entities at those points.

Remove	Removes specific entities from the selection set.
Add	Adds entities to the selection set.
Undo	Removes the last group of selected entities.

Tips

◻ BOX, AUto, and SIngle work best with menu macros. Combining SIngle and AUto lets you select a single entity if the pickbox is on an entity, or use standard window or crossing window selection methods.

◻ Previous selects all the points or blocks drawn by the DIVIDE or MEASURE commands.

Warning(s)

▪ You cannot use the Previous option when moving back and forth from model space and paper space.

▪ You cannot select objects from model space that were created in paper space and vice versa.

SETVAR

Screen [* * * *] [SETVAR:]
Screen [SETTINGS] [next] [SETVAR:]
Pull down [Settings] [Set SysVars]

The SETVAR command is used to modify system variables. Most system variables are modified through AutoCAD commands. A few system variables are "read-only." System variables are stored as integers, reals, points, or text strings. Most are saved in the drawing file, and a few in the general configuration file, but some are only retained for the current editing session. 'SETVAR is a transparent command. See individual commands for associated system variables. See Appendix B for a complete listing.

Prompts

Variable name or ?:
New value for *varname* <*current*>:

Options

Variable name   Enter the name of a variable to change.

?   Activates the wild-card options for reviewing variable settings. The default, an asterisk, displays a sorted listing of all variables. You can use any of the wild-card options to create a more specific list.

Tips

▫ Scripts, macros, and AutoLISP routines frequently access system variables.

▫ Most variables can be modified in Release 11 by typing the variable name at the command prompt. Owners of Release 10 (or earlier releases) must use the SETVAR command. A variable with the same name as a command name must be changed with the SETVAR command.

See also: Transparent Commands, Wild-Card Characters, Appendix B

SHADE

Screen **[DISPLAY] [SHADE:]**
Pull down **[Display] [Shade]**

Produces a shaded rendering of the current viewport. SHADE (Release 11 only) produces the same results as the AutoSHADE 2.0 command Quick Shade. Only one light source is used. The only control over this command is by changing the settings of the system variables SHADEDGE and SHADEDIF.

Related System Variable(s)

SHADEDGE, SHADEDIF

Tips

▫ You can change the SHADEDGE and SHADEDIF settings from the [Settings] - [Shade Style] pull-down menu or from the [DISPLAY] - [SHADE:] screen menu.

▫ SHADEDGE specifies how faces and edges are displayed. Some methods require a 256-color display.

▫ SHADEDIF specifies how the model is illuminated. SHADE DIFfuse defaults to 70. That is, 70 percent of the light is diffuse reflection from the light source and 30 percent is ambient light. The value can be set anywhere from 1 to 100. A higher setting increases diffuse lighting and adds more reflectivity and contrast to the image.

▫ Create slides of shaded viewports for later viewing.

▫ The SHADE command takes about twice as long as single regenerations of the same viewport.

Warning(s)

■ You can't plot a shaded viewport.

■ You can't select entities in a shaded image.

See also: MSLIDE, VSLIDE

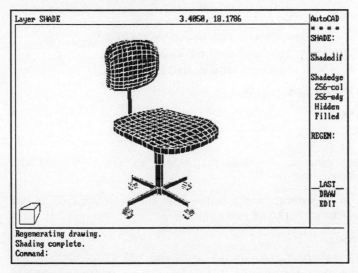

SHADE Example

SHAPE

Screen [DRAW] [next] [SHAPE:]

Shapes are an alternative to blocks. Shape definitions are stored in shape files. Each shape file can contain numerous symbol definitions. The shape file (extension .SHP) must be compiled from AutoCAD's main menu option 7. The extension for a compiled shape file is .SHX. Once the shape file is compiled, it must be loaded with the LOAD command before it can be used. The SHAPE command inserts a defined shape into the drawing.

Prompts

```
Shape name (or ?):
Starting point:
Height <1.0>:
Rotation angle <0>:
```

Options

?	Activate wild-card options for reviewing the names of shapes defined in the drawing. The default, an asterisk, displays a listing of all loaded shapes. You can use any of the wild-card options to create a more specific list.
LOAD	Load a shape (.SHX) file.
LOAD ?	List currently loaded shape files.

Related System Variable(s)

FILEDIA

Tips

▫ Shape files can be used to produce special text fonts and symbols.

▫ Shapes regenerate much faster than the same symbols stored as blocks and take up less space.

Warning(s)

▪ Even though shape definitions require less memory, they are not as desirable as block definitions. They cannot be exploded or scaled differently in X,Y directions. Shape files are external to the drawing file and must always accompany the drawing file in a drawing exchange.

▪ If the File dialogue box is enabled (FILEDIA set to 1), you cannot use the ? option with the LOAD command.

▪ You can only osnap to a shape's insertion point.

▪ Shapes cannot include attribute definitions, but blocks may contain both shapes and attdefs.

- Complex shape definitions are tedious and time-consuming to create.

See also: BLOCK, PURGE, Wild-Card Characters

Example

Some sample shape files come with your AutoCAD software. Copy the file ES.SHP into your ACAD directory if you want to examine shapes.

SHELL / SH

Screen [UTILITY] [External Commands] [SH:] *or* [SHELL:]

SHELL (or SH) functions as a gateway between AutoCAD, the operating system (such as DOS), and other external programs. Pressing <RETURN> once after typing SHELL or SH allows you to issue a single operating system command and immediately return to AutoCAD. If you press <RETURN> while at the OS Command prompt, you will stay in the operating system until you type EXIT to return to AutoCAD. Once in the operating system, you can execute most operating system commands. It is also possible to access other software programs via SHELL, depending on their memory requirements.

Prompt

OS Command:

Options

It is easy to forget you have shelled out of AutoCAD and into the operating system or another program. If you are shelled to the operating system, you will see a double greater than symbol (>>) at the command prompt instead of the normal single greater than symbol.

Tips

- If the message Unknown command appears, make sure the file ACAD.PGP exists in your AutoCAD directory. If you still have problems, check your *AutoCAD Reference Manual.*

- AutoCAD 386 Release 11 owners can use the SHROOM utility included with AutoCAD to release the maximum amount of memory for external programs. See the AutoCAD README.DOC and SHROOM.DOC.

Warning(s)

- Make sure you exit the SHELL command from the same directory as you entered.

- Don't issue a CHKDSK/F while you are shelled out of AutoCAD.

- Don't delete any temporary AutoCAD files — they usually have a $ symbol in the file name — or extension or lock files where the last character in the extension is a K (.??K).

- Don't load any RAM-resident programs while in the shell; they should be loaded before you enter AutoCAD.

- When re-entering the drawing editor, you may notice some display debris. Issue a redraw to clean up the graphics display; reload the menu to clean up the screen menu area.

- Don't run programs (such as BASIC) that reset the I/O ports.

- On systems not based on DOS, the SHELL command may behave differently. Check your *AutoCAD Reference Manual.*

SKETCH

Screen **[DRAW] [next] [SKETCH:]**

The SKETCH command enables you to draw freehand in contiguous short line segments with an imaginary pen. You first specify line segment length, then sketch temporary line segments. A Record option stores the line segments when you are finished. You have the option of setting a system variable (SKPOLY) to sketch either lines or polylines. The default setting is to sketch lines with a record increment of .1. You must have a pointing device, such as a mouse or digitizer, to use SKETCH.

Prompts

```
Record increment <0.1000>:
Sketch.  Pen eXit Quit Record Erase Connect .
```

Options

Pen	Is a toggle switch for the up or down pen position. Sketching proceeds while the pen is down until you press P on the keyboard, or release the pick button on your pointing device.
eXit	Records temporary line segments and exits the SKETCH command.
Quit	Discards temporary line segments and exits the SKETCH command.
Record	Records temporary line segments and remains in the SKETCH command.
Erase	Erases temporary line segments in the opposite order in which they were entered as you move your pointing device back over the line segments.
Connect	By moving your pointing device close to the endpoint of the last temporary line segment, you can connect to that endpoint and continue sketching.
. (period)	Draws a single line segment from the last point to the current pointing device location.

You can press <^C> to cancel SKETCH.

The buttons on a pointing device are redefined during the sketch mode to the following:

Puck	Keyboard Command	Function
Pick	P	pen up/down
1	.	single line
2	R	record lines
3	X	exit
4	Q	quit (<^C>)
5	E	erase
6	C	connect

System variables

SKETCHINC, SKPOLY

Tips

□ You can toggle snap, grid, and ortho on and off while sketching. To get smoother sketch lines, keep snap off.

▫ If an extrusion value (thickness) is set, line segments are extruded once the record option is selected. You can also extrude SKETCH lines by using the CHANGE or CHPROP commands.

Warning(s)

▪ You cannot turn tablet mode on and off while sketching.

▪ If you sketch too fast, you may hear a beep indicating that AutoCAD is using all available memory. Slow down and proceed.

Example

```
Command: SKETCH
Record increment <0.1000>: ↵
Sketch.  Pen eXit Quit Record Erase Connect . P
<Pen down>                                    Sketch lines.
P
<Pen up> ↵
30 lines recorded.
```

```
Layer SKETCH                    1.1145,4.1089      AutoCAD
                                                   * * * *
                                                   SKETCH:

                                                   Connect
                                                   Erase
                                                   Record

                                                   eXit
                                                   Quit

                                                   SKPOLY:
                                                   SKLINE:
                                                   ____

                                                   _LAST_
                                                    DRAW
                                                    EDIT

Command: SKETCH
Record increment <0.1000>:
Sketch.  Pen eXit Quit Record Erase Connect .
```

SKETCH Example

SNAP

Type <^B> *or* <F9>
Screen [SETTINGS] [next] [SNAP:]
Pull down [Settings] [Snap On/Off   ^B]

SNAP is a drawing aid. It restricts your crosshairs movement to a specified increment. You can modify the increment value and turn SNAP on or off as needed. The default is a SNAP increment of 1.0000 and off. On DOS systems, <^B> and <F9> will toggle SNAP on or off. You can also change your snap settings with the DDRMODES dialogue box.

Prompts

Snap spacing or ON/OFF/Aspect/Rotate/Style <1.0000>:

Options

Snap spacing	Set the XY snap increment values. Changing snap settings turns SNAP On.
ON	Turn snap on.
OFF	Turn snap off.
Aspect	Set individual horizontal (X) and vertical (Y) snap increments. This option is not available if you are in isometric mode. (See below.)
Rotate	Rotate the snap (and grid) by any specified angle about a base point.
Style	Allows selection of the standard or isometric styles.
Iso	Set isometric SNAP and GRID style.
Standard	Return from isometric mode to normal SNAP (and GRID) style.

Related System Variable(s)

SNAPANG, SNAPBASE, SNAPISOPAIR, SNAPMODE, SNAPSTYL, SNAPUNIT

Tips

▫ Typed coordinates, distances, and OSNAPs override SNAP.

▫ Each viewport retains its own SNAP setting.

▫ You will not snap to a grid point unless SNAP is on and is set to an even multiple of the grid increment.

▫ To specify a SNAP aspect ratio from the pull-down menu, you must first set the X spacing and then the Y spacing.

▫ Screen crosshairs are oriented to the current snap rotation angle. ORTHO forces lines to be drawn orthogonally in relation to the crosshair orientation.

▫ If you want to create an array at an angle, rotate the snap angle.

▫ You can check current SNAP settings with the STATUS command.

Warning(s)

■ SNAP is inactive during perspective views.

See also: DDRMODES, GRID, ISOPLANE, OSNAP

SOLAREA

Screen **[SOLIDS] [INQUIRY] [SOLAREA:]**
Pull down **[Sol-Prim's] [INQUIRY >] [Solid Area]**

The SOLAREA (SOLid AREA) (Release 11 only) command calculates the surface area of solid entities. Picking more than one solid results in the sum of all solids picked.

Area calculations are derived from meshing the surfaces of the selected solids and then adding the area of the faces of the mesh. The areas of curved surfaces are only an approximation. Therefore, increasing the wire mesh density improves the accuracy.

Prompts

Select solids for surface area computation...
Select objects:

Related System Variable(s)

SOLAREAU, SOLWDENS

Warning(s)

■ SOLAREA results for curved surfaces are only approximate.

See also: AMELITE

Example

```
Select objects:
1 object selected.
Surface area of solids of 84.6 sq cm
```

SOLBOX

Screen **[SOLIDS] [SOLBOX:]**
Pull down **[Sol-Prim's] [Box]**

The SOLBOX (SOLid BOX) command (Release 11 only) creates 3D solid boxes. The defaults expect you to define two diagonal corner points and a height.

Prompts

```
Corner of box:
Cube/Length/<Other corner>:
Height:
```

Options

Cube	All sides (length, width, depth) of the box are equal.
Length	You individually define the length (X axis), width (Y axis), and height (Z axis).
Other corner	Specify a diagonal corner point by entering a coordinate or by picking a point on the drawing. Once you have specified the corner point, you are asked to determine the height. If the second corner point coordinates contained a Z value, the prompt uses that Z value as its default.

See also: AMELITE

Example

```
Command: SOLBOX
Corner of box:                         Point ①.
Cube/Length/<Other corner>:            Point ②.
Height: 1
```

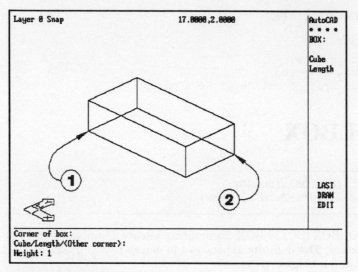

```
Layer 0 Snap                    17.0000,2.0000        AutoCAD
                                                      * * * *
                                                      BOX:

                                                      Cube
                                                      Length




                                                      LAST
                                                      DRAW
                                                      EDIT

Corner of box:
Cube/Length/<Other corner>:
Height: 1
```

SOLBOX Example

SOLCONE

Screen **[SOLIDS] [SOLCONE:]**
Pull down **[Sol-Prim's] [Cone]**

The SOLCONE (SOLid CONE) command (Release 11 only) creates
a 3D solid cone. You define the center point, radius (default) or
diameter, and height.

Prompts

Center point:
Diameter/<Radius>:
Height of cone:

Options

Diameter   Specify the diameter by entering a value or by
            picking two points.

Radius   Specify the radius by entering a value or by
            picking two points.

Warning(s)

■ The elliptical selection [Elliptcl] on the screen menu is only available with full AME.

See also: AMELITE

Example

```
Command: SOLCONE
Elliptical/<Center point>:                     Point ①.
Diameter/<Radius>: @3<0
Height of Cone: 6
```

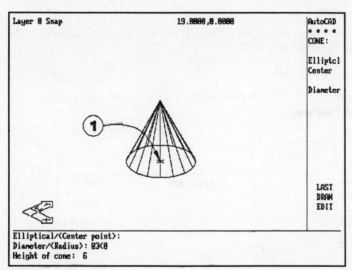

SOLCONE Example

SOLCYL

Screen **[SOLIDS] [SOLCYL:]**
Pull down **[Sol-Prim's] [Cylinder]**

The SOLCYL (SOLid CYLinder) command (Release 11 only) creates a 3D solid cylinder column. You specify the center point, radius (default) or diameter, and height.

Prompts

```
Center point:
Diameter/<Radius>:
Height of cylinder:
```

Options

Diameter   Specify the diameter by inputting a value or by
                 picking two points.

Radius   Specify the radius by inputting a value or by
                 picking two points.

Warning(s)

- The elliptical selection [Elliptcl] on the screen menu is only
  available with full AME.

See also: AMELITE

Example

```
Command: SOLCYL
Elliptical/<Center point>:              Point ①.
Diameter/<Radius>: @3<0
Height of cylinder: 6
```

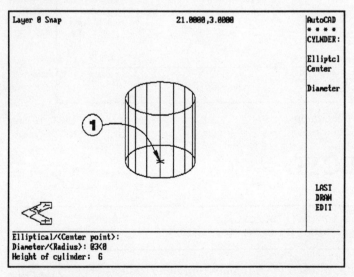

SOLCYL Example

SOLEXT

Screen **[SOLIDS] [SOLEXT:]**
Pull down **[Sol-Prim's] [Extrude]**

The SOLEXT (SOLid EXTrude) command (Release 11 only) lets you create unique solid entities by extruding existing polyline, polygon, circle, ellipse, and 3Dpoly entities.

Prompts

```
Select polylines and circles for extrusion...
Height of extrusion:
Extrusion taper angle from Z <0>:
```

Related System Variable(s)

SOLDELENT

Tips

▫ The SOLDELENT system variable controls whether the selected entities are deleted (the default) or kept in the drawing file after being extruded.

▫ You can taper the sides of the extrusion with the AME program.

▫ If the entity has an assigned thickness the same as the desired extrusion height, you can use the SOLIDIFY command instead.

Warning(s)

■ Polyline segments must contain at least three vertexes. If the segments overlap, they cannot be extruded. Open polyline segments are automatically closed when extruded.

■ Wide polylines are extruded based on the center of the polyline. The width is converted to 0.

See also: AMELITE, SOLIDIFY

Example

```
Command: SOLEXT
Select polylines and circles for extrusion...
Select objects:                              Point ①.
1 selected, 1 found
Select objects:
```

Height of extrusion: **6**
Extrusion taper angle from Z <0>: ⏎

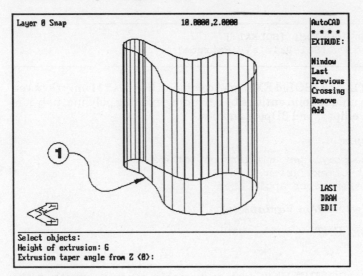

Extruded Solid

SOLID

Screen **[DRAW] [next] [SOLID:]**

SOLID draws solid filled areas. These areas can be triangular or quadrilateral. You enter points in a triangular order. The first two points are the endpoints of a starting edge. The next point defines the endpoint of a triangle, or you can enter two more points to define a second (quadrilateral) edge. If FILL or the system variable FILLMODE is on, the areas are filled.

Prompts

First point:
Second point:
Third point:
Fourth point:

Related System Variable(s)

FILLMODE

Tips

▫ You can save time during regenerations and redraws by turning FILL off. To see the results of turning FILL on or off requires a drawing regeneration.

See also: FILL

Example

```
Command: SOLID
First point:                    Point ①.
Second point:                   Point ②.
Third point:                    Point ③.
Fourth point:                   Point ④.
Third point:                    Point ⑤.
Fourth point: ↵                 Defines triangular area.
Third point: ↵
```

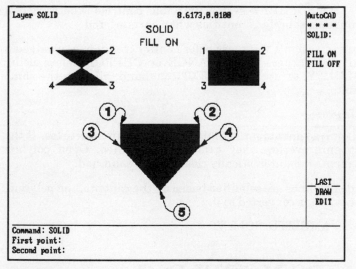

SOLID Examples

SOLIDIFY

Screen **[SOLIDS] [SOLIDIFY]**
Pull down **[Sol-Prim's] [Solidify]**

SOLIDIFY (Release 11 only) converts 2D entities (polyline, polygon, circle, ellipse, trace, donut, and solid) into unique solid entities by extruding them to the value of their thickness.

Related System Variable(s)
SOLDELENT, SOLSOLIDIFY

Tips

▫ The SOLDELENT system variable controls whether the selected entities are deleted (the default) or kept in the drawing file after being extruded.

▫ The SOLSOLIDIFY system variable controls whether solid commands solidify 2D entities when encountered.

▫ You can assign a thickness before entity creation, or change an entity's thickness with CHANGE or CHPROP before using SOLIDIFY, or use the SOLEXT command, all with the same results.

Warning(s)

■ Polyline segments must contain at least three vertexes. If the segments overlap, they cannot be solidified. Open polyline segments are automatically closed when solidified.

■ Wide polylines are solidified based on the center of the polyline. The width is converted to 0.

See also: AMELITE, SOLEXT

SOLIDS MODELING   See AMElite

SOLLIST

Screen **[SOLIDS] [INQUIRY] [SOLLIST:]**
Pull down **[Sol-Prim's] [INQUIRY >] [List Solid]**

The SOLLIST (SOLid LIST) command (Release 11 only) provides solid type, area, and material information about selected solids.

Prompts

Tree/<Solid>:

Options

Tree   Display the definition of a solid model's Constructive Solid Geometry (CSG) tree.

Solid   Display information about the top level of a solid's Constructive Solid Geometry (CSG) tree.

Related System Variable(s)

SOLPAGELEN

See also: AMELITE

Example

```
Command: SOLLIST
Tree/<Solid>: S
Select objects: 1 selected, 1 found
Select objects:
1 solid selected.
Solid type = BOX (2.000, -2.000, 2.000)   Handle = 1B
Area = 24.000        Material = MILD_STEEL
Representation = PMESH   Shade type = CSG
Rigid motion:
+1.000                +0.000 +0.000 +3.000
+0.000                +1.000 +0.000 +8.000
+0.000                +0.000 +1.000 +0.000
+0.000                +0.000 +0.000 +1.000
Command: SOLLIST
Tree/<Solid>: T
Select objects: 1 selected, 1 found
Select objects:
1 solid selected.
Solid type = BOX (2.000, -2.000, 2.000)   Handle = 1B
Area = 24.000        Material = MILD_STEEL
Representation = PMESH   Shade type = CSG
```

SOLMAT

Screen **[SOLIDS] [UTILITY] [SOLMAT:]**
Pull down **[Sol-Prim's] [UTILITY >] [Material]**

The SOLMAT (SOLid MATerial) command (Release 11 only) maintains a list of materials and assigns their properties to solid entities. You can append new materials to the list and modify existing properties. The following properties are maintained for each material:

Density	kg/cu_m
Young's Modulus	GN/sq_m
Poisson's ratio	
Yield strength	MN/sq_m
Ultimate strength	MN/sq_m
Thermal conductivity	
Linear expansion coeff.	alpha/1e6
Specific heat	kJ/(kg deg_C)

Prompt

Change/Edit/<eXit>/LIst/LOad/New/Remove/SAve/SEt/?:

Options

Change	Change the material assigned to existing solids.
Edit	Edit the definition of a material loaded in the current drawing.
eXit	Leave the SOLMAT command and return to the command prompt. You can also press <^C> to cancel.
LIst	Display the definition of a material. You can use wild-card options for reviewing the names of materials defined in the drawing or in files with the extension .MAT.
LOad	Load a material definition into the drawing from an external file.
New	Define a new material. If the material already exists in the current drawing, you are prompted to use the Change option on existing solids with that material.
Remove	Deletes a material definition from your drawing. You can enter the name or use a ? and receive a list of current material definitions.

SAve   Saves a material definition from your drawing
                    into a file. You are warned if the material already
                    exists in that file.
SEt   Specifies a default material for new solids.
?   Lists the materials currently defined in your
                    drawing and external file.

See also: AMELITE

Example

```
Command: SOLMAT
Change/Edit/<eXit>/LIst/LOad/New/Remove/SAve/SEt/?: LI
Material to list <MILD_STEEL>/?: ?
List materials from file <acad> : ↵
Defined in drawing:
            MILD_STEEL
Defined in file:
            ALUMINUM
            BRASS   Soft Yellow Brass
            BRONZE  Soft Tin Bronze
            COPPER
            GLASS
            HSLA_STL High Strength Low Alloy Steel
            LEAD
            MILD_STEEL
            NICU            Monel 400
            STAINLESS_STL Austenic Stainless Steel
Material to list <MILD_STEEL>/?: ↵

Material:           MILD_STEEL
Density:            7860 kg/cu_m
Young's modulus: 220 GN/sq_m
Poisson's ratio:       0.275
Yield strength:        207 MN/sq_m
Ultimate strength:     345 MN/sq_m
Thermal conductivity:  56
Linear expansion coefficient:  12 alpha/1e6
Specific heat:         0.46 kJ/(kg deg_C)
Change/Edit/<eXit>/LIst/LOad/New/Remove/SAve/SEt/?: ↵
```

SOLMESH

Screen [SOLIDS] [DISPLAY] [SOLMESH:]
Pull down [Sol-Prim's] [DISPLAY >] [Mesh]

The SOLMESH (SOLid MESH) command (Release 11 only) displays a solid object as a PFACE entity. The mesh approximates the surfaces of solids by creating multi-edged faces.

You can convert a mesh (SOLMESH) to a wireframe (SOLWIRE) and back. However, the solid can only be displayed as a mesh or wireframe, not both at the same time.

The mesh model is considered a block reference.

Prompts
```
Select solids to be meshed...
Select objects:
```

Related System Variable(s)
SOLWDENS

Tips
▫ Use the SHADE command to produce a shaded rendering of the solid. This is equivalent to the Quick Shade command in AutoShade 2.0.

▫ You can perform hidden line removal on a solid mesh.

Warning(s)
■ Curved surfaces are actually a series of straight edges representing the curve and therefore only approximations.

■ You cannot use OSNAP on circles and arcs unless you convert the model back to a wireframe.

See also: AMELITE, BLOCK, HIDE, SHADE, SOLWIRE

Example
```
Command: SOLMESH
Select solids to be meshed ...
Select objects:
```

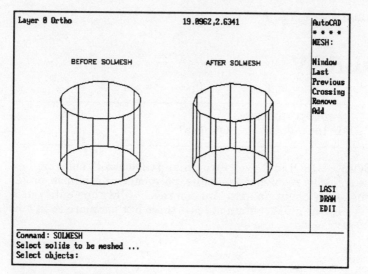

```
Layer 0 Ortho            19.0962,2.6341          AutoCAD
                                                 * * * *
                                                 MESH:

       BEFORE SOLMESH           AFTER SOLMESH    Window
                                                 Last
                                                 Previous
                                                 Crossing
                                                 Remove
                                                 Add




                                                 LAST
                                                 DRAW
                                                 EDIT

Command: SOLMESH
Select solids to be meshed ...
Select objects:
```

SOLMESH Example

SOLPURGE

Screen **[SOLIDS] [UTILITY] [SOLPURG:]**
Pull down **[Sol-Prim's] [UTILITY >] [Purge Solids]**

The SOLPURGE (SOLid PURGE) command (Release 11 only) lets you decrease your drawing size and conserve memory by purging selected solid information.

Prompt

Memory/Bfile/Pmesh/<Erased>:

Options

Memory	Purge memory associated with AME.
Bfile	Purge Bfile entities on a selective basis and reduce the drawing size.
Pmesh	Purge Pmesh entities from the drawing on a selective basis.
Erased	Purge secondary entities associated with erased AME solids.

See also: AMELITE

SOLREV

Screen **[SOLIDS] [SOLREV:]**
Pull down **[Sol-Prim's] [Revolve]**

The SOLREV (SOLid REVolve) command (Release 11 only) creates unique solids by revolving a polyline, polygon, circle, ellipse, or 3D polyline entity about an axis. You can revolve only one entity at a time. A polyline must contain at least three but not more than 500 vertexes.

Prompts

```
Select polyline or circle for revolution...
Select objects:
Axis of revolution - Entity/X/Y/<Start point of axis>:
Included angle <full circle>:
```

Options

Entity   The nearest endpoint of the entity becomes the origin of the axis that determines the positive direction of the rotation.

X   The positive X axis of the current UCS is the axis of revolution.

Y   The positive Y axis of the current UCS is the axis of revolution.

Start point of axis
           The start point of the axis determines the positive direction of rotation.

Related System Variable(s)

SOLDELENT

Tips

□ The SOLDELENT system variable controls whether the selected entities are deleted (the default) or kept in the drawing file after being extruded.

Warning(s)

- Polyline segments must contain at least three vertexes. If the segments overlap, they cannot be revolved. Open polyline segments are automatically closed when revolved.

- Wide polylines are revolved based on the center of the polyline. The width is converted to 0.

See also: AMELITE

Example

```
Command: SOLREV
Select polyline or circle for revolution...
Select objects:                                    Point ①.
1 selected, 1 found
Select objects: ↵
Axis of revolution - Entity/X/Y/<Start point of axis>: E
Entity to revolve about:                           Point ②.
Included angle <full circle>: ↵
```

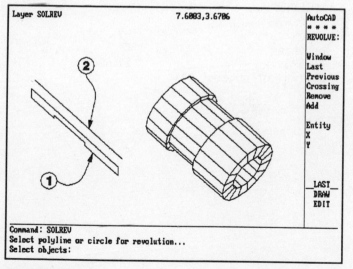

SOLREV Example

SOLSPHERE

Screen **[SOLIDS] [SOLSPH:]**
Pull down **[Sol-Prim's] [Sphere]**

The SOLSPHERE (SOLid SPHERE) command (Release 11 only) creates 3D solid spheres in which all the surface points are equidistant from the center.

Prompts

```
Center of sphere:
Diameter/<Radius> of sphere:
```

Options

Diameter   Create the sphere by specifying its diameter.

Radius   Create the sphere by specifying its radius.

See also: AMELITE

Example

```
Command: SOLSPHERE
Center of sphere:                          Point ①.
Diameter/<Radius> of sphere: @3<0
```

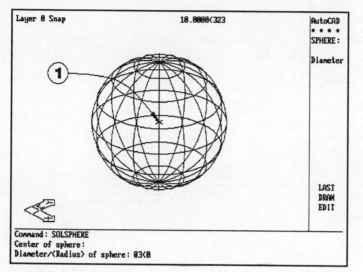

SOLSPHERE Example

SOLTORUS

Screen [SOLIDS] [SOLTORS:]
Pull down [Sol-Prim's] [Torus]

The SOLTORUS (SOLid TORUS) command (Release 11 only) creates solid 3D donut-shaped entities. After specifying the center of the torus, you enter two radius or two diameter values, one for the tube and the other for the torus.

Prompts

Center of torus:
Diameter/<Radius> of torus:
Diameter/<Radius> of tube:

Options

Diameter   Create the torus by specifying its diameter.

Radius   Create the torus by specifying its radius.

See also: AMELITE

Example

```
Command: SOLTORUS
Center of torus:                          Point ①.
Diameter?<Radius> of torus: @3<0
Diameter/<Radius> of tube: 1
```

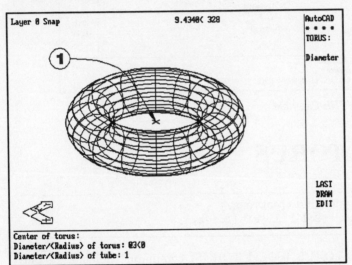

SOLTORUS Example

SOLVAR

Screen **[SOLIDS] [UTILITY] [SOLVAR:]**
Pull down **[Sol-Prim's] [UTILITY >] [Solvars]**

The SOLVAR (SOLid VARiables) command (Release 11 only) lets you set variables controlling the solid modeling environment, similar to the SETVAR command.

Prompt

Variable name or ?:

Options

Variable name   Enter a variable name.
?   List the variables.

Tips

▫ You can enter the variable name directly at the command prompt.

See also: AMELITE

SOLWEDGE

Screen **[SOLIDS] [SOLWEDGE:]**
Pull down **[Sol-Prim's] [Wedge]**

The SOLWEDGE (SOLid WEDGE) command (Release 11 only) creates a wedge. The default expects you to define two diagonal points and the height.

Prompts

Corner of wedge:
Length/<Other corner>:
Height:

Options

Length   You specify the length (X axis), width (Y axis), and height (Z axis) individually.

Other corner Specify the opposite corner point by entering a coordinate or by picking a point on the drawing. Once you have defined the base of the wedge, you are prompted for the height. If the <other corner> coordinate contained a Z value, the prompt uses that Z value as its default.

See also: AMELITE

Example

```
Command: SOLWEDGE
Corner of wedge:                     Point ①.
Length/<Other corner>:               Point ②.
Height: 1
```

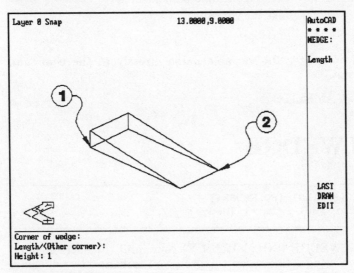

SOLWEDGE Example

SOLWIRE

Screen **[SOLIDS] [DISPLAY] [SOLWIRE:]**
Pull down **[Sol Prim's] [Sol-DISPLAY] [Wireframe]**

The SOLWIRE (SOLid WIREframe) command (Release 11 only) displays a solid object as a wireframe. The wireframe approximates solids by displaying the edges of faces and the tessellation lines of curved surfaces.

You can convert a wireframe (SOLWIRE) to a mesh (SOLMESH) and back. However, the solid can only be displayed as mesh or wireframe, not both at the same time.

Prompts

```
Select solids to be wired...
Select objects:
```

Related System Variable(s)

SOLWDENS

Warning(s)

- Solids must be converted to a mesh (SOLMESH) before shading and hidden line removal can be performed.

See also: AMELITE, SOLMESH

Example

```
Command: SOLWIRE
Select solids to be wired ...
Select objects:
```

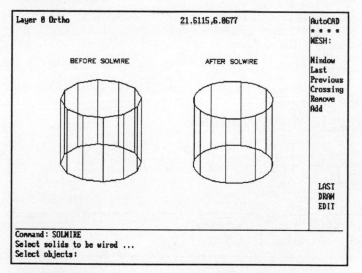

SOLWIRE Example

STATUS

Screen [INQUIRY] [STATUS]
Pull down [Utility] [Status]

STATUS displays a text screen of information on the current drawing's limits, extents, display, drawing tool settings, and some system information.

Tips

□ The STATUS numeric display format is based on the current units system.

□ Drawing extents specify the actual size of the drawing regardless of the limits setting.

□ To get status reports on the current dimensioning variables, layers, styles, and system variables, use those individual commands with the ? option.

Warning(s)

▪ You cannot issue a transparent help ('HELP or '?) for the STATUS command.

See also: LAYER, SETVAR, UNITS

STRETCH

Screen [EDIT] [next] [STRETCH:]
Pull down [Modify] [Stretch]

STRETCH lets you dynamically lengthen or shorten entities by placing a crossing window around the endpoints of the entities to be stretched and specifying displacement by keyboard entry or dragging.

You can stretch lines, arcs, traces, solids, polylines, and 3D faces. Entity endpoints that lie outside the crossing window remain fixed. Endpoints inside the window change. Text, blocks, and circles move if their definition points are within the crossing window. The definition point for blocks, shapes, and text is the insertion point; for circles the center point. Unlike other editing commands, you must use a crossing window in selecting objects.

Prompts

```
Select objects to stretch by window...
Select objects:
First Corner:
Other Corner:
Select Objects:
Base point:
New point:
```

After you specify the base point, you can pick a new point to stretch or move the selected objects. Or you can type an absolute or relative coordinate.

Tips

▢ Polyline width, tangent, and curve fitting information is not modified when a polyline is stretched.

▢ If dimension text was created with associative dimensioning (DIMASO) on, then STRETCH updates the dimension text. The definition point for dimension text is its middle center point. You can restore dimension text position with Hometext.

▢ The EXTEND and TRIM commands are similar to STRETCH, but they require a boundary line.

▢ Using CHANGE to a point is also similar to using STRETCH. However, if you change to a point with ORTHO off, all the selected lines will converge at one point.

▢ Unless you leave one endpoint outside the crossing window, STRETCH acts just like the MOVE command.

▢ Stretching a viewport border in paper space increases or decreases the area of model space that is visible in the viewport.

Warning(s)

▪ If you use the screen menu, a C for crossing is automatically entered at the select objects prompt. If you enter the STRETCH command from the keyboard, or repeat the command by pressing <RETURN>, you must enter crossing selection mode to select objects.

▪ If you pick more than one crossing window, STRETCH only uses the last crossing selection.

See also: CHANGE, EXTEND, TRIM

Example

```
Command: STRETCH
Select objects to stretch by window...
Select objects: C
First corner:          Point ①.
Other corner:          Point ②.
8 found.
Base point:            Pick any point.
New point: @1'<180
```

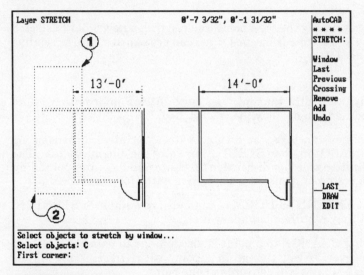

STRETCH Example

STYLE

```
Screen [DRAW] [DTEXT:] [STYLE:]
Screen [DRAW] [TEXT:] [STYLE:]
Screen [SETTINGS] [next] [STYLE:]
Pull down [Options] [DTEXT OPTIONS >] [Text font...]
```

The STYLE command lets you create, modify, or list text styles. A style name can be up to 31 characters long. Each text style must reference a font file. Compiled font files have the extension .SHX.

Prompts and Options

```
Text style name (or ?) <STANDARD>:
Font file <txt>:
Height <0.0000>:
Width factor <1.00>:
Obliquing angle <0>:
Backwards? <N>
Upside-down? <N>
Vertical? <N>
```

Style name	Create a new style or edit an existing style. Once you end the command, this style becomes the default style.
?	Activate the wild-card options for reviewing the names of styles defined in the current drawing. The default displays a sorted listing of all named styles. Use any wild-card option to create a more specific list.
Font	You supply a font name as the basis for the style. (See example below.) The default is <TXT>.
Height	Set a fixed height, or 0 for a variable height.
Width factor	Specify a width factor to expand or compress text.
Obliquing angle	Slant the text angle. A positive number slants towards the right; a negative number slants towards the left.
Backwards	Mirrors text horizontally.
Upside-down	Mirrors text vertically.
Vertical	Text is drawn vertically.

The default settings are:

STANDARD	Obliquing angle = 0
Font = TXT	Backwards = No
Height = 0	Upside-down = No
Width factor = 1	Vertical = No

Related System Variable(s)

TEXTSTYLE, TEXTSIZE, FILEDIA

Tips

□ If you set the text height to 0, you will be prompted for the text height of each text object during the DTEXT or TEXT commands.

□ You can change the current style in the STYLE, TEXT, DTEXT, and dimensioning commands.

▢ You can redefine individual text object styles with CHANGE.

▢ Specify your text height based on your plotting scale factor.

▢ The LIST command will display the style settings of a text object.

▢ You can purge any unused text styles except for STANDARD.

Warning(s)

■ If you redefine a style's font and/or its horizontal or vertical orientation, all text strings created with that style will globally update. If you change the other settings, they only affect new text.

■ You are not prompted for a style name if you select a font from the icon menu. The style name defaults to the font name.

■ Unlike blocks, font file definitions (.SHX) are stored external to the drawing file and must accompany the drawing file in a drawing exchange.

■ Fonts take up different amounts of horizontal space. The more complex the font, the longer it takes to display.

See also: CHANGE, DIM, DTEXT, PURGE, RENAME, TEXT, Wild-Card Characters

```
Layer STYLE                    8.7221, 8.9364 ·          AutoCAD
                                                         * * * *
      STYLE DEFAULT  OBLIQUING ANGLE SET TO 15°          STYLE:
      WIDTH SET TO .75   OBLIQUING ANGLE SET TO -15°      ?
      BACKWARDS       UPSIDE DOWN                   V     Fonts
        WIDTH SET TO 1.5                            E
                                                    R     Yes
   CYRILLIC   В111СИЛЛИВ  ROMAND   ROMAND           T     No
   CYRILTLC   ЧЙРИЛТЛЧ    ROMANS   ROMANS           I
   GOTHICE    ООТВ1СЕ     ROMANT   ROMANT           C     DTEXT:
   GOTHICG    СОТ9SЕ9     SCRIPTC  SCRIPTC          A     TEXT:
   GOTHICI    ООВ1IOI     SCRIPTS  SCRIPTS          L
   GREEKC     ГРЕЕКХ      SYASTRO  ΒΨΘΩΩΧΥ
   GREEKS     ГРЕЕКΣ      SYMAP
   ITALICC    ITALICC     SYMATH   √→<ЖC·
   ITALICT    ITALICT     SYMETEO
   MONOTXT    MONOTXT     SYMUSIC  ---ᐱ---b♪        ___LAST___
   ROMANC     ROMANC      TXT      TXT              DRAW
                                                    EDIT
Text style name (or ?) <STANDARD>:
Existing style.
Font file <TXT>:
```

Style

TABLET

Screen [SETTINGS] [next] [TABLET:]

The TABLET command lets you configure and calibrate a digitizing tablet. Configuring defines tablet areas for tablet menus and the screen pointing area. Calibrating aligns the tablet to a paper drawing for digitizing. The tablet and screen menus are interactive; you can pick commands off the tablet that activate screen menus. The tablet menu supplied with AutoCAD works in conjunction with the menu file ACAD.MNX. When digitizing, use <^T> to toggle the tablet mode on and off. On DOS-based systems, you can also use the <F10> function key.

Prompt

Option (ON/OFF/CAL/CFG):

Options

ON	Enables tablet (digitizing) mode.
OFF	Disables tablet (digitizing) mode.
CAL	Calibrates the tablet with the coordinates of a paper drawing. Calibration is only effective in the space where the calibration took place.
CFG	Reserves portions of the tablet for menus and the screen pointing area. You can have a maximum of four tablet menu areas. The screen menu option [re-cfg] activates a macro to automatically configure the tablet menu supplied with AutoCAD.

Tips

- The current UCS is the digitizing plane when calibrating a tablet. You will need to recalibrate the tablet if you change the UCS, or digitized points will be projected onto the UCS.

- Before calibrating, configure for 0 tablet menu areas and enlarge the screen pointing area. This will give you more digitizing space for your paper drawing.

- Snap, ortho, and grid remain active when digitizing.

Warning(s)

- You cannot change viewports or select commands from the screen while tablet mode is on.

- Tablet calibration is lost between editing sessions.

TABSURF

```
Screen [DRAW] [next] [3D Surfs] [TABSURF:]
Screen [SURFACES] [TABSURF:]
Pull down [Draw] [Surfaces...] [TABULATED]
```

TABSURF (TABulated SURFace) generates a 3D polygon mesh by extruding a path curve through space along a direction vector. (See example.)

The path curve can be a line, arc, circle, 2D, or 3D polyline. The direction vector can be a line or an open 2D or 3D polyline. The surface starts at the endpoint nearest your pick point on the path curve. If you use a polyline for the direction vector, only the first and last vertexes are recognized.

Prompts
```
Select path curve:
Select direction vector:
```

Related System Variable(s)
SURFTAB1

Tips

□ A TABSURF mesh can be exploded into individual 3D faces.

See also: EXPLODE, PEDIT, 3DFACE, 3DMESH

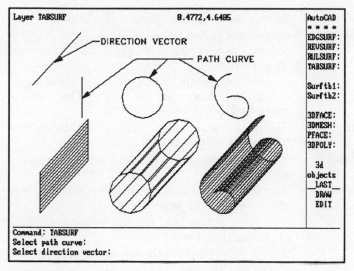

TABSURF Examples

TEXT

Screen **[DRAW] [next] [TEXT]**

TEXT is AutoCAD's basic text command. It is an older command than DTEXT and does not dynamically show text characters on the screen as you enter them. It places a single text string when you end text input.

Prompts

```
Justify/Style/<Start point>:
Height <default>:
Rotation angle <default>:
Text:
```

Options

Start point   Default text justification is at the bottom left corner of the first character for each line of text.

Justify	Specify one of the following text justifications:
Align	Specify the beginning and ending point of a line of text. The text height is adjusted to fit between these points.
Fit	Specify the beginning and ending point of a line of text. You determine the height. The width is controlled by the two endpoints.
Center	Specify the center of the text horizontally and the base of the text vertically.
Middle	Specify the middle of the text line horizontally and vertically.
Right	Text justification is at the bottom right of the last character for each line of text.
TL	Text justification is at the top left of the tallest character (Release 11 only).
TC	Text justification is at the top center of the tallest character (Release 11 only).
TR	Text justification is at the top right of the tallest character (Release 11 only).
ML	Text justification is at the middle left, between the top of the tallest character and the bottom of lowest descender (Release 11 only).
MC	Text justification is at the middle center, between the top of the tallest character and the bottom of the lowest descender (Release 11 only).
MR	Text justification is at the middle right, between the top of the tallest character and the bottom of the lowest descender (Release 11 only).
BL	Text justification is at the bottom left of the lowest descender (Release 11 only).
BC	Text justification is at the bottom center of the lowest descender (Release 11 only).
BR	Text justification is at the bottom right of the lowest descender (Release 11 only).
Style	Change the current style. The style must have been created with the STYLE command.
↵	If you press <RETURN>, the last text entered is highlighted. You are then prompted for a new text string. The new text is placed directly below the highlighted text with the same style, height, and rotation as the highlighted text.

Height   Assign a text height. You are not prompted for
                          this when using Align or defaulting to a text style
                          with a predefined height.

Rotation angle   Specify the text angle.

Text   Supply the text string.

The default settings are:

Start point	Left justified
Height	0.2000
Rotation angle	0

Special Character Codes

You can code your text string to obtain the following special
characters:

%%o	Toggle overscore mode on/off
%%u	Toggle underscore mode on/off
%%d	Draw degrees symbol
%%p	Draw plus/minus tolerance symbol
%%o	Draw diameter symbol
%%%	Draw a single percent symbol

When you are entering text, the control characters appear in
the drawing. Once you end the command, the appropriate
characters replace the control codes.

Related System Variable(s)

TEXTSIZE, TEXTSTYLE

Tips

▫ You can preset the font, alignment, height, and rotation of text
  by selecting [Options] - [Dtext Options >] from the pull-down
  menu. These preset variables are automatically activated when
  you pick [Draw] - [Dtext] from the pull-down menus. When using
  the screen menus, the text variables are based on the last text
  inserted during the drawing session. The next drawing session
  defaults to the preset height and font; however, you must
  redefine the rotation angle and text justification.

▫ When using the same block of text for multiple drawings, save
  time by wblocking the text from DTEXT.

▫ You can assign a thickness to text, but only after the text is
  inserted. Do this with the CHANGE or CHPROP command.

▫ OSNAP INSert locates the insertion point of text.

□   Edit text strings with the DDEDIT or CHANGE commands.

□   The spacing between multiple lines of text is determined by the individual text font definition files.

□   You can also import ASCII text from a separate file on disk with the ASCTEXT.LSP program from the BONUS disk. If installed, you can select it with [BONUS] - [ASCTEXT] from the screen menu, or [File] - [EXCHANGE   >] - [Import Text] on the pull-down menus.

Warning(s)

■   Base your text height on the scale you plan to plot the drawing. The text height you specify in AutoCAD should be the height of plotted text multiplied by the plot scale factor.

■   You cannot use the Fit option for text styles assigned a vertical orientation.

See also: CHANGE, DDEDIT, DTEXT, QTEXT, STYLE

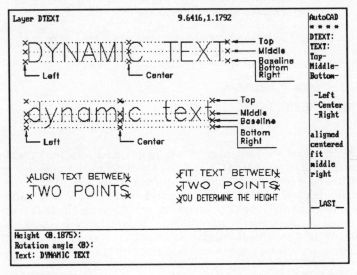

TEXT Examples

TIME

Screen **[INQUIRY] [TIME:]**

The TIME command displays: the current date and time; the date and time the drawing was created; the date and time the drawing was last updated; and the amount of time spent in the current editing session. In addition, you can set an elapsed timer. The default turns the elapsed timer on.

Prompt

Display/ON/OFF/Reset:

Options

Display	Current status of the time command.
ON	Activates the elapsed timer.
OFF	Stops the elapsed timer.
Reset	Resets the elapsed timer to zero.

Related System Variable(s)

CDATE, DATE, TDCREATE, TDINDWG, TDUPDATE, TDUSRTIMER

Tips

□ Time is displayed to the nearest millisecond using military format.

□ The date and time are based on the date and time maintained by your computer.

Warning(s)

■ Inserting a drawing or block does not add to the existing time.

■ The time you work on a drawing won't be saved if you quit.

TRACE

TRACE creates line segments with width, similar to the PLINE command. TRACE also automatically calculates the miter for adjacent segments, but only after the endpoint of the next segment is entered. If FILL is on, a trace is displayed as solid-filled. The default trace width is .05.

Prompts

```
Trace width <0.0500>
From point:
To point:
To point:
To point:
```

Related System Variable(s)

TRACEWID

Tips

□ Polylines are much more flexible and versatile than traces.

□ Object snap modes treat traces the same as solid fills. You can osnap to the endpoints and midpoint of traces.

□ While drawing a trace, you do not have Undo and Close options like those in the LINE and POLYLINE commands.

□ You cannot assign tapers to trace segments.

□ You cannot use the following editing commands on a trace: OFFSET, EXTEND, TRIM, CHANGE point, and EXPLODE.

See also: FILL, POLYLINE

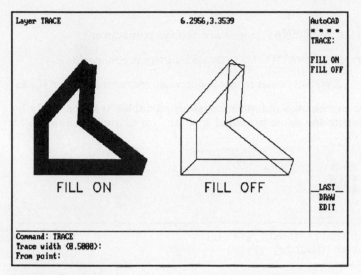

```
Layer TRACE                    6.2956,3.3539         AutoCAD
                                                     * * * *
                                                     TRACE:

                                                     FILL ON
                                                     FILL OFF




      FILL ON              FILL OFF                   LAST
                                                     DRAW
                                                     EDIT

Command: TRACE
Trace width <0.5000>:
From point:
```

TRACE Example

Transparent Commands

Transparent commands can be accessed while in the middle of other commands. An apostrophe must precede the command name. You cannot use transparent commands during TEXT, DTEXT, ATTDEF, SKETCH, PLOT, PRPLOT, VPOINT, DVIEW, ZOOM Dynamic, in dimensioning, or while you are in another transparent command. You can't perform a transparent ZOOM, VIEW, or PAN in paper space. Transparent commands will not work if the command would cause a regeneration.

The following commands can be transparent:

'DDEMODES	'PAN	'SETVAR
'DDLMODES	'?	'TEXTVAR
'DDRMODES	'REDRAW	'TEXTSCR
'GRAPHSCR	'REDRAWALL	'VIEW
'HELP	'RESUME	'ZOOM (Except ALL
		and Extents)

Tips

□   Filters and OSNAP modes are always transparent.

□   Turn REGENAUTO off to avoid lengthy regenerations.

□   Set VIEWRES to fast zooms to decrease redraw and regen times.

□   You can change individual system variables transparently by entering the name preceded with an ' (apostrophe) (Release 11 only).

TRIM

Screen **[EDIT] [next] [TRIM:]**
Pull down **[Modify] [Trim]**

TRIM lets you clip the portions of entities that cross another entity selected as a cutting edge. You can have more than one cutting edge, and an entity can be both a cutting edge and an object to trim. Lines, arcs, circles, and 2D polylines can act as cutting edges and objects to trim. When you're working in paper space, viewport borders can be cutting edges.

Prompts

```
Select cutting edge(s)...
Select objects:
<Select object to trim>/Undo:
```

Options

Select object to trim
            Select the part of the entity you want to delete.

Undo   Restore the last entity trimmed.

Tips

□   The extrusion direction of entities that are cutting edges and the entities to trim must be parallel to the Z axis of the current UCS.

▫ It is possible to select more than one cutting edge per object. The entity will trim to the first edge and stop. Pick the object again and it will trim to the next cutting edge.

▫ Trimming circles requires two intersections with a cutting edge.

▫ Entities trim to the center of wide polyline cutting edges.

▫ Ends of wide polylines are always square. If you trim a polyline at an angle, a portion of the polyline width may extend past the cutting edge.

▫ When trimming a linear dimension, the entire dimension updates.

Warning(s)

■ You can only trim one entity at a time.

■ Blocks, text, and traces cannot be cutting edges nor objects to trim.

■ You cannot decurve a splined polyline that has been trimmed. The polyline becomes permanently curved polyline segments.

See also: CHANGE, EXTEND, STRETCH

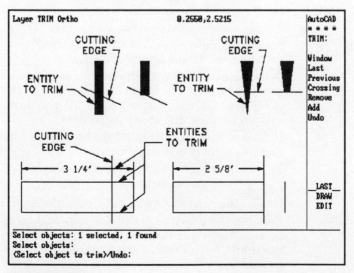

TRIM Examples

U

See UNDO

UCS

Screen **[UCS:]**
Pull down **[Settings] [UCS Control...]** *or*
[UCS Options...] *or* **[UCS Previous]**

The UCS (User Coordinate System) lets you redefine the location of 0,0 and the direction of the X, Y and Z axes. You can also set your UCS with the DDUCS dialogue boxes. The default UCS is the World (WCS).

Prompt

```
Origin/ZAxis/3point/Entity/View/X/Y/Z/Prev/Restore/
Save/Del/?/<World>:
```

Options

Origin	Specify a new origin point while retaining the direction of the X, Y, and Z axes.
ZAxis	Specify a new origin point and a positive Z axis.
3point	Specify an origin, one point on the positive X axis, and one point in the positive X,Y plane.
Entity	Defines a new UCS with the same orientation as a selected entity. The origin is determined by the entity type. It does not work for 3D polylines, polygon meshes, and viewport borders.
View	Defines a new UCS parallel to the screen. The point of origin is unchanged.
X	Rotates the current UCS around the X axis.
Y	Rotates the current UCS around the Y axis.
Z	Rotates the current X and Y axes about the Z axis.
Previous	Restores the previous UCS. You can backtrack up to ten previous coordinate systems for paper space and ten previous coordinate systems for model space.
Restore	Retrieve a previously saved UCS. Responding with a question mark (?) is the same as UCS ?.

Save	Stores the current UCS with a name you specify, up to 31 characters long. Responding with a question mark (?) is the same as UCS ?.
Delete	Deletes a saved UCS. Responding with a question mark (?) is the same as UCS ?.
?	Activates the wild-card options for reviewing the names of UCSs defined in the current drawing. The default, an asterisk, gives a sorted listing of the named UCS. You can use any of the wild-card options to create a more specific list. If the current UCS is unnamed, it is listed as *WORLD* or *NO NAME*, depending on its orientation.
World	Restores the WCS.

Related System Variable(s)

UCSFOLLOW, UCSICON, UCSORG, UCSXDIR, UCSYDIR, VIEWMODE, WORLDUCS

Tips

□ Only one UCS can be current.

□ If you get lost when locating a UCS, return to the WCS and start over.

See also: DDUCS, DVIEW, PLAN, UCSICON, VPOINT, Wild-Card Characters

Example

```
Command: UCS
Origin/ZAxis/3point/Entity/View/X/Y/Z/Prev/
Restore/Save/Del/?/<World>: 3
Origin point <0,0,0>:                          Point ①.
Point on positive portion of the X-axis
<3.00,1.00,0.00>:                              Point ②.
Point on positive-Y portion of the UCS X-Y plane
<2.00,2.00,0.00>:                              Point ③.
Command: UCS
Origin/ZAxis/3point/Entity/View/X/Y/Z/Prev/
Restore/Save/Del/?/<World>: S
?/Name of UCS: RIGHT
```

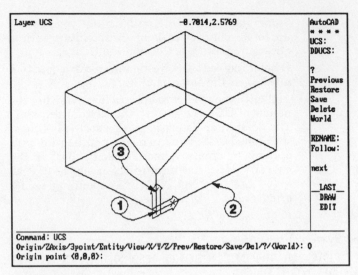

UCS Example

UCSICON

Screen **[SETTINGS]** **[next]** **[UCSICON:]**
Pull down **[Settings]** **[Ucsicon On/Off/OR]**

The UCSICON is a marker used to graphically display the origin and viewing plane of the current UCS. When the marker is L-shaped, you are in model space; when the marker is triangular, you are in paper space. The default for the icon is <ON>, Noorigin, and model space.

Prompts

ON/OFF/All/Noorigin/ORigin <ON>:

Options

ON	Displays the UCSICON.
OFF	Turns the UCSICON display off.
All	Display changes to the UCSICON in all viewports.

Noorigin   Display the UCSICON at the lower left side of the viewport regardless of the current UCS definition.

ORigin   Displays the UCISICON at the origin of the current UCS (0,0,0). If the origin is off the screen viewing area, the icon is shown in the lower left corner.

Following are the different icon features:

W   The UCS is the same as the WCS.

+   The icon is located at the origin point of the UCS.

Box   You are viewing the UCS from a positive Z direction.

Box with a broken pencil
                  The X,Y plane of the UCS is perpendicular to your viewing plane.

The icon is drawn as a cube in perspective
                  Perspective viewing is on.

Related System Variable(s)

UCSICON

Tips

□ Selecting UCSICON from the pull-down menus acts as a three-way toggle switch - ON/OFF/OR.

□ When the origin is near the edge or off the display screen, the icon is shown in the lower left corner.

See also: UCS

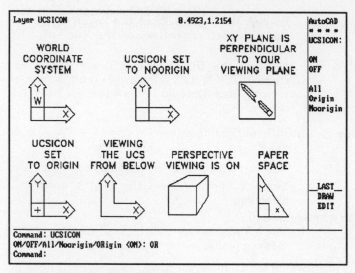

UCSICON Display Examples

UNDEFINE   See REDEFINE

UNDO / U / REDO

Screen [EDIT] [next] [UNDO:]
Screen [* * * *] [U:]
Screen [* * * *] [REDO:]
Pull down [Utility] [U]
Pull down [Utility] [Redo]

The UNDO command lets you sequentially reverse previous commands individually, in groups, or to the beginning of the current editing session. The default setting is the number of commands to undo at one time.

The U command is a subset of the UNDO command. U only reverses the effects of the last command. This is the same as using the UNDO command and entering the number 1.

REDO reverses the effects of the last UNDO command. You can redo only once, and it must be the first command after UNDO.

Prompts

`Auto/Back/Control/End/Group/Mark/<number>:`

Options

Auto	Auto ON marks a menu macro as one command. Auto OFF treats each command in a menu macro as individual commands.
Back	Used in conjunction with the Mark option. You can undo to a marker with the Back option.
Control	Limits or disables the UNDO command.
All	Enables all the undo prompts and options.
None	Disables the UNDO and U commands.
One	Allows only the last command to be undone.
End	Terminates the UNDO group option.
Group	Treats a sequence of commands as one. Places an ending marker with the Mark option. This is similar to the way Auto behaves with menu macros.
Mark	Sets a marker before issuing a series of commands. You can have as many markers as you want. The Back option undoes commands back to the last marker. Once you reach the first marker, you will see the following message: `This will undo everything. OK? <Y>.`
Number	Enter the number of commands to undo.

Tips

▫ The U options of the LINE and PLINE command undo to the previous point. Entering a U during the TRIM command will restore the last entity trimmed.

▫ Issuing a U at the DIM: prompt reverses the last dimensioning command. Issuing a U at the command prompt after dimensioning undoes everything done while in dimensioning mode.

Warning(s)

▪ Issuing the PLOT or PRPLOT command during a drawing session resets UNDO.

▪ The UNDO command views a script command sequence as a group. Therefore, you can reverse the whole script with one U command.

See also: OOPS

UNITS

Screen [SETTINGS] [next] [UNITS:]

The UNITS command controls the input and display format of coordinates, distances, and angles. You specify the system of units, the precision, the system of angle measure, the precision of angle display, and the direction of angles.

Options

Format   Specify the units of measure – Scientific, Decimal (the default), Engineering, Architectural, or Fractional.

Precision   The number of digits past the decimal place or the smallest fraction of an inch to display. The default is 4.

Systems of angle measure
                Specify the format for angle measurements; Decimal degrees (the default), Degrees/minutes/seconds, Grads, Radians, or Surveyor's units.

Number of fractional places for display of angles:
                Select the precision with which angles are displayed. The default is 0 (no fractions)

Direction for angle 0
                Set angle 0 equal to East (the default), North, West or South.

Do you want angles measured clockwise?
> No — measures angles counterclockwise (the default); Yes — measures angles clockwise.

Related System Variable(s)

ANGBASE, ANGDIR, AUNITS, AUPREC, LUNITS, LUPREC, UNITMODE

Tips

□ You can change units settings after you begin a drawing.

□ You can globally update associative dimension text to show a change in units settings.

□ The format for entering 3'-5 1/2" is 3'5-1/2 or 3'5-1.5. The inch character is optional.

□ You can enter fractions with denominators other than those with a power of 2 (ex. 2/3) and improper fractions (ex. 6/4). You can refer to decimal feet such as 4.6' when working with architectural or engineering units. You cannot have improper fractions mixed with whole numbers such as 2-5/4.

□ You can enter angles in radians or grads format even if the current units setting is for another format. Enter the suffix "r" for radians or "g" for grads. Do not include the suffix if the format is current.

□ You can override the current angle format and enter angles in decimal degrees relative to AutoCAD's default orientation (zero degrees equals 3 o'clock) and direction (counterclockwise) by preceding the angle with two angle brackets (<<). Preceding the angle with three angle brackets (<<<) overrides only the orientation and direction and allows the angle to be specified in the current angle units format.

Warning(s)

■ Civil engineering drawings are usually created in decimal units with the intention that 1.0 equals 1'-0". If you change the units to architectural, 1.0 becomes 1". If necessary, you can scale the drawing 12 times to have 1.0 equal to 1'-0".

See also: DIMENSIONING, SCALE

VIEW

Screen [DISPLAY] [VIEW:]

The VIEW command can save the current viewport or a user-definable window to a name, for future retrieval. The view name can be up to 31 characters long. VIEW may be executed transparently by entering 'VIEW within another command.

Prompts

?/Delete/Restore/Save/Window:

Options

?	Activates the wild-card options for reviewing the names of views defined in the drawing. The default, an asterisk, displays a sorted listing of all named views. You can enter view names separated by commas or you can use any of the wild-card options to create a more specific list. An M (model space) or P (paper space) indicates in which space the view was defined.
Delete	Removes a defined view. You can enter view names separated by commas or you can use any of the wild-card options to create a more specific list.
Restore	Displays a saved view in the current viewport. If you restore a model space view while working in paper space, you are asked to select a viewport. The viewport must be on and active. You are then switched to model space.
	If you restore a paper space view while working in model space, you are switched to paper space. If tilemode is on, you cannot restore a paper space view.
Save	Saves the current viewport display.
Window	Specify a window area to save as a view. Restoring the view may display more than the windowed area up to the current display size; plotting the view only plots the windowed area.

Related System Variable(s)

VIEWCTR, VIEWDIR, VIEWMODE, VIEWSIZE, VIEWTWIST

V

Tips

□ The PLOT command gives you the option of plotting a saved view.

□ You can specify a predefined view for display before beginning a drawing session. At the Enter name of drawing prompt, type the drawing name followed by a comma and the view name.

□ ZOOM Previous includes restored views.

□ Rename views with the RENAME command.

Warning(s)

■ You receive no warnings when naming a view to the same name as an existing view.

■ If you have difficulty accessing the view as a transparent command, check the VIEWRES and REGENAUTO settings. Set VIEWRES to fast zooms and REGENAUTO to Off.

■ Most views can be restored transparently. However, you cannot execute a transparent view when working in paper space or during the following commands: VPOINT, DVIEW, ZOOM, VIEW, or PAN.

See also: REGENAUTO, RENAME, TILEMODE, Transparent Commands, VIEWRES, Wild-Card Characters, ZOOM

Example

```
Command: 'VIEW
?/Delete/Restore/Save/Window: W
View name to save: OFFICE
First corner:                      Point ①.
Other corner:                      Point ②.
```

Make lower right viewport active.

```
Command: 'VIEW
?/Delete/Restore/Save/Window: R
View name to restore: OFFICE
```

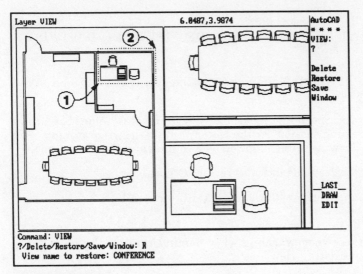

VIEW Example

VIEWPORTS   See VPORTS

VIEWRES

Screen **[DISPLAY] [VIEWRES:]**

VIEWRES controls zoom speeds and the display resolution of arcs, circles, and linetypes. The default is for fast zooms. With this setting, most zooms, pans, and view restores are done at redraw, not regeneration, speed.

Prompts

```
Do you want fast zooms? <Y>:
Enter circle zoom percent (1-20000) <100>:
```

Options

Entering a value greater than 100 for the circle zoom percent gives you better circle and arc displays, but increases regeneration times. Lower values decrease the display resolution, but also decrease regeneration time.

Tips

▫ Regardless of the VIEWRES setting, circles and arcs are always plotted at the plotter's resolution.

Warning(s)

▪ Broken linetypes can appear as continuous lines due to VIEWRES and the current zoom level. Forcing a regeneration or zooming in closer may display the linetype correctly.

See also: REGEN

VPLAYER

Screen **[MVIEW] [VPLAYER:]**
Pull down **[Display] [Mview] [Vplayer]**

VPLAYER (Release 11 only) controls layer freeze state per viewport. TILEMODE must be set to 0 (off) in order to activate this command.

Prompts

?/Freeze/Thaw/Reset/Newfrz/Vpvisdflt:
All/Select/<Current>:

Options

All	Selects *all* paper space viewports including those that aren't visible.
Select	Select paper space viewports using standard object selection methods. If you are in model space, you are temporarily switched to paper space for viewport selection.
Current	Selects the current viewport.
?	Displays a listing of the frozen layers for the current viewport. If you are in model space, you are temporarily switched to paper space for viewport selection.
Freeze	Specify layers to freeze. You can list layer names separated by commas or use wild-card characters. Once you name the layers, you select the viewport(s).

Thaw	Select layers to thaw. You can list layer names separated by commas or use wild-card characters. You can use the DDLMODES command. Once you name the layers, you select the viewport(s).
Reset	Restores the default visibility setting for layers based on the Vpvisdflt setting.
Newfrz	Create new layers that are frozen in all viewports. Create more than one layer at a time by separating each layer name with a comma.
Vpvisdflt	ViewPort VISibility DeFauLT — determines layer visibility defaults before creating viewports. You can set more than one layer by using wild-card characters.

Related System Variable(s)

TILEMODE

Warning(s)

- VPLAYER cannot override LAYER command settings. Layers must be thawed and on in order to be affected by the VPLAYER command.

See also: DDLMODES, LAYER, Wild-Card Characters

VPOINT

```
Screen [DISPLAY] [VPOINT:]
Pull down [Display] [Vpoint 3D...]
```

VPOINT (ViewPOINT) lets you specify the direction and angle for viewing a drawing by selecting a 3D viewpoint. Issuing the command regenerates the drawing in parallel projection from the 3D point that you specify. The default creates a plan view <0.0000,0.0000,1.0000> of the current UCS. You have three ways to define a viewpoint: enter X,Y,Z values; supply an angle in the X,Y plane and from the X,Y plane; or pick a point on the compass icon.

VPOINT can only display parallel projection. To generate perspectives, use the DVIEW command. VPOINT has been superseded by the DVIEW command, which lets you dynamically select and control a 3D viewpoint.

Prompt

```
Rotate/<View point> <0.0000,0.0000,1.0000>:
```

Options

Rotate   Specify the viewpoint by entering two angles – the angle in the X,Y plane from the X axis and the Z angle from the X,Y plane.

View point   Specify a view direction by entering X,Y,Z coordinates relative to 0,0,0.

If you enter a <RETURN> at the prompt, a compass and axes tripod are displayed to assist in selecting a viewpoint.

Related System Variable(s)

WORLDVIEW

Tips

▫ Specify your viewpoint of 0,0,1 to return to plan view, or use the PLAN command.

Warning(s)

▪ You cannot control the distance you are viewing an object, only the orientation. To control the distance, use the DVIEW command.

▪ The viewpoint is always viewed through 0,0,0 of the WCS or UCS depending on the setting of the WORLDVIEW system variable. If you want to view your drawing through a different point, use the DVIEW command.

See also: DVIEW, PLAN

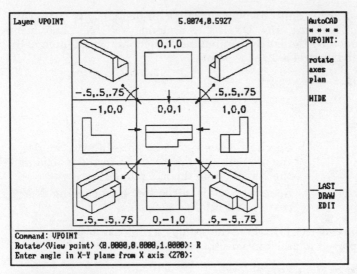

VPOINT Example

VPORTS / VIEWPORTS

Screen **[SETTINGS] [next] [VPORTS:]**

In model space, the VPORTS command lets you divide your screen into several viewing areas commonly referred to as tiled viewports. Depending on your hardware, you can define up to four or sixteen viewports at any one time. Each viewport can display a different view of your drawing and has independent Viewpoint, Snap, Grid, Viewres, Ucsicon, Dview, and Isometric settings. You can independently zoom, regenerate, and redraw in each viewport.

Model space viewports are interactive. You can begin most drawing and editing commands in one viewport and click into another viewport to complete the drawing or editing command. Only one viewport can be current at a time. The current viewport is surrounded by a wider border and the crosshairs are only present within that viewport. You can only plot the current viewport.

Paper space (Release 11 only) lets you create unlimited viewports. These viewports are not tiled. In other words, the viewports can overlap one another and your crosshairs can span the entire display screen. You can control layer visibility per viewport and plot multiple viewports at multiple scales.

The following information is for tilemode viewports. See PSPACE, MVIEW, and VPLAYER for more information about paper space viewports.

Prompt

```
Save/Restore/Delete/Join/SIngle/?/2/<3>/4:
```

Options

Save	Save the current viewport configuration with a name. A viewport name can be 31 characters long.
Restore	Retrieve a saved viewport configuration. Responding with a ? activates the wild-card options for reviewing the names of viewports defined in the current drawing. The default, an asterisk, displays a listing of the saved viewport configurations. You can use any of the wild-card options to obtain a more specific list.
Delete	Delete a saved viewport configuration.
Join	Combine two adjacent viewports into one viewport provided they form a rectangle.
SIngle	Turn multiple viewports off and return to one viewport. The current viewport is the default.
?	Activates the wild-card options for reviewing the names of viewports defined in the current drawing. The default, an asterisk, gives a complete listing of all saved viewport configurations. You can use any of the wild-card options to create a more specific list.
2	Splits the current viewport into two horizontal or vertical viewports.
3	Splits the current viewport into any one of a variety of three-viewport configurations. This is the default.
4	Splits the current viewport into four viewports.

Related System Variable(s)

CVPORT, MAXACTVP, TILEMODE

Tips

▫ REDRAW and REGEN only affect the current viewport. You can redraw and regenerate all the displayed viewports with the REDRAWALL and REGENALL commands.

▫ Highlighting and dragging occur only in the current viewport.

▫ Create viewports in paper space with the MVIEW command.

▫ Viewports in model space are non-overlapping tiled divisions of your graphics screen. Viewports in paper space can overlap.

▫ You can plot multiple viewports from paper space.

▫ You can use the edges of viewports in paper space as hatching boundaries.

Warning(s)

■ You can't switch viewports during the following commands: SNAP, GRID, VPORTS, ZOOM, PAN, VPOINT, and DVIEW.

■ You can only plot from the current viewport.

See also: MSPACE, MVIEW, PSPACE, REDRAWALL, REGENALL, TILEMODE, Wild-Card Characters

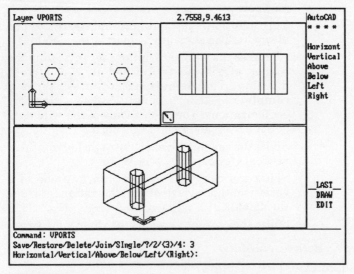

VPORTS Example

VSLIDE

Screen **[UTILITY] [SLIDES] [VSLIDE:]**

VSLIDE (View SLIDE) displays a slide file in the current viewport. A slide file has the extension .SLD. You create slides with the MSLIDE command. The default slide name is the current drawing file name. If a slide has been stored in a slide library, the format is: *library-name (slide-name)*.

Use REDRAW, or any command that causes a redraw, to clear the slide. Placing an asterisk before the slide name causes the slide file to be read but not displayed until the next VSLIDE command. This is used in script files to rapidly load and display slides. See SCRIPT.

Prompt
Slide file <*dwg-name*>:

Related System Variable(s)
FILEDIA

Tips
□ Slides are often used for slide show presentations and as references.

□ Since slide files do not retain any of the data associated with entities, recalling slides is equivalent to redraw speed.

□ Slides can be used as an invisible "layer" to trace over onto the current drawing.

Warning(s)
■ Slides cannot be edited or plotted.

See also: DELAY, Dialogue Boxes, MSLIDE, SCRIPT

WBLOCK

Screen [BLOCKS] [WBLOCK:]

WBLOCK (Write BLOCK) writes a drawing, part of a drawing, or a block to a disk file as a new drawing. The WBLOCK is assigned to model space. This file can be inserted (using the INSERT command) into other drawings, or can be recalled from the main menu option number 2 – Edit an existing drawing.

Prompts

```
File name:
Block name:
Insertion base point:
```

Options

File name
: The name can be up to eight characters for DOS-based systems and include a drive and path specification. The file extension .DWG is applied automatically.

Block name
: Specify the name of the block in the current drawing to be written to the disk file.

=
: If you respond with an = to the Block name prompt, any existing block in the current drawing with the same name as the wblock file name is written to the file. You cannot use this method on DOS-based systems if the block name contains more than eight letters.

*
: If you respond with an asterisk, WBLOCK writes the entire drawing to the disk. This purges any unused blocks, layers, linetypes, text styles, named views, UCS, viewport configurations, and unreferenced symbols. Model space entities are written to model space, and paper space entities are written to paper space.

W

<RETURN>   If you do not give a Block name, you are prompted
to enter an insertion base point and to select the
entities to wblock. This is similar to creating a
block, except the block definition is saved to disk
instead of saved within the current drawing. Use
the OOPS command to restore the deleted
entities.

Related System Variable(s)

FILEDIA

Tips

▫ Wblocking in paper space only writes those entities created in
paper space. Wblocking in model space only writes those entities
created in model space. Using the * option writes those entities
created in model space to model space and those entities created
in paper space to paper space.

Warning(s)

■ You can't wblock an external reference or one of its dependent
blocks in response to the Block name prompt.

■ Make sure the desired UCS or WCS setting is current before
wblocking entities.

■ WBLOCK doesn't write the entities' handles to the output file.

See also: BASE, BLOCK, Dialogue Boxes, HANDLES

Example

```
Command: WBLOCK
File name: PUMP
Block name: ↵
Insertion base point:          Point ①.
Select objects:                Select pump entities.
```

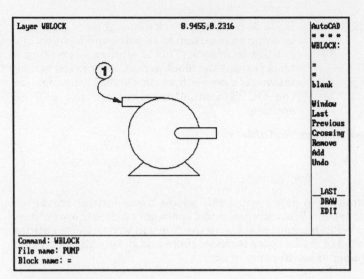

WBLOCK Example

Wild-Card Characters

Wild-card characters are available for certain commands that retain lists of information. You can retrieve complete or partial lists of information. These lists are presented in alphanumeric order (except with VPORTS and SHAPE).

The commands taking advantage of wild-card characters are: BLOCK, DIM: SAve, DIM: REStore, DIM: VAriables, INSERT, LAYER, SETVAR, STYLE, UCS, and VIEW.

A? (question mark) is the option that activates use of wild cards. The default, an asterisk, displays a complete list of information. There are 10 different wild-card characters, which can be used to form specific search patterns.

Options

?	Matches any single character.
* (asterisk)	Matches any string. It can be used anywhere in the search pattern.

X

~ (tilde)	When used as the first character in the pattern, it matches everything but the characters in the string.
# (pound)	Matches any numeric character.
@ (AT)	Matches any alpha character.
. (period)	Matches any non-alphanumeric character.
[...]	Matches any of the characters enclosed in the brackets.
[~...]	Matches any of the characters not enclosed in the brackets.
- (hyphen)	Specifies a range for a character. Used within brackets.
' (reverse quote)	Reads the next character literally.

Related System Variable(s)

MAXSORT

Warning(s)

■ Entering a ? at the command prompt will display AutoCAD's general help text screens. Using an '? in the middle of a command will provide help on that particular command.

See also: BLOCK, DIM: SAve, DIM: REStore, DIM: VAriables, DVIEW, INSERT, LAYER, SETVAR, STYLE, UCS, VIEW, VPORTS

XBIND

Screen **[BLOCKS]** **[XBIND:]**

The XBIND command (Release 11 only) makes selected external reference (xref) file information a permanent part of the current drawing file. When specifying the referenced items, you can type in the name, list multiple names separated with commas, or use wild-card characters. A similar command, XREF Bind, adds the entire external reference file to your drawing.

Prompt

Block/Dimstyle/LAyer/LType/Style:

Options

Block	Adds selected xref blocks permanently to your drawing file.
Dimstyle	Adds selected xref dimstyles permanently to your drawing file.
LAyer	Adds selected xref layers permanently to your drawing file.
LType	Adds selected xref linetypes permanently to your drawing file.
Style	Adds selected xref styles permanently to your drawing file.

Tips

▫ The added items are given names made up of the external reference file name followed by a dollar sign ($), a sequential number, and another dollar sign. The number is incremented if an item by the same name already exists.

Warning(s)

■ If the XBIND command needs more than 31 characters for renaming an item, the command ends and undoes the effects of the entire XBIND command.

See also: XREF

XREF

Screen **[BLOCKS]** **[XREF:]**

The EXREF (eXternal REFerence) command (Release 11 only) lets you attach external drawing files to your current drawing. These references are loaded into your drawing file each time you open the file for editing or request a plot from the main menu.

You cannot edit reference files indirectly, but you can osnap to referenced entities and control layer visibility, color, and linetype. Each time you make changes directly to the reference file, the latest version is loaded when you edit drawings referencing them.

You can easily locate referenced items in lists because their name
is modified in the drawing reference to the file name followed by a
vertical bar (I) symbol and the item name. This keeps any symbols,
linetypes, styles, etc. containing the same names in both files from
conflicting.

Prompt

```
?/Bind/Detach/Path/Reload/<Attach>:
```

Options

?	Lists the xrefs in a drawing file. You can use wild-card characters to specify a subset or press <RETURN> and receive a complete listing.
Bind	Makes the xref a permanent part of the drawing file. You can enter a single xref name, multiple names separated by commas, or wild-card characters. Nested xrefs are also included.
Detach	Remove xrefs from the drawing. You can enter a single xref name, multiple names separated by commas, or wild-card characters. Nested xrefs are also detached.
Path	Modify the path to search for reference file names. You can enter a single xref name, multiple names separated by commas, or wild-card characters.
Reload	Reload reference files without exiting the drawing editor. You can enter a single xref name, multiple names separated by commas, or wild-card characters. Nested xrefs are also reloaded.
Attach	Attach a reference drawing to your current drawing. This activates the File dialogue box if it is enabled and your system supports the dialogue box feature.

Related System Variable(s)

FILEDIA

Tips

▫ If you want to selectively bind items, not the entire reference file, use the XBIND command.

▫ Binding a reference file causes the names of referenced items to change. The referenced items are the given names made up of external reference file name followed by a dollar sign ($), a sequential number, and another dollar sign. The number is incremented if an item by the same name already exists.

▫ Reference files can be nested. In other words, one reference file can reference another.

▫ You can use most editing commands such as copy, scale, and rotate on xref objects.

▫ External reference files help keep individual file sizes to a minimum.

▫ You can assign another name to referenced drawings with the format: *xref name=file name*. Xref name is the new name for the external reference only within the current drawing. The actual file name remains unchanged. You may want to do this when attaching references with the same name located in different directories, or when an item exceeds the 31-character limit. You can request the File dialogue box by using the format: *xref name=~*.

Warning(s)

■ Any changes you make to the color, linetype, or visibility of referenced items are only retained for the current session. To make permanent changes, open the referenced file directly and make the changes.

■ You cannot explode reference files.

■ If you encounter an error when using the Path or Reload option, the XREF command is terminated and the entire sequence is undone.

■ A log file is maintained each time you use the Attach, Detach, and Reload options. This file contains a log of actions for those commands. The file (in ASCII format) has the same name as the current drawing, with the file extension .XLG. You may want to periodically print and/or erase these files.

- Only model space entities can be referenced; paper space entities are ignored.

- If the Bind option needs more than 31 characters for renaming an item, the command ends and undoes the effects of the Bind up to that point.

See also: XBIND

ZOOM

Screen [DISPLAY] [ZOOM:]
Pull down [Display] [Zoom Window] *or* [Zoom Previous]
or [Zoom All] *or* [Zoom Dynamic] *or* [Zoom Vmax]

The ZOOM command magnifies (zooms in) or shrinks (zooms out) the display in the current viewport. It does not physically change the size of the drawing; rather, it lets you view a small part of the drawing in detail, or look at a greater part with less detail.

Prompts

All/Center/Dynamic/Extents/Left/Previous/Vmax/Window/
<Scale(X/XP)>:

Options

All
In plan view, All displays the drawing to the limits or to the drawing extents, whichever is greater. In 3D, All displays the Extents.

Center
Specify a center point and a new display height or magnification in drawing units. If you pick a new center and press <RETURN>, the new point will become the center of the screen without changing the zoom magnification. If you enter a magnification value, it is considered an absolute zoom. Entering a magnification value followed by an X zooms relative to the current factor. Entering a magnification value followed by an XP scales the magnification of the model space view relative to paper space.

Dynamic
Dynamic is a graphical combination of the ZOOM All, Pan, and Window prompts and options. The entire generated portion of your drawing is

displayed with a box representing the last zoom magnification. This box can be moved around the screen to simultaneously pan to another drawing area. You can change the size of the box by toggling the pick button and moving the pointing device to resize the zoom box. Once the box size and location are satisfactory, press <RETURN>.

If you have a color monitor, you will see a solid white or black box indicating the current drawing extents. A dotted green box depicts the area that was last displayed in the current viewport. Red lines outline four corners indicating the limits of the virtual screen that may be displayed without requiring regeneration. If an hourglass appears in the lower left corner of the monitor, regeneration is required. The hourglass appears when the zoom box is outside the red border markers (the virtual screen).

Extents	Displays all of the drawing entities as large as possible in the current viewport.
Left	Specifies a lower left corner and a new display height or magnification in drawing units. If you pick a new lower left corner and press <RETURN>, the new point becomes the lower left corner of the screen without changing the zoom magnification. If you enter a magnification value, it is considered an absolute zoom factor. Entering a magnification value followed by an X zooms relative to the current value. Entering a magnification value followed by an XP scales the magnification of the model space view relative to paper space.
Previous	Restores a previous ZOOM, PAN, VIEW, or DVIEW. The ZOOM command retains the last ten views for each viewport.
Vmax (Release 11 only)	Zooms to the limits of the virtual screen's display space. This displays the maximum drawing area possible without causing a regeneration.
Window	Specifies a window area for the new display. Often you will see more than the window area because the display area is extended to fill the graphics screen.

Scale	Scale is the default option. Enter a magnification number. A scale factor of 1 displays the drawing limits, 2 displays the drawing twice as big, and .5 displays the drawing half its size.
ScaleX	Zooms relative to the current viewport display. Enter the value followed by an X (times). The display center remains fixed.

ScaleXP (Release 11 only)

Scales the magnification of a model space view relative to paper size. Tilemode must be set to 0 or off.

Related System Variable(s)

TILEMODE, VIEWCTR, VIEWSIZE, VSMAX, VSMIN

Tips

▫ Each viewport retains its own zoom setting.

▫ All zooms work transparently except All, Extents, or zooms that cause a regeneration. Make sure VIEWRES is set to fast zooms and turn REGENAUTO off.

▫ Plot multiple scaled views of the same drawing on a drawing by setting up viewports in paper space and using the ScaleXP option.

Warning(s)

■ You cannot invoke a transparent ZOOM while using VPOINT, DVIEW, VIEW, PAN, or another ZOOM command.

See also: LIMITS, PAN, Transparent Commands, VIEW, REGENAUTO, VIEWRES

Example

```
Command: 'ZOOM
All/Center/Dynamic/Extents/Left/Previous/Window/
<Scale(X)>: C
Center point:                                 Point ①.
Magnification or Height <4.0000> : 1.25
```

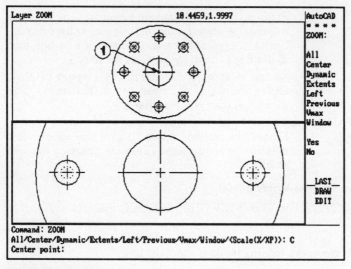

```
Layer ZOOM                        18.4459,1.9997         AutoCAD
                                                         * * * *
                                                         ZOOM:

                                                         All
                                                         Center
                                                         Dynamic
                                                         Extents
                                                         Left
                                                         Previous
                                                         Vmax
                                                         Window

                                                         Yes
                                                         No


                                                          LAST
                                                          DRAW
                                                          EDIT


Command: ZOOM
All/Center/Dynamic/Extents/Left/Previous/Vmax/Window/<Scale(X/XP)>: C
Center point:
```

ZOOM Example

3DFACE

Screen **[DRAW] [next] [3DFACE:]**
Screen **[SURFACES] [3DFACE:]**
Pull down **[Draw] [3D Face]**

3DFACE creates opaque objects defined by either three or four corner points entered in circular fashion. You can specify varying Z coordinates for the corner points, thereby creating nonplanar faces. You can specify individual visible or invisible edges. The default is visible.

Prompts

First point:
Second point:
Third point:
Fourth point:

Options

I   Enter an I before specifying the first point of an invisible edge. Enter the I before any coordinate input, filters, or osnaps.

Related System Variable(s)

SPLFRAME

Tips

◻ 3D faces are displayed as edges; they are never filled.

◻ Planar 3D faces are considered opaque by the HIDE command.

Warning(s)

■ You cannot extrude a 3D face.

See also: EDGESURF, PEDIT, PFACE, REVSURF, RULESURF, TABSURF, 3DMESH

Example

```
Command: 3DFACE
First point:            Point ①.
Second point:           Point ②.
Third point: I          Make next edge invisible. Point ③.
Fourth point:           Point ④.
Third point:            Point ⑤.
Fourth point:           Point ⑥.
Third point: ↵
```

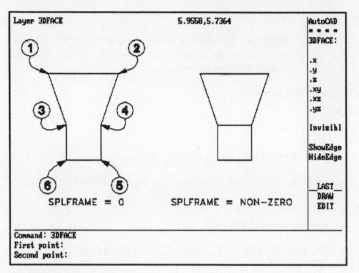

3DFACE Example

3DMESH

Screen **[DRAW] [next] [3D Surfs] [3DMESH:]**
Screen **[SURFACES] [3DMESH:]**
Pull down **[Draw] [Surfaces...]** *click 3DMesh icon*

3DMESH creates open three-dimensional polygon meshes. You specify the mesh size and location in terms of the number of vertexes in two directions, M and N. 3D meshes act like multiple 3D faces fused together and are treated as one entity. You specify the mesh size and the vertexes as 2D or 3D points. You can close a 3D mesh by editing it with the PEDIT command. Since the 3DMESH command requires inputting individual vertex points, we recommend using the automated mesh commands: EDGESURF, REVSURF, RULESURF, and TABSURF.

Prompts

```
Mesh M size:
Mesh N size:
Vertex (#, #):
```

Options

Mesh M size   Specify the number of vertexes on the M direction.

Mesh N size   Specify the number of vertexes on the N direction. The N direction is considered the direction in which you begin to define the mesh.

Tips

▫ You can fit a smooth surface or other edits to a polygon mesh with the PEDIT command.

▫ Exploding a 3D mesh will result in individual 3D faces.

See also: EDGESURF, EXPLODE, PEDIT, PFACE, REVSURF, RULESURF, TABSURF, 3DFACE

Example

```
Command: 3DMESH
Mesh M size: 3
Mesh N size: 3
Vertex (0, 0): 0,0,0
Vertex (0, 1): 0,1,.5
Vertex (0, 2): 0,2,0
Vertex (1, 0): 1,0,.5
Vertex (1, 1): 1,1,1
Vertex (1, 2): 1,2,.5
Vertex (2, 0): 2,0,0
Vertex (2, 1): 2,1,.5
Vertex (2, 2): 2,2,0
```

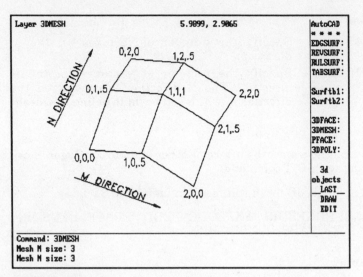

3DMESH Example

3DPOLY

Screen **[DRAW] [next] [3D Surfs] [3DPOLY:]**
Screen **[SURFACES] [3DPOLY:]**
Pull down **[Draw] [3D Poly]**

The 3DPOLY command creates a 3D polyline where each vertex can be located anywhere in 3D space. 3D polylines cannot have arc segments, width, or taper. Use the PEDIT command to edit 3D polylines.

Prompts

```
From point:
Close/Undo/<Endpoint of line>:
```

Options

Close   Closes the polyline segments created during the command by connecting the start point to the endpoint.

Undo   Undoes the last polyline segment.

Endpoint of line   Specify an endpoint. This is the default option. If you press <RETURN> at the endpoint prompt, the command is terminated.

Tips

▫ The PEDIT options available for 3D polylines are: Close, Edit vertex, Spline, Decurve, and Undo.

Warning(s)

■ 3D polylines only support continuous linetypes.

See also: PEDIT, POLYLINE

Example

```
Command: 3DPOLY
From point: 0,0,0
Close/Undo/<Endpoint of line>: 1,0,1
Close/Undo/<Endpoint of line>: 1,1,0
Close/Undo/<Endpoint of line>: 0,1,1
Close/Undo/<Endpoint of line>: C
```

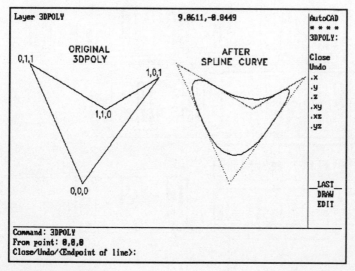

3DPOLY Example

Assist
- Help!
- Cancel
- Osnap: <mode>
- CENter
- ENDpoint
- INSert
- INTersection
- MIDpoint
- NEArest
- NODe
- PERpendicular
- QUAdrant
- Quick,<mode>
- NONE
- FILTERS ^
- Filters Sub Menu

Draw
- Line
- Point
- Circle
- Arc
- 3D Face
- Polyline
- 3D Poly
- Donut
- Ellipse
- Polygon
- Insert
- Xref
- Surfaces...
- Objects...
- DText
- Hatch
- Dim...
- Dimensions Icon Menu
- Objects Icon Menu
- Surfaces Icon Menu

Modify
- Erase
- Oops!
- Move
- Rotate
- Scale
- Stretch
- Trim
- Extend
- Break
- Chamfer
- Fillet
- Copy
- 2D Array
- 3D Array
- Mirror
- Offset
- Divide
- Measure
- PolyEdit

Display
- Redraw
- Mview ^
- Zoom Window
- Zoom Previous
- Zoom All
- Zoom Dynamic
- Zoom Vmax
- Pan
- Dview
- Dview Options...
- Vpoint 3D...
- Plan View (UCS)
- Plan View (World)
- Shade
- Hide
- Vpoint 3D Icon Menu
- Dview Options Icon Menu
- Mview Sub Menu

Settings
- Snap On/Off
- Grid On/Off
- Ortho On/Off
- Layer Control...
- Drawing Tools...
- Set SysVars
- Set Dim Vars...
- UCS Control...
- UCS Options...
- UCS Previous
- Ucsicon On/Off/OR
- Shade Style
- UCS Options Icon Menu
- UCS Control Dialogue Box
- Dim Variables Icon Menu
- Drawing Tools Dialogue Box
- Layer Control Dialogue Box

Options
- Entity Creation...
- 2D Polyline Width
- Polygon Creation
- Donut Diameters
- INSERT OPTIONS >
- DTEXT OPTIONS >
- HATCH OPTIONS >
- Point Size
- Point Type...
- Linetype Scale
- Chamfer Distances
- Fillet Radius
- Offset Distance
- Divide Units
- Measure Distance
- D/M Block Name
- Dimension Style
- Hatch Options Sub Menu
- Text Options Sub Menu
- Insert Options Sub Menu
- Entity Creation Dialogue Box

Utility
- U
- Redo
- Undo Mark
- Undo Back
- Area
- Distance
- ID Point
- List
- Status
- Limits
- Load LTypes
- AutoShade...
- RenderMan...
- RenderMan Icon Menu
- AutoShade Icon Menu

File
- Save
- End
- Quit
- Files
- Plot
- Print
- EXCHANGE >
- Exchange Sub Menu

Solids
- Load AME
- Load AMElite
- Sol — Prim's
- Box
- Cone
- Cylinder
- Sphere
- Torus
- Wedge
- Extrude
- Revolve
- Solidify
- MODIFY ^
- INQUIRY ^
- DISPLAY ^
- UTILITY ^
- Utility Sub Menu
- Display Sub Menu
- Inquiry Sub Menu
- Modify Sub Menu

AutoCAD Release 11 Pull-Down Menu, Courtesy Autodesk, Inc.

Appendix A

This appendix shows the AutoCAD Release 11 pull-down menu and provides a few "trivial facts" about different commands.

Pull-Down Menus

The illustration on the facing page shows the Release 11 pull-down menu, courtesy of Autodesk, Inc.

Commands With an Extra <RETURN>

The following list shows commands requiring an extra <RETURN> or cancel to return to the command prompt:

```
CHANGE              LAYER
CHPROP              VPLAYER
DTEXT
```

Commands With an Exit

The following list shows commands requiring eXit or cancel to return to the command prompt:

```
DVIEW               PEDIT Edit vertex option
PEDIT               DIM:
```

Commands Requiring a Regeneration

The following commands require a regeneration in order to see modifications:

```
BLOCK (Redefined)   PDMODE
COLOR               PDSIZE
FILL                QTEXT
LINETYPE            STYLE
LTSCALE
```

Commands With a Question Mark

The following commands allow a question mark at the prompt, to give you a listing or status of that command:

BLOCK	LOAD
DIM	MINSERT
DIM SAve	SETVAR
DIM REStore	STYLE
DIM Variables	UCS
INSERT	VIEW
LAYER	VPLAYER
LINETYPE	VPORTS
HATCH	XREF

Transparent Commands

Transparent commands can be accessed while in the middle of other commands. An apostrophe must precede the command. You cannot use transparent commands during TEXT, DTEXT, ATTDEF, SKETCH, PLOT, PRPLOT, VPOINT, DVIEW, and DIMensioning. Transparent commands will not work if the drawing requires a regeneration. The following commands can be transparent:

'DDEMODES	'REDRAW
'DDLMODES	'REDRAWALL
'DDRMODES	'RESUME
'GRAPHSCR	'SETVAR
'HELP	'TEXTSCR
'?	'VIEW
'PAN (see below)	'ZOOM (except ZOOM All
	and ZOOM Extents)

However, you cannot activate a transparent pan during the following commands: VPOINT, DVIEW, ZOOM, VIEW, and PAN, or in paper space. Filters and OSNAP are always transparent.

Set REGENAUTO to OFF. Set VIEWRES to fast zooms.

Commands Using the File Dialogue Box

The following commands will display a file dialogue box for file selection if the system variable FILEDIA is set to 1 or if you enter a tilde (~) in response to the file name prompt.

ATTEXT	LOAD
DXBIN	MENU
DXFIN	MSLIDE
DXFOUT	SAVE
FILMROLL	SCRIPT
IGESIN	STYLE
IGESOUT	VSLIDE
LINETYPE	WBLOCK

Prototype Drawings

A prototype drawing is a default drawing that is loaded into the drawing editor when you start an editing session. The initial default drawing is ACAD.DWG. The following is a list of variables, including command and system variables, that you may want to preset in your own prototype drawings:

UNITS	PDMODE
LIMITS	PDSIZE
LAYERS	SNAP
LINETYPE	GRID
COLOR	MIRRTEXT
LTSCALE	STYLES
VIEWS	FILLMODE
VIEWPORTS	REGENAUTO
DIM VARS	VIEWRES

Appendix B (the next Appendix) contains a complete list of system variables. See the individual commands for tips and warnings.

AutoCAD BONUS Disk AutoLISP ROUTINES

The following AutoLISP routines are on the BONUS disk that came with your AutoCAD program:

ASCTEXT	Imports ASCII files into AutoCAD.
ATTREDEF	Updates and redefines attributes.
AXROT	Rotates entities around an axis.
CALC(ulator)	Full-featured calculator (Release 11 only).
CHBlock	Lets you change the location, rotation and X, Y, Z scales of blocks.
CHFACE	Moves the vertexes of a 3D face.
CHTEXT	Modifies text characters individually or as a group (Release 11 only).
CL	Constructs center lines through circles and arcs.
DELLAYER	Deletes all entities on a layer.
DLINE	Constructs continuous double (parallel) lines and arcs.
EDGE	Changes the visibility of 3D face edges.
END	Adds a prompt to the END command.
FACT	Illustrates the use of recursion to compute factorials.
LLOAD	AutoLISP and ADS application loader (Release 11 only).
MFACE	Creates PFACE entities (Release 11 only).
MVSETUP	Assists in setting up a new drawing. Replaces and enhances the SETUP.LSP routine shipped

with earlier releases of AutoCAD (Release 11 only).

PROJECT	Projects 3D models into 2D entities.
PTEXT	Creates and edits paragraphs of text.
RECTANG	Constructs a 2D rectangle or square.
RPOLY	Refines a random polygon by iteratively replacing its vertexes with the midpoint of its edges.
SPIRAL	Constructs a 2D spiral.
SSX	Selects entities based on entity type, color, layer, linetype, block name, text style, and thickness.
TABLES	Displays and sorts tables (layer, linetype, view, block, style, UCS, and viewport).
XDATA	Lists extended entity data (Release 11 only).
XPLODE	Modifies the EXPLODE command. Replaces the LEXPLODE.LSP routine shipped with earlier releases of AutoCAD (Release 11 only).
XREFCLIP	Inserts and clips xref blocks (Release 11 only).

Command Aliases

You can activate commands by entering these individual aliases at the command prompt.

Alias	Command	Alias	Command
A	ARC	MS	MSPACE
C	CIRCLE	P	PAN
CP	COPY	PS	PSPACE
DV	DVIEW	PL	PLINE
E	ERASE	R	REDRAW
L	LINE	Z	ZOOM
LA	LAYER	3DLINE	LINE
M	MOVE		

Solids

BOX	SOLBOX	CYLINDER	SOLCYL
WED	SOLWEDGE	SPH	SOLSPHERE
WEDGE	SOLWEDGE	SPHERE	SOLSPHERE
CON	SOLCONE	TOR	SOLTORUS
CONE	SOLCONE	TORUS	SOLTORUS
CYL	SOLCYL		

Complex Solids

FIL	SOLFILL	EXTRUDE	SOLEXT
SOLF	SOLFILL	REV	SOLREV
CHAM	SOLCHAM	REVOLVE	SOLREV
SOLC	SOLCHAM	SOL	SOLIDIFY
EXT	SOLEXT		

Boolean Operations

UNI	SOLUNION	DIF	SOLSUB
UNION	SOLUNION	DIFF	SOLSUB
INT	SOLINT	DIFFERENCE	SOLSUB
INTERSECT	SOLINT	SEP	SOLSEP
SUB	SOLSUB	SEPARATE	SOLSEP
SUBTRACT	SOLSUB		

Modification and Query Commands

SCHP	SOLCHP	SLIST	SOLLIST
CHPRIM	SOLCHP	MP	SOLMASSP
MAT	SOLMAT	MASSP	SOLMASSP
MATERIAL	SOLMAT	SA	SOLAREA
MOV	SOLMOVE	SAREA	SOLAREA
SL	SOLLIST	SSV	SOLVAR

Documentation Commands

FEAT	SOLFEAT	SU	SOLUCS
PROF	SOLPROF	SUCS	SOLUCS
PROFILE	SOLPROF		

Model Representation Commands

SW	SOLWIRE	SM	SOLMESH
WIRE	SOLWIRE	MESH	SOLMESH

FILE LOCKING

Lock files always reside in the same directory as the open file. If the open file is in a read-only directory, AutoCAD can't lock it and won't allow you to edit it or write to it with commands such as WBLOCK.

Open File Extension	Lock File Extension	Function
.adt	.adk	Audit report file.
.bak	.bkk	Drawing file backup.
.bkn		Emergency backup file incremented. sequentially to next unique name.
.cfg	.cfk	Configuration file.
.dwg	.dwk	Drawing file.
.dxb	.dxk	Binary drawing interchange file.
.dxf	.dxk	Drawing interchange file.
.flm	.flk	Filmroll file (AutoShade).
.hlp		Help file.
.hdx		Help index file.
.igs	.igk	IGES interchange file.
.lin	.lik	Linetype library file.

Open File Extension	Lock File Extension	Function
.lsp		AutoLISP program library file.
.lst	.ltk	Printer plot output file.
.mat		Materials file.
.mnu		Menu file.
.mnx	.mnk	Compiled menu file.
.msg		Message file.
.old	.olk	Original version of converted drawing file.
.pat		Hatch pattern library file.
.pgp		Program parameters file.
.plt	.plk	Plot output file.
.prp	.prk	ADI printer plotter output file.
.pwd	.pwk	Login file.
.scr		Command script file.
.shx	.sxk	Shape/font definition source file.
.slb		Slide library file.
.sld	.sxk	Slide file.
.txt	.txk	Attribute extract or template file (CDF/SDF format).
.unt		Units file.
.xlg	.xlk	External references log file.
.$ac	.$ak	Temporary file.
.ac$		Temporary file.
.$a		Temporary file.

Appendix B

AutoCAD System Variables

This appendix contains a table of all AutoCAD system variables. Use this table to find AutoCAD's environment settings and their values. All the variable settings available through AutoCAD's SETVAR command at the Release 11 command prompt or AutoLISP's SETVAR and GETVAR functions are shown. If you enter an apostrophe before the variable name, it will be treated as a transparent command (Release 11 only).

The system variable name and the default AutoCAD prototype drawing (ACAD.DWG) settings are shown. A brief description is given for each variable, and the meaning is given for each code flag.

All values are saved with the drawing unless noted with <CFG> for ConFiGuration file, or <NS> for Not Saved. Variables marked <RO> are read only, meaning you can't use SETVAR or the setvar function to change them. Variable names shown in bold are new in Release 11.

Solid variables (beginning with the letters "SOL") cannot be used unless the Advanced Modeling Extension (AME) or AMElite is loaded.

AutoCAD System Variables

VARIABLE NAME	DEFAULT SETTING	DEFAULT MEANING	COMMAND NAME	VARIABLE DESCRIPTION
ACADPREFIX	"C:\ACAD\"			AutoCAD directory path **\<NS\>, \<RO\>**
ACADVER	"10"			AutoCAD release version **\<RO\>**
AFLAGS	0		ATTDEF	Sum of: Invisible=1 Constant=2 Verify=4 Preset=8
ANGBASE	0	EAST	UNITS	Direction of angle 0
ANGDIR	0	CCW	UNITS	Clockwise=1 Counter clockwise=0
APERTURE	10	10	APERTURE	Half of aperture height in pixels **\<CFG\>**
AREA	0.0000		AREA,LIST	Last computed area **\<NS\>, \<RO\>**
ATTDIA	0			Insert uses: DDATTE dialogue box=1 Attribute prompts=0
ATTMODE	1	ON	ATTDISP	Attribute display Normal=1 ON=2 OFF=0
ATTREQ	1	PROMPTS		Insert uses: Prompts=1 Defaults=0
AUNITS	0	DEC. DEG.	UNITS	Angular units Dec=0 Deg=1 Grad=2 Rad=3 Survey=4
AUPREC	0	0	UNITS	Angular units decimal places
AXISMODE	0	OFF	AXIS	Axis ON=1 Axis OFF=0
AXISUNIT	0.0000,0.0000		AXIS	Axis X,Y Increment
BACKZ	0.0000		DVIEW	Back clipping plane offset - See VIEWMODE **\<RO\>**
BLIPMODE	1	ON	BLIPMODE	Blips=1 No Blips=0
CDATE	19881202.144648898		TIME	Date.Time **\<NS\>, \<RO\>**
CECOLOR	"BYLAYER"		COLOR	Current entity color **\<RO\>**
CELTYPE	"BYLAYER"		LINETYPE	Current entity linetype **\<RO\>**
CHAMFERA	0.0000		CHAMFER	Chamfer distance for A
CHAMFERB	0.0000		CHAMFER	Chamfer distance for B
CLAYER	"0"		LAYER	Current layer **\<RO\>**
CMDECHO	1	ECHO	SETVAR	Command echo in AutoLISP Echo=1 No Echo=0 **\<NS\>**
COORDS	0	OFF	[^D] [F6]	Update display Picks=0 ON=1 Dist>Angle=2
CVPORT	1		VPORTS	Identification number of the current viewport
DATE	2447498.61620926		TIME	Julian time **\<NS\>, \<RO\>**
DTASTAT	1	OK	DD???	Dialogue box exit code 0=cancel 1=OK **\<RO\>**

VARIABLE NAME	DEFAULT SETTING	DEFAULT MEANING	COMMAND NAME	VARIABLE DESCRIPTION
DIMALT	0	OFF	DIMALT	Use alternate units ON=1 OFF=0
DIMALTD	2	0.00	DIMALTD	Decimal precision of alternate units
DIMALTF	25.4000		DIMALTF	Scale factor for alternate units
DIMAPOST	""	NONE	DIMAPOST	Suffix for alternate dimensions **<RO>**
DIMASO	1	ON	DIMASO	Associative=1 Line,Arrow,Text=0
DIMASZ	0.1800		DIMASZ	Arrow Size=Value (also controls text fit)
DIMBLK	""	NONE	DIMBLK	Block name to draw instead of arrow or tick **<RO>**
DIMBLK1	""	NONE	DIMBLK1	Block name for 1st end, see DIMSAH **<RO>**
DIMBLK2	""	NONE	DIMBLK2	Block name for 2nd end, see DIMSAH **<RO>**
DIMCEN	0.0900	MARK	DIMCEN	Center mark size=Value Add center lines=Negative
DIMCLRD	0	COLOR	DIMCLRD	Dimension line, arrow, and dim line leader color
DIMCLRE	0	COLOR	DIMCLRE	Dimension extension line color
DIMCLRT	0	COLOR	DIMCLRT	Dimension text color
DIMDLE	0.0000	NONE	DIMDLE	Dimension line extension=Value
DIMDLI	0.3800		DIMDLI	Increment between continuing dimension lines
DIMEXE	0.1800		DIMEXE	Extension distance for extension lines=Value
DIMGAP	0.0900		DIMGAP	Gap between text and dimension line
DIMEXO	0.0625		DIMEXO	Offset distance for extension lines=Value
DIMLFAC	1.0000	NORMAL	DIMLFAC	Overall linear distance factor=Value
DIMLIM	0	OFF	DIMLIM	Add tolerance limits ON=1 OFF=0
DIMPOST	""	NONE	DIMPOST	User defined dimension suffix (eg: "mm") **<RO>**
DIMRND	0.0000	EXACT	DIMRND	Rounding value for linear dimensions
DIMSAH	0	OFF	DIMSAH	Allow separate DIMBLKS ON=1 OFF=0
DIMSCALE	1.0000		DIMSCALE	Overall dimensioning scale factor=Value
DIMSE1	0	OFF	DIMSE1	Suppress extension line 1 Omit=1 Draw=0
DIMSE2	0	OFF	DIMSE2	Suppress extension line 2 Omit=1 Draw=0
DIMSHO	0	OFF	DIMSHO	Show associative dimension while dragging
DIMSOXD	0	OFF	DIMSOXD	Suppress dim. lines outside extension lines Omit=1 Draw=0
DIMSTYLE	*UNNAMED		Dim: SAVE	Current dimension style **<RO>**
DIMTAD	0	OFF	DIMTAD	Text above dim. line ON=1 OFF(in line)=0

VARIABLE NAME	DEFAULT SETTING	DEFAULT MEANING	COMMAND NAME	VARIABLE DESCRIPTION
DIMTIH	1	ON	DIMTIH	Text inside horizontal ON=1 OFF(aligned)=0
DIMTIX	0	OFF	DIMTIX	Force text inside extension lines ON=1 OFF=0
DIMTM	0.0000	NONE	DIMTM	Minus tolerance=Value
DIMTOFL	0	OFF	DIMTOFL	Draw dim. line even if text outside ext. lines
DIMTOH	1	ON	DIMTOH	Text outside horizontal ON=1 OFF(aligned)=0
DIMTOL	0	OFF	DIMTOL	Append tolerance ON=1 OFF=2
DIMTP	0.0000	NONE	DIMTP	Plus tolerance=Value
DIMTSZ	0.0000	ARROWS	DIMTSZ	Tick size=Value Draw arrows=0
DIMTVP	0.0000		DIMTVP	Text vertical position
DIMTXT	0.1800		DIMTXT	Text size=Value
DIMZIN	0		DIMZIN	Controls leading zero (see AutoCAD manual)
DISTANCE	0.0000		DIST	Last computed distance **<NS>,<RO>**
DRAGMODE	2	AUTO	DRAGMODE	OFF=0 Enabled=1 Auto=2
DRAGP1	10		SETVAR	Drag regen rate **<CFG>**
DRAGP2	25		SETVAR	Drag input rate **<CFG>**
DWGNAME	"TEST"			Current drawing name **<RO>**
DWGPREFIX	"C:\IA-ACAD\"			Directory path of current drawing **<NS>, <RO>**
ELEVATION	0.0000		ELEV	Current default elevation
ERRNO	0	NONE	SETVAR	Error code caused by ADS or AutoLISP program
EXPERT	0	NORMAL	SETVAR	Suppresses "Are you sure" prompts
				(See AutoLisp or ADS Programmer's Reference Manual)
EXTMAX	-1.0000E+20,-1.0000E+20			Upper right drawing extents X,Y **<RO>**
EXTMIN	1.0000E+20,1.0000E+20			Lower left drawing extents X,Y **<RO>**
FILEDIA	1	ON	SETVAR	Enables/disables dialogue box for filenames **<CFG>**
FILLETRAD	0.0000		FILLET	Current fillet radius
FILLMODE	1		FILL	Fill ON=1 Fill OFF=0
FLATLAND	0		SETVAR	Temporary 3D compatibility setting
				act like Release 9=1 R10=0
FRONTZ	0.0000		DVIEW	Front clipping plane offset - See VIEWMODE **<RO>**
GRIDMODE	0	OFF	GRID	Grid ON=1 Grid OFF=0
GRIDUNIT	0.0000,0.0000		GRID	X,Y grid increment

VARIABLE NAME	DEFAULT SETTING	DEFAULT MEANING	COMMAND NAME	VARIABLE DESCRIPTION
HANDLES	0		HANDLES	Entity handles Enabled=1 Disabled=0 <RO>
HIGHLIGHT	1		SETVAR	Highlight selection ON=1 OFF=0 <NS>
INSBASE	0.0000,0.0000		BASE	Insert base point of current drawing X,Y
LASTANGLE	0		ARC	Last angle of the last arc <NS>,<RO>
LASTPOINT	0.0000,0.0000			Last @ pickpoint X,Y <NS>
LASTPT3D	0.0000,0.0000,0.0000			Last @ pickpoint X,Y,Z <NS>
LENSLENGTH	50.0000		DVIEW	Length of lens in perspective in millimeters <RO>
LIMCHECK	0	OFF	LIMITS	Limits error check ON=1 OFF=0
LIMMAX	12.0000,9.0000		LIMITS	Upper right X,Y limit
LIMMIN	0.0000,0.0000		LIMITS	Lower left X,Y limit
LTSCALE	1.0000		LTSCALE	Current linetype scale
LUNITS	2	DEC.	UNITS	Linear units: Scientific=1 Dec=2 Eng=3 Arch=4 Frac=5
LUPREC	4	0.0000	UNITS	Unit precision decimal places or denominator
MAXACTVP	16		SETVAR	Max. no. of viewports to regen <NS>,<RO>
MAXSORT	200		SETVAR	Max. no. symbol/filenames sorted by commands <CFG>
MENUECHO	0	NORMAL	SETVAR	Normal=0 Suppress echo of menu items=1 No prompts=2 No input or prompts=3 <NS>
MENUNAME	"ACAD"		MENU	Current menu name <RO>
MIRRTEXT	1	YES	SETVAR	Retain text direction=0 Reflect text=1
ORTHOMODE	0	OFF	[^O] [F8]	Ortho ON=1 Ortho OFF=0
OSMODE	0	NONE	OSNAP	Sum of: Endp=1 Mid=2 Cen=4 Node=8 Quad=16 Int=32 Ins=64 Perp=128 Tan=256 Near=512 Quick=1024
PDMODE	0	POINT	SETVAR	Controls style of points drawn
PDSIZE	0.0000	POINT	SETVAR	Controls size of points
PERIMETER	0.0000		AREA,LIST	Last computed perimeter <NS>,<RO>
PFACEVMAX	4		SETVAR	Maximum number of vertexes per face <NS>,<RO>
PICKBOX	3		SETVAR	Half the pickbox size in pixels <CFG>
PLATFORM	varies		SETVAR	Stores string showing type of system, such as "DOS", "386 DOS Extender", "OS/2", or "Sun 3".

VARIABLE NAME	DEFAULT SETTING	DEFAULT MEANING	COMMAND NAME	VARIABLE DESCRIPTION
POPUPS	1			AUI Support=1 No Support=0 **<NS>**, **<RO>**
QTEXTMODE	0	OFF	QTEXT	Qtext ON=1 Qtext OFF=0
REGENMODE	1	ON	REGENAUTO	Regenauto ON=1 Regenauto OFF=0
SCREENSIZE	570.0000,410.0000			Current size of viewport in pixels, X and Y **<RO>**
SHADEDGE	3		SETVAR	Display of edges and faces by SHADE command
SHADEDIF	70		SETVAR	Ratio of ambient light to diffuse light
SKETCHINC	0.1000		SKETCH	Recording increment for sketch
SKPOLY	0	LINE	SETVAR	Polylines=1 Sketch with Line=0
SNAPANG	0		SNAP	Angle of SNAP/GRID rotation
SNAPBASE	0.0000,0.0000		SNAP	X,Y base point of SNAP/GRID rotation
SNAPISOPAIR	0	LEFT	SNAP [^E]	Isoplane Left=0 Top=1 Right=2
SNAPMODE	0	OFF	SNAP [^B] [F9]	Snap ON=1 Snap OFF=0
SNAPSTYL	0	STD	SNAP	Isometric=1 Snap standard=0
SNAPUNIT	1.0000,1.0000		SNAP	Snap X,Y increment
SOLAMEVER	1.0			AME version and release number **<RO>**
SOLAREAU	sq cm			Unit of measure for area calculations.
SOLAXCOL	3		SOLMOVE, SOLCHP	Color of coordinate system icon (AME); 1 - 8.
SOLDECOMP	X			Mass properties decomposition direction; X,Y, or Z.
SOLDELENT	3	ALWAYS		Delete 2D entities automatically 1 = never, 2 = ask, 3 = always.
SOLDISPLAY	wire			Solids default display: wireframe or mesh.
SOLHANGLE	0.000000		SOLSECT	Angle of hatch pattern (AME).
SOLHPAT	NONE		SOLSECT	Hatch pattern used to crosshatch sections (AME).
SOLHSIZE	1.000000		SOLSECT	Scale of hatch pattern used to crosshatch (AME).
SOLLENGTH	cm			Unit of measure for length of solid entity.
SOLMASS	gm			Unit of measure for mass of solid entity.
SOLMATCURR	MILD_STEEL			Name of default material **<RO>**.
SOLPAGELEN	25		[several]	Page length for messages; 0 = continuous scrolling
SOLRENDER	CSG		SHADE	Color of shading; CSG or Uniform.
SOLSERVMSG	3		ALL	Messages displayed; 0 = None, 1 = Errors only, 2 = Errors and start/end = All

VARIABLE NAME	DEFAULT SETTING	DEFAULT MEANING	COMMAND NAME	VARIABLE DESCRIPTION
SOLSOLIDIFY	2		ALL	Converts 2D into solid; 1=never, 2=ask, 3=always.
SOLSUBDIV	3			Subdivision level for mass properties calc.; 1-8.
SOLVOLUME	cu cm			Unit of measure for volume calculations.
SOLWDENS	4			Wireframe and mesh density for new solids; 1 - 8.
SPLFRAME	0		SETVAR	Display spline frame ON=1 OFF=0
SPLINESEGS	8		SETVAR	Number of line segments in each spline segment
SPLINETYPE	6	CUBIC	SETVAR	Pedit spline generates: Quadratic B-Spline=5 Cubic B-Spline=6
SURFTAB1	6		SETVAR	Rulesurf and tabsurf tabulations, also revsurf and edgesurf M density
SURFTAB2	6		SETVAR	Revsurf and edgesurf N density
SURFTYPE	6	CUBIC	SETVAR	Pedit smooth surface generates: Quadratic B-Spline=5 Cubic B-Spline=6 Bezier=8
SURFU	6		SETVAR	M direction surface density
SURFV	6		SETVAR	N direction surface density
TARGET	0.0000,0.0000,0.0000		DVIEW	UCS coords of current viewport target point **<RO>**
TDCREATE	2447498.61620031		TIME	Creation time (Julian) **<RO>**
TDINDWG	0.00436285			Total editing time **<RO>**
TDUPDATE	2447498.61620031		TIME	Time of last save or update **<RO>**
TDUSRTIMER	0.00436667		TIME	User set elapsed time **<RO>**
TEMPPREFIX	""			Directory location of AutoCAD's temporary files, defaults to drawing directory **<NS>**, **<RO>**
TEXTEVAL	0	TEXT	SETVAR	Evaluate leading "(" and "!" in text input as: Text=0 AutoLISP=1 **<NS>**
TEXTSIZE	0.2000		TEXT	Current text height
TEXTSTYLE	"STANDARD"		TEXT,STYLE	Current text style **<RO>**
THICKNESS	0.0000		ELEV	Current 3D extrusion thickness
TILEMODE	1	ON	TILEMODE	Enables/disables paper space and viewport entities
TRACEWID	0.0500		TRACE	Current width of traces
UCSFOLLOW	0		SETVAR	Automatic plan view in new UCS=1 Off=0
UCSICON	1		UCSICON	Sum of: Off=0 On=1 Origin=2

VARIABLE NAME	DEFAULT SETTING	DEFAULT MEANING	COMMAND NAME	VARIABLE DESCRIPTION
UCSNAME	""		UCS	Name of current UCS Unnamed="" **<RO>**
UCSORG	0.0000,0.0000,0.0000		UCS	WCS origin of current UCS **<RO>**
UCSXDIR	1.0000,0.0000,0.0000		UCS	X direction of current UCS **<RO>**
UCSYDIR	0.0000,1.0000,0.0000		UCS	Y direction of current UCS **<RO>**
UNITMODE	0		SETVAR	0=Display units standard 1=display in input mode
USERI1 - 5	0			User integer variables USERI1 to USERI5
USERR1 - 5	0.0000			User real variables USERR1 to USERR5
VIEWCTR	6.2518,4.5000		ZOOM,PAN,VIEW	X,Y center point of current view **<RO>**
VIEWDIR	0.0000,0.0000,1.0000		DVIEW	Camera point offset from target in WCS **<RO>**
VIEWMODE	0		DVIEW,UCS	Perspective and clipping settings, see AutoCAD Reference Manual **<RO>**
VIEWSIZE	9.0000		ZOOM,PAN,VIEW	Height of current view **<RO>**
VIEWTWIST	0.0000		DVIEW	View wist angle **<RO>**
VPOINTX	0.0000		VPOINT	X coordinate of VPOINT **<RO>**
VPOINTY	0.0000		VPOINT	Y coordinate of VPOINT **<RO>**
VPOINTZ	1.0000		VPOINT	Z coordinate of VPOINT **<RO>**
VSMAX	12.5036,9.0000,0.0000		ZOOM,PAN,VIEW	Upper right of virtual screen X,Y **<NS>**, **<RO>**
VSMIN	0.0000,0.0000,0.0000		ZOOM,PAN,VIEW	Lower left of virtual screen X,Y **<NS>**, **<RO>**
WORLDUCS	1		UCS	UCS equals WCS=1 UCS not equal to WCS=0 **<RO>**
WORLDVIEW	1		DVIEW,UCS	Dview and VPoint coordinate input: WCS=1 UCS=0

<NS> Not Saved   **<CFG>** Configure File   **<RO>** Read Only

Appendix C

How to Use the AREF Disk

The optional AutoCAD reference disk, called the AREF disk, puts the *AutoCAD Reference Guide* on-line within AutoCAD. This ready-to-use disk contains all the material in the reference guide. The disk loads and appends the reference guide to the regular AutoCAD help system, letting you access the guide from within AutoCAD. If you don't have the disk yet, an order form is provided in the back of this book. If you already have the AREF disk, the following instructions will tell you how to load and use it.

Copying the AREF DISK

Before starting, make a backup copy of the AREF disk using the DOS DISKCOPY command. Store the original in a safe place, and use the copy as your working disk. After making a backup copy, you are ready to install the files onto your hard disk.

What Files Are on the AREF Disk?

You will find the following files on the AREF disk.

README.DOC	Instructions for installing and using the AREF disk.
AREF.BAT	Executes AREFX.EXE to decompress the AREF files onto your hard disk.
AREFX.EXE	A compressed file containing the following files:
INSTALL.BAT	An automatic setup routine for completing the installation of AREF files on your computer.
AREF.HLP	AREF help text file.
AREF.SLB	AREF slide library.
AREF.LSP	The AREF AutoLISP program.

Installing the AREF Files on Your Hard Disk

The AREF.BAT file decompresses the files contained in AREFX.EXE, copying them into the current directory of your hard disk. It assumes that your current directory is your AutoCAD program or support directory containing your ACAD.HLP file, and that the AREF disk is in drive A.

- Log into your AutoCAD directory.

- Verify that the ACAD.HLP file exists in the directory. If it doesn't, and it doesn't exist anywhere else on your hard disk, copy the file from your original AutoCAD disks.

- Place the AREF disk in drive A: or B:. (Be sure to specify the correct size disk when you order.)

- At the DOS prompt, type A:AREF   (or B:AREF if you're using Drive B:). It decompresses and copies the following files into your AutoCAD directory:

```
README.DOC
INSTALL.BAT
AREF.HLP
AREF.SLB
AREF.LSP
```

- Once the decompression process is complete, remove the AREF disk and store it in a safe place.

Continue the AREF disk installation using the batch file INSTALL.BAT.

The installation batch file program automatically configures the AREF program files in your current AutoCAD directory. Here are the steps to run the INSTALL program.

- Log into your AutoCAD directory if you're not already there.

- Verify that the ACAD.HLP file exists in the directory. If it doesn't, and it doesn't exist anywhere else on your hard disk, copy the file from your original AutoCAD disks.

- At the DOS prompt, type: INSTALL

INSTALL.BAT performs the following functions:

- Deletes ACAD.HDX. A new ACAD.HDX index file will automatically be generated when you first access help in AutoCAD.

- Renames your original ACAD.HLP as ACADHLP.OLD

- Creates a new ACAD.HLP file consisting of the standard ACAD.HLP and the AREF.HLP file.

Installation is now complete.

How to Load the AREF Program

The AREF.LSP program provides the interface for accessing the AREF.HLP file and its supporting slide library AREF.SLB. In order to use the on-line reference guide, you must first load the AREF.LSP program.

The easiest way to load the program is to type at the AutoCAD command prompt:

(load "AREF")

Once the program is loaded, you can access the reference guide as if it were any other AutoCAD command. Type AREF at the command prompt or add it to a menu selection.

There are a number of ways you can automate the loading of AREF.LSP. You can add the following macro to your menu(s).

[Load REF]^C^C^C(load "AREF")

Once you select the macro, AREF will be available throughout the editing session.

If you don't have an ACAD.LSP file, you can rename AREF.LSP to ACAD.LSP, and it will automatically load each time you enter the drawing editor. If you have an ACAD.LSP file, you can append the AREF.LSP file to it and get the same results.

How to Use the AREF Program

When you access the on-line *AutoCAD Reference Guide* program by typing AREF at the command prompt, you will receive the command prompt:

Enter command name or topic:

Pressing <RETURN> will bring up a text screen with an explanation of how AREF works. Typing a command name results in the following prompt and options:

Command/Quit/Slide/Tips/Example/<Description>:

Command	Enter a new command name.
Quit	Returns to AutoCAD's Command: prompt.

Slide	If a slide example is available for that command, it will appear in your current viewport to graphically describe the command. We recommend using multiple viewports and bringing the slide into a portion of your screen or your current viewport.
Tips	Displays Tip(s), Warning(s), and cross-references for that command.
Example	The example provides a command prompt and response sequence showing how to use the command. The results of the example often are shown graphically in the slide.
Description	The default provides you with the following information:

Description of command

Menu access (shows how to access the command)

Command prompts and options

System variable(s)

You access AutoCAD's help file by typing HELP or ? at the command prompt. AutoCAD's help command is transparent by typing an apostrophe before the word help or ?. Unlike AutoCAD's help command, AREF's help cannot be used transparently. You must type AREF at the command prompt to access the help file. To exit the AREF program, either type Q to quit, or press <^C> to cancel. When you exit AREF, you are returned to the regular AutoCAD command prompt.

The New Riders Library

New Riders Publishing consistently delivers the best tutorials and references for understanding your personal computer and its programs.

INSIDE AutoCAD   6th Edition/Releases 10, 11
The Complete AutoCAD Guide

By Rusty Gesner and Jim Boyce
928 pages, over 400 illustrations
ISBN 0-934035-55-5 **$34.95**

INSIDE AutoCAD, the best-selling book on AutoCAD, is entirely new and rewritten for users of AutoCAD Releases 10 and 11. This easy-to-understand book serves as both a tutorial and a lasting reference guide. Learn to use every single AutoCAD command as well as time-saving drawing techniques and tips. Includes coverage of 3D modeling features, AutoShade, and AutoLISP. This is the book that lets you keep up and stay in control with AutoCAD.

Optional Productivity Disk available.

CUSTOMIZING AutoCAD®
A Complete Guide to AutoCAD Menus, Macros and More!

By J. Smith and R. Gesner
480 Pages, 100 illustrations
ISBN 0-934035-45-8, **$27.95**

Uncover the hidden secrets of AutoCAD in this all new edition. Discover the anatomy of an AutoCAD menu and build a custom menu from start to finish. Manipulate distance, angles, points, and hatches — ALL in 3D! Customize hatches, text fonts, and dimensioning for increased productivity. Buy *CUSTOMIZING AutoCAD* today and start customizing AutoCAD tomorrow!

Optional Productivity Disk available.

INSIDE AutoLISP®

The Complete Guide to Using AutoLISP for AutoCAD Applications

By J. Smith and R. Gesner
736 pages, over 150 illustrations
ISBN: 0-934035-98-9, **$34.95**

Introducing the most comprehensive book on AutoLISP for AutoCAD. Learn AutoLISP commands and functions and write your own custom AutoLISP programs. Numerous tips and tricks for using AutoLISP for routine drawing tasks. Import and export critical drawing information to/from Lotus 1-2-3 and dBASE. Automate the creation of scripts for unattended drawing processing. *INSIDE AutoLISP* is the book that will give you the inside track to using AutoLISP.

Optional Productivity Disk available.

STEPPING INTO AutoCAD®
A Guide to Technical Drafting Using AutoCAD

By Mark Merickel
544 pages, over 140 illustrations
ISBN 0-934035-51-2, **$29.95**

This popular technical drafting tutorial is organized to lead you step by step from the basics to production of industry standard dimensioned drawings. Handy references provide quick setup of the AutoCAD environment. Improve your drawing accuracy through AutoCAD's dimensioning commands. It also includes extensive support for ANSI Y14.5 level drafting.

Optional ANSI Y14.5 Tablet Menu Disk available.

AutoCAD® for Architects and Engineers
A Practical Guide to Design, Presentation and Production

By John Albright and Elizabeth Schaeffer
544 pages, over 150 illustrations
ISBN 0-934035-53-9 **$29.95**

Master your AutoCAD project using high-powered design development. Learn to construct working drawings using techniques from real-life projects. Export crucial data for credible report generation. Generate stunning computer presentations with AutoLISP, AutoShade, and AutoFlix. The ONLY AutoCAD book specifically written for the architectural, engineering, and construction community.

Optional Productivity Disk available.

AutoCAD® Reference Guide   2nd Edition/Releases 10, 11
Everything You Wanted to Know About
AutoCAD — FAST!

By Dorothy Kent
256 pages, over 50 illustrations
ISBN: 0-934035-02-4, **$14.95**

All AutoCAD commands are arranged alphabetically and described in just a few paragraphs. Includes tips and warnings from experienced users for each command. This is the instant-answer guide to AutoCAD.

Also available on disk.

INSIDE AutoSketch®   2nd Edition – Version 3.0
A Guide to Productive Drawing Using AutoSketch

By Frank Lenk
240 pages, over 120 illustrations
ISBN: 0-934035-96-2, **$24.95**

INSIDE AutoSketch gives you real-life mechanical parts, drawing schematics, and architectural drawings. Start by learning to draw simple shapes such as points, lines and curves, then edit shapes by moving, copying, rotating, and distorting them. Explore higher-level features to complete technical drawing jobs using reference grids, snap, drawing layers, and creating parts. *INSIDE AutoSketch* will help you draw your way to succes.

Optional Productivity Disk available.

INSIDE AutoDesk Animator®
The Complete Guide to Animation on a PC

By Leah Freiwald and Lee Marrs
480 pages, over 500 illustrations
ISBN 0-934035-76-8 **$29.95**

Exploit the power of the Autodesk Animator program, guided by an Emmy-winning graphics animator and a computer training expert. With a series of hands-on tutorials, they take you from basic to advanced animations so that you will be capable of producing professional animated graphics for everything from presentations to your own cartoons. The book also includes coverage of the Autodesk ATK to easily create animated presentations from your 3D AutoCAD drawings. With the help of *INSIDE AUTODESK ANIMATOR,* you can tame this exciting program and make it work for you in real world presentations!

Optional Productivity Disk available.

INSIDE CompuServe®
The Easy Start Guide to Online Information and Communication

By Julie Anne Arca and Richard T. Lindstrom
320 pages, includes communication programs disks
ISBN 0-934035-83-0, **$29.95** (Book/Disk Set)

INSIDE CompuServe will escort you through today's largest and most diverse information source. This book and disk set contains all the guidance you need to connect your telephone, modem, and PC to CompuServe's on-line telecommunications service. Whether you're just getting started or exploring new realms, *INSIDE CompuServe* is a valuable resource to help you get the best out of the most popular computer information service, CompuServe.

Shareware communication program disks available with book.

Inside CorelDRAW!™
The Practical Guide to Computer-Aided Graphic Design

By Daniel Gray
424 pages, over 175 illustrations including eight pages in full color
ISBN: 0-934035-33-4, **$24.95**

Make impressive graphic design easy with *INSIDE CorelDRAW!* This handy, by-your-side tutorial shows you how to get the most from Corel's fabulous graphic arts and typography software for the PC. Learn how to produce your own projects by following the hands-on practice examples and by studying the full-color samples from the CorelDRAW! masters. Whether you're an artist, a designer, or a PC enthusiast, you'll quickly be creating eye-catching artwork of your own.

Add to Your New Riders Library Today
with the Best Books for the Best Software

Add to Your New Riders Library Today
with the Best Books for the Best Software

Yes, please send me the productivity-boosting material I have checked below. Make check payable to New Riders Publishing.

❑ **Check enclosed.**

Charge to my credit card:

❑ **VISA**   ❑ **MasterCard**

Card # _____

Expiration date: _____

Signature: _____

Name: _____

Company: _____

Address: _____

City: _____

State: _____ ZIP: _____

Phone: _____

The easiest way to order is to pick up the phone and call 1-800-541-6789 between 9:00 a.m. and 5:00 p.m., EST. Please have your credit card available, and your order can be placed in a snap!

Quantity	Description of Item	Unit Cost	Total Cost
	Inside CorelDRAW!, 2nd Edition	$29.95	
	AutoCAD 3D Design & Presentation*	$29.95	
	Maximizing Windows 3 (Book-and-Disk set)	$39.95	
	Inside AutoCAD, Special Edition (for Releases 10 and 11)*	$34.95	
	Maximizing AutoCAD: Volume I (Book-and-Disk set) Customizing AutoCAD with Macros and Menus	$34.95	
	AutoCAD for Beginners	$19.95	
	Inside Autodesk Animator*	$29.95	
	Maximizing AutoCAD: Volume II (Book-and-Disk set) Inside AutoLISP	$34.95	
	Inside AutoSketch, 2nd Edition*	$24.95	
	AutoCAD Reference Guide, 2nd Edition	$14.95	
	AutoCAD Reference Guide on Disk, 2nd Edition	$14.95	
	Inside CompuServe (Book-and-Disk set)	$29.95	
	Managing and Networking AutoCAD*	$29.95	
	Inside AutoCAD, Release 11, Metric Ed. (Book-and-Disk set)	$34.95	
	Maximizing MS-DOS 5 (Book-and-Disk set)	$34.95	
	Inside Generic CADD*	$29.95	
	Inside Windows	$29.95	
	AutoCAD Bible	$39.95	
	*Companion Disk available for these books	$14.95 ea.	
❑ 3½" disk	Shipping and Handling: See information below.		
❑ 5¼" disk	TOTAL		

Shipping and Handling: $4.00 for the first book and $1.75 for each additional book. Floppy disk: add $1.75 for shipping and handling. If you need to have it NOW, we can ship product to you in 24 to 48 hours for an additional charge, and you will receive your item overnight or in two days. Add $20.00 per book and $8.00 for up to three disks overseas. Prices subject to change. Call for availability and pricing information on latest editions.

New Riders Publishing • 11711 N. College Avenue • P.O. Box 90 • Carmel, Indiana 46032
1-800-541-6789   1-800-448-3804
Orders/Customer Service   FAX

To order: Fill in the reverse side, fold, and mail

‖‖‖‖

NEW RIDERS PUBLISHING

P.O. Box 90

Carmel, Indiana 46032